Smallmouth
BASS
An In-Fisherman
Handbook of Strategies

Smallmouth
BASS
An In-Fisherman
Handbook of Strategies

Al Lindner
    Dave Csanda
        Bob Ripley
            Ron Lindner
                Doug Stange
                    Dan Sura
                        Larry Dahlberg

Published by
Al Lindner's Outdoors, Inc.

IV

Book Compiled by Bob Ripley and Dan Sura
Cover Art by Larry Tople
Artwork by Dan Vickerman
Typesetting by Type/Graphics
Litho Prep by Quality Graphics
Printing by Bang Printing
Copyright 1984 by Al Lindner
All rights reserved
Published by Al Lindner's Outdoors, Inc.
P.O. Box 999, Brainerd, Minnesota 56401
Printed in the United States of America

ISBN 0-9605254-3-2 (Volume 4)

ISBN 0-9605254-7-5 (6 Volume Set)

First Edition, 1984
Second Printing, 1985
Third Printing, 1985

Library of Congress Catalogue
Card Number 84-81854

ISBN 0-9605254-3-2 (Volume 4)
ISBN 0-9605254-7-5 (6 Volume Set)

ACKNOWLEDGEMENT

Most fishing books contain very little information that is truly new. At best, they may introduce one or two new concepts. Most of the information in this book, however, is not only new, but of *breakthrough* status. Credit for these new smallmouth concepts belongs not only to the authors, but also to the many additional, knowledgeable persons consulted.

We are very grateful to persons like Mike Radulovich and Doug Loehr for their input on bass in pits. Rich Zaleski shed additional light on the smallmouth's lifestyle in northeastern lakes and reservoirs, while John Herrick detailed bass action on the Canadian Shield. Michigan biologist, Asa Wright, supplied invaluable information on the location of Great Lakes' smallmouth bass, and fisheries researcher, Ralph Manns, provided insight into smallmouth temperature preferences. In the realm of rivers, Dan Gapen and Bill Lindner offered invaluable assistance. Guides like Jim Fofrich, and promoters like Gary Roach, added their knowledge and help.

Then, too, we gleaned knowledge from anglers themselves. Some of these anglers have attained a nationwide reputation, while others are less well-known, yet knowledgeable. We appreciate the help of fishing educators like Bill Dance for his unique presentation tips, and Steve Price for reservoir bass information. Men like the legendary Bill Binkelman, who helped devise the Calendar Periods, certainly deserve credit—and the list goes on and on.

Beyond this background material, each of the authors has shared in breakthroughs of major importance. Their on-the-water experience, both individually and along with great smallmouth bass anglers from around the world, enables them to pass on to you their many secrets, tricks and tips in this original edition to *SMALLMOUTH BASS: A HANDBOOK OF STRATEGIES.*

TABLE OF CONTENTS

INTRODUCTION

The smallmouth bass is easily one of the favorite sportfish pursued by North American anglers. "Everybody loves a smallie" is surely a hard-to-debate statement.

Anglers fish for smallmouths in everything from large, Great Lakes craft to small canoes. They wade small, shallow streams with fly rods. In the huge, deep reservoirs of the South, they resort to fully-rigged, ultra-sophisticated bass boats, armed with every conceivable type of electronic equipment. Smallies are caught on top water popping bugs, and are enticed from depths of 50-60 feet with live bait. In rivers, they are fished from Jon boats, as well as from the riverbank using only a cane pole.

Smallmouths are found as far south as Texas, and as far north as the Canadian river systems. Smallies are a sought-after sportfish in California, as well as in Maine.

Why the interest? In one word, *fight*. And fight, the smallie does! This robust gamefish has been proclaimed, ". . . inch for inch, pound for pound, the gamest fish that swims."

A number of major advancements in smallmouth fishing have occurred in the last decade. Among these are the use of depth finders, and new back-trolling and deep-water fishing systems popularized by Ron and Al Lindner. However, smallmouth fishing is more than just plug or jig pitching and structure fishing. We now know that smallmouths use weed cover in certain lakes, and that predictable bass movements occur in some rivers. We've determined that smallmouths use timber as cover in some reservoirs, and in other reservoirs avoid such areas. We are aware that the predator/prey relationship affects not only the health of a smallmouth bass fishery, buy also fish location and how fish react in a particular body of water. We have also cracked their seasonal code—how smallmouths will most likely respond in spring, summer or fall. We definitely know that they react differently in lake, river, pit or reservoir environments.

Until now, no one has put together a book containing these new aspects of smallmouth bass fishing. All you have to do is sit back, read, enjoy, and above all else, learn.

x

Chapter 1
THE SMALLMOUTH BASS
FISH OF MYSTERY AND MAGIC

Of the six species of black bass, only two command widespread angling enthusiasm. The widely distributed largemouth, of course, is the fish of the masses—the most popular gamefish in North America. But the smallmouth epitomizes both beast and beauty in one dynamite package of mystery and might. Only the bronzeback, as it's often called, commands instant respect from each and every angler.

The smallmouth is a true all-American. Originally absent in other parts of the world, smallmouths may have first been identified in literature in 1664, when French settlers along the St. Lawrence River wrote of a fish called "Ouchigan"—the Algonquin Indian word for "ferocious." How simple, and how fitting!

The smallmouth has charisma, that certain something, which instantly endears. Perhaps Dr. J. A. Henshall said it all in the oft-repeated, 1881 description: ". . . inch for inch and pound for pound the gamest fish that swims." Powerful, robust, brutish, yet projecting dazzling grace and beauty in its consecutive head-shaking, gill-rattling leaps—the smallmouth fascinates anglers.

Minnesota Historical Society photo

These old-timers fishing in the Park Rapids area of Minnesota used to do a real number on the smallmouths. But catching and killing this many good-sized fish in any outing has to have a tremendous detrimental effect on a fish population. With the primitive equipment and methods available to these folks at this time, it just goes to show how vulnerable the smallmouth really is.

The smallmouth grows to impressive size, too. The present world record weighed 11 lbs. 15 oz., was 27 inches long, and had a girth of 21⅔ inches. It was caught in Dale Hollow Lake, on the Kentucky/Tennessee border in 1955. Most fish, however, run less than 3 pounds, and a 5-pounder is almost always considered a trophy. Its normal lifespan is 8-10 years, with 15 being about the maximum.

HOMEBODY AND COMPETITOR

Despite numerous attempts to transplant it, the smallie is still (with few exceptions) primarily found in the Great Lakes, and the lakes, rivers and reservoirs of the St. Lawrence, Upper Mississippi, Ohio and Tennessee drainage systems. This is pretty much its natural range. Today, by way of introduction, it is also found in parts of the Canadian Shield, in certain watersheds of the upper Northeast, and very select waters in the West.

Obviously, the smallmouth has a defined range. Even within this range, it does not enjoy widespread distribution. More than this, even in the waters it is •

found in, it is seldom what you'd term a *dominant* species. Because it is seldom the *primary* gamefish in any environment, understanding its lifestyle has a tremendous bearing on your angling approach.

Why a fish's range is limited, or why one species of fish becomes dominant or another secondary in an environment, can be difficult to understand. The complex interactions within various environments would overload even the best computer.

If we deal only with simple, observable information, it's easy to see why a fish like a lake trout is present in a body of water. Lake trout have very specific temperature and water quality demands. But that's not true for smallmouths, because they don't seem that specialized. In fact, you'd think they'd be more widespread.

Again, the factors involved are complex. Habitat is critical at all stages of the smallmouth's life. Available and appropriate food sources are also important at each life stage. Competition for food and living space plays a part. There is probably no single reason why smallmouths exist in such seemingly select, but widely varying, waters.

One thing is certain: The smallmouth is not just a fish of cool, clear, deep, rocky lakes and rivers. Certainly they exist—often thrive—in such waters; but many of these waters don't hold smallmouths, either. And many other smallmouth waters are far different from such cool, clean, deep environments.

Why, then, does the smallmouth bass do well in certain waters?

As we said, fish need certain conditions from birth to death. The entire life-to-death process is like a series of doors along the life path of a fish. First the doors must be there, and second, the fish must be able to move through them.

The first door could be spawning habitat; a second, rearing areas for young fish; and a third, living areas for adult fish. Available food, adequate water quality, fishing pressure and competing species all have a bearing on whether the doors ultimately open or not, or how far they open. This affects the smallmouth's ability to thrive.

Environmental Doors

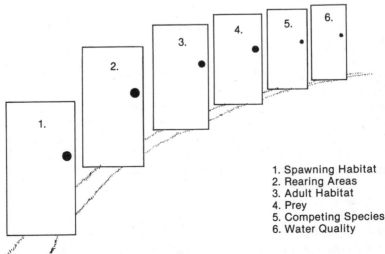

1. Spawning Habitat
2. Rearing Areas
3. Adult Habitat
4. Prey
5. Competing Species
6. Water Quality

For a body of water to support a strong, stable population of smallmouths, it must offer fish the opportunity to reproduce, find comfort (quality habitat, adequate water quality and temperature), and obtain sufficient food. But for the smallmouth, these conditions must be found within a fairly limited area.

Generally, smallmouths are *homebodies.* They seldom roam all over a lake or reservoir during the year the way a walleye or pike might. Instead, they remain in fairly limited areas. Thus, a good smallmouth area must provide all the fish's requirements within a short distance.

For example, if an area only has smallmouth spawning habitat, but doesn't offer food or comfort during the rest of the year, smallmouths probably won't be present—at least in any number. Likewise, plenty of food may be available in some distant lake section far removed from the smallmouth's usual home area. But smallmouths aren't likely to travel to those areas to utilize those food sources.

In short, smallmouths prefer to stay at home, providing "home" offers food, security, comfort and adequate spawning habitat. If these factors aren't available in some lake areas, there may be no smallmouths—or only a marginal population. Remember our "door" example. If the doors are wide open, the fish easily pass through life growing and thriving. But when the doors are squeezed partly shut, or shut tightly, few fish can progress to trophy size.

Time and time again, we also see competition playing a part in smallmouth success. Even in waters where suitable environmental conditions exist, smallmouth habitat may be occupied by competing species.

Indeed, the smallmouth's lifestyle often puts it at odds with other predators. Being something of both a cool- and warm-water fish, rather than strictly one or the other, the smallmouth must compete for living and reproduction sites with many other species of fish. At one time or the other during the season, adult smallmouths may have to lock horns with largemouths, spotted bass, walleyes, northern pike, muskies and lake trout. Newly-hatched or young-of-the-year smallmouths must also compete with these fish—and even panfish.

On a seasonal basis, throughout its entire life, the smallmouth almost always has other species to compete against. There are simply few waters that provide both optimum habitat and lack of competition at the same time.

In areas where transplanted smallmouths have fared well, most notably in states like Maine or in the wilderness lakes of the Canadian Shield, there are few competing predators. Many such lakes were lake trout waters with marginal largemouth bass, walleye, musky, or even northern pike populations. Environmentally, the habitat and water conditions in these pristine lakes isn't optimum for smallmouths. Adequate, yes, but optimum, no. But, relatively speaking, smallmouths thrive there without the *competition* present in most of their natural waters. So it is that the very bodies of water where smallmouths were not natural, have some of the best bass populations, and are the ones people identify as classic smallmouth waters today!

In one of our favorite Canadian lakes, smallmouths are the dominant, shallow-water fish. There are no incoming streams for walleye spawning, and main-lake walleye spawning grounds aren't present, either. Few marshes result in poor northern pike spawning. In addition, muskies were never introduced,

Early stocking efforts were rather primitive, but they got the job done. Often smallmouths were carried to lakes in milk cans. Usually, lakes along railway lines were planted first because it was convenient. The smaller photo shows Ontario's official bass stocking rail car in the 1920's. It initially stocked Lake of the Woods, an act that changed the face of angling in the Kenora region. Natural dispersion through rivers and streams spread the smallmouths and continues even today.

and there are almost no largemouth bass or sunfish. The two primary food sources are small perch and crayfish.

Obviously, this is rather a unique situation. Shallow, rocky lips and drop-off areas are adequate to support smallmouths, while the deep holes in this late-stage oligotrophic lake are home to lake trout, whitefish and ciscoes. The only competition is lake trout—a deep-water fish that's far removed from the smallmouths for much of the year.

Smallmouths introduced into such bodies of water quickly expand to fill the unused, shallow habitat. Unfortunately, there are few waters, or sections of larger bodies of water, where smallmouths can become the dominant gamefish. Thus they normally fill a supporting, rather than a leading role. Time and again they win the Oscar for best supporting actor, but seldom for the best performance in a leading role.

MOVEMENT

Earlier, we mentioned smallmouth home areas. Again, although there are exceptions, most smallmouth groups are based in distinct areas of bodies of water.

Smallmouths seldom do a lot of long-distance moving, although, of course, conditions often force smallmouths to move. In rivers, for example, smallmouths must move during low water conditions, and may move during flood conditions. There are also examples of fish following open-water forage in the Great Lakes and reservoirs. Typically, however, long distance movement to fulfill food, comfort and reproductive needs is *not* part of the smallmouth's lifestyle. Rather, it appears that if smallmouths must move on a continual basis, the smallmouth population suffers.

Tagging studies also offer circumstantial evidence that smallmouths are generally homebodies. Fish removed from a home range and released at distant points usually return to the home area. So, when you assess the smallmouth potential of a lake, or a portion of some large lake, river or reservoir, keep in mind that smallmouth bass are reluctant to roam. The smallmouth does best when everything it needs is in a small area within a body of water. If you think in terms of locating small, localized "families" of fish, rather than intermingling populations, you've got the concept.

In the final assessment, few environments offer conditions conducive to overwhelming smallmouth success. The smallmouth bass has a fairly wide range today, but isn't a predominant fish within that range. You'll find lakes, rivers or reservoirs with smallmouths present, but they're rarely the principal fish.

CATCH AND RELEASE

Like all freshwater bass, the smallmouth is a nest builder and protective spawner. This behavior is a sword that cuts two ways. In one regard, this trait helps protect the eggs and newly-hatched fry from predators like rock bass, perch, suckers and the like, because the male fish will drive off most intruders.

At the same time, it makes the smallmouth very vulnerable to angling during the spawning cycle. Once a male is removed from the nest, the eggs and fry have little chance of survival. As early as 1894, an International Anglers Com-

mission meeting in Niagara Falls, Ontario spoke of the rapid extinction of bass by angling overharvest during spawning times, and recommended a closed angling season until spawning was complete, and fish moved into different habitats.

A wealth of experience and research clearly shows that smallmouth bass are prime candidates for catch and release. Their tendency to use limited areas, coupled with extreme angling vulnerability during spawning, often allows unknowing anglers to overharvest them to a dangerous degree. It takes surprisingly few big fish "kills"—stringers of 3 to 5 pound bass killed for pictures or food—before the trophy potential of even the best smallmouth areas begins to nosedive.

We at IN-FISHERMAN have a loving respect for smallmouth bass. They

Early smallmouth bass anglers. Circa 1890.

either are, or are very near, everyone's favorite gamefish. Thus, throughout this book, we will constantly stress the necessity to treat them like the trophies they are, and not as "food" fish. You can catch and re-catch big smallmouths from the same areas for years, providing you return most of them, to keep the local population at a healthy level. Keep too many fish, however, and you're usually in for a sad lesson. So take photos of individual large fish, but please, leave your stringer at home.

This introduction should give you an excellent idea of what makes a smallmouth "tick." As you proceed through this book, you'll continually add new levels of knowledge to this foundation. By the time you're done, you'll be able to catch smallmouth bass anywhere in North America. Bet you can hardly wait!

Chapter 2

This is Your Life...
SMALLMOUTH
BASS

Despite its name, the smallmouth bass (*Micropterus dolomieui*) is not a true bass. It is a member of the sunfish family (*Centrarchidae*), along with the other species of black bass, as well as crappies, rock bass and the numerous sunfish. This classification will seem strange to the many anglers who regard black bass among the finest of all freshwater gamefish, and condemn the smaller species of the family as less glamorous.

Scientific classifications are not based on reputations and appearances, but on true relationship, as indicated by similarities in structure, habits and distribution. Smallmouths differ from other basses chiefly by the following characteristics: (1) There is no dark horizontal band along the side, (2) the upper jaw never extends beyond the eye, and (3) there are 13-15 soft rays on the back dorsal fin.

The smallmouth bass is a longer and thinner fish compared to most other members of the sunfish family, but is rather robust when compared to the

SMALLMOUTH BASS

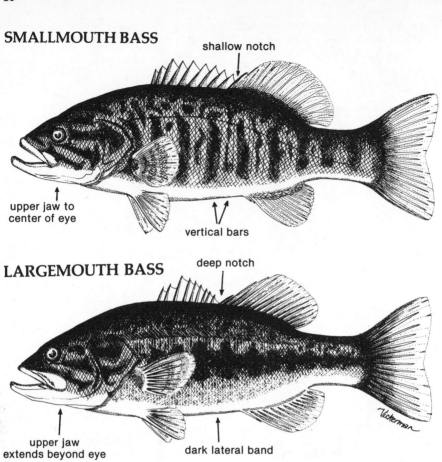

shallow notch

upper jaw to
center of eye

vertical bars

LARGEMOUTH BASS

deep notch

upper jaw
extends beyond eye

dark lateral band

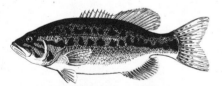

SPOTTED BASS

GUADALUPE BASS

SUWANEE BASS

REDEYE BASS

spotted bass. The adults are much heavier built than the young. The depth of body in the young is much less than the length of the head, and measures about 3.2 to 3.8 times the fish's length. Adult body depth is about equal to the head length, and is about one-third the length of the body. The body is about one-half as wide as it is deep.

The mouth is large, but not nearly so large as in the largemouth; the maxillary (upper jaw) extends at least to the center of the pupil, but does not extend behind the back of the eye as it does in all ages of largemouth bass except the very young. The eye is much larger (about one-fourth of the head length) in young specimens than in adults, where the eye is one-seventh as long as the head.

The small scales of a smallmouth number about 15-18 in a row across the cheek; the largemouth has only about 10 or 11. The outline of the erect dorsal fin is only slightly depressed in the center, rather than being cut so deeply as it is in the largemouth, where it almost divides the dorsal into two fins. The shortest (next to the last) dorsal spine is always more than half the length of the longest. The pectoral fins are short and rounded and have 16-18 rays; largemouths have 14-15 rays. Membranes of the soft dorsal and anal fins bear scales —sometimes difficult to see—near the base. These are absent in the largemouth.

Smallmouths are usually greenish-bronze in color on the sides and back, with a white belly. However, there are marked differences in the color of bass from varying waters. Individual fish living in the vicinity of a dark background are usually dark, while those in muddy or silty water are light with a yellowish tinge that is especially pronounced on the belly. The young have dusky spots on their sides which are more or less united to form dark, vertical bars, but they never show the dark, longitudinal streak that is characteristic of young largemouth bass and spotted bass.

Even when swimming, young smallmouths can be distinguished from other fish in the northern states by a characteristic pattern of the caudal fin, which is yellowish at the base, blackish in a distinct band across the middle of the fin, and whitish on the margin of each lobe. This pattern fades with increasing age, so that adults have a uniformly greenish-olive tail fin. Usually, the entire body color becomes uniform in adults, but under certain conditions the vertical blotches and other dark markings on the sides may show very distinctly in adults. Such contrasting colors become especially evident in spawning females, and in either males or females living in extremely clear water or kept in aquariums.

DISTRIBUTION

The native range of the smallmouth bass originally extended through the Ohio and Mississippi River drainages and the Great Lakes. As the accompanying map shows, smallmouths have been stocked in many waters, expanding the original native range.

Actually, the expansion of the smallmouth follows the history and growth of American railroads. Stories of wildcat stocking are plentiful.

In 1854, General William Schriver brought 12 fish from Wheeling, West Virginia over the mountains in a bucket aboard a locomotive tender. These fish

Smallmouth Bass Distribution

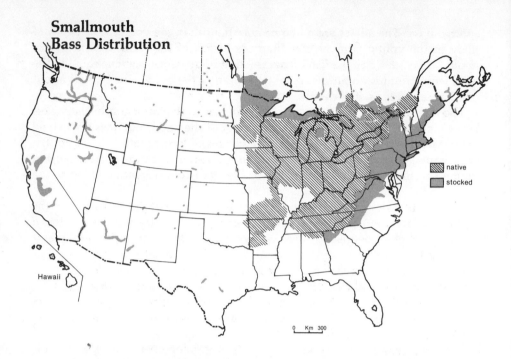

native
stocked

Hawaii

0 Km 300

were placed in the Chesapeake and Ohio Canal basin leading to the Potomac River at Cumberland, Maryland. In 1870, citizens of Pennsylvania stocked smallmouths from Harpers Ferry on the Potomac into the Delaware River.

Between 1857 and 1880, many smallmouths were stocked by state fisheries commissions in New York, Rhode Island, Pennsylvania, New Jersey, Connecticut, Massachusetts and Maine. In the western United States, several state fish commissioners sponsored the introduction of smallmouths into their waters. Prior to 1890, California, Kansas, Nevada and Wyoming had at least attempted introductions. Nebraska began planting smallmouths in 1898.

The United States Fish Commission began rearing smallmouths at its Neosho, Missouri; Wytheville, Virginia; and Washington, D.C. hatcheries in 1892. Only a few thousand were produced prior to 1895, and these all appear to have been stocked in eastern waters already containing smallmouths. Records of both the United States Fish Commission and state fish commissioners in the western United States indicate that smallmouths probably were not obtained from federal fish hatcheries until 1904. By 1916, however, nearly every state had received at least one shipment of smallmouth bass.

The range of the smallmouth in Canada has increased considerably since 1873, when the Federal Government introduced the first plantings of bass into unstated waters. However, very little stocking was done until after 1900, when a jurisdictional dispute over inland fisheries was decided in favor of the provinces.

Early plantings were done by cooks from logging camps who wanted easier access to fish for feeding hungry lumberjacks. These stocking efforts were unsophisticated by today's standards; fish were simply put into barrels and shipped by rail. On arrival, they were carried to various lakes in milk cans or even buckets.

One of the early extensions of the smallmouth's range occurred in the highlands of central Ontario, north of Toronto. Here, in 1901, fish were placed in the Lake of Bays, Fairy and Vernon Lakes, and the Opeongo chain of Algonquin Park. The stocking of Cache Lake followed in 1912.

After the decline of the early logging era, the tree-stripped landscape regenerated itself with smaller, short-life trees. Since these trees die quicker and are more easily felled by beavers and storms than the original hardwood trees, they provide cover that's easily utilized by smallmouth bass.

As the accompanying stocking records show, the smallmouth is a fighter and sportfish all around the world. Its ability to adjust to varying types of habitat is still expanding many fisheries.

Some of the First Plantings in U.S.

State	First Known Introduction	State	First Known Introduction
Alabama	1906	New Hampshire	1864-5
Arizona	1941	New Jersey	1866
California	1874	New Mexico	1913
Colorado	1912	New York	1825-42-71
Connecticut	pre-1842	North Carolina	1868-88
Delaware	about 1872	North Dakota	1905
Florida	1912	Oklahoma	1906
Georgia	1895	Oregon	1912
Idaho	1905	Pennsylvania	1870
Kansas	pre-1886	Rhode Island	1870
Louisiana	1915	South Carolina	1895
Maine	1866	South Dakota	1905
Maryland	1854	Texas	1916
Massachusetts	1850	Utah	1912
Mississippi	1907	Vermont	about 1870
Montana	1913	Virginia	early 1800's
Nebraska	1898	Washington	1904
Nevada	1888	Wyoming	1889

Origins and Status of Smallmouth Bass in Europe

Country	Year of Introduction First	Successful	Original Source	Self-sustaining Population	Regular Stocking Program
Austria	1884-90	None	Germany	No	No
Belgium	1885-90	1885-90	Germany	Limited	No
British Isles	1889	None	U.S.A.	No	No
Czechoslovakia	post 1884	None	Germany	No	No
Denmark	1958	None	Canada	No	No
Finland	1890	None	Canada	No	No
France	1869	None	U.S.A.	No	No
Germany	1883	None	U.S.A.	No	No
Hungary	1884-90	None	Germany	No	No
Italy	1884-90	None	Germany	No	No
Netherlands	1884-90	None	Germany	No	No
Norway	1887	None	Germany	No	No
Poland	1884-90	None	Germany	No	No
Sweden	1884-90	1958	Germany	Limited	No
Switzerland	1885-90	None	Germany	No	No

Origins and Status of Smallmouth Bass in Africa

Country/ Province	Year of Introduction First	Successful	Original Source	Natural- ized	Regular Stocking Program
Rhodesia	1940	Unknown	Cape Prov.	Doubtful	No
South Africa					
Cape Province	1937	1937	Maryland(U.S.A.)	Yes	900-1,500
Natal	1938	1938	Cape Prov.	Yes	No
Orange Free State	1945	None	Cape Prov.	No	No
Transvaal	1938	Yes	Cape Prov.	Yes	2,500-6,500
Swaziland	1938	None	Cape Prov.	No	No
Uganda	Unknown	None	Unknown	—	—
Mauritius	1949	Unknown	Cape Prov.	Doubtful	—

SMALLMOUTH BASS DIET—AN OVERVIEW

Just what does a smallmouth bass eat? In order to understand predator/prey relationships, we'll look at several typical food chains. This information will help you realize how various aquatic environments affect the smallmouth and its prey. In the end, a basic knowledge of the smallmouth's diet will help you catch more fish!

Beneath the surface of any lake, river or reservoir exists a relentless struggle of life and death—a survival of the fittest. This endless struggle is known as *predation*—the devouring of one living animal by another. To put it simply, all fish are predators. Big fish eat smaller fish, and so on, with the smallest fish eating a multitude of microscopic plants and animals called plankton. This entire sequence is called a food chain.

As you would expect, the smallmouth bass's food chain varies in different bodies of water, and even seasonally within the same body of water. Some food chains are short and simple, while others are long and complex. For example, in a reservoir, if smallmouth bass are feeding predominantly on shad, which feed on plankton, the food chain is short. However, in a lake where smallmouths are eating perch, which prey on minnows that eat invertebrates, and so on, the food chain is long and complex.

Many scientific studies have been conducted on the stomach contents of smallmouth bass. Some of these indicate that smallmouth bass consume numerous crayfish; thus, the logical conclusion is that smallmouths *prefer* crayfish to other types of prey. In reality, however, this is not necessarily true. Hard crayfish shells take a long time to dissolve in a fish's stomach. Crayfish may appear to be the most prevalent food item, even though the fish may be eating as many or more minnows.

The smallmouth bass is actually a middle-of-the-road feeder. Smallmouths are neither completely selective, nor are they indiscriminate about what they prey upon. They can be selective at times, yet will smack an easy target of nearly any description at other times.

Smallmouths are really opportunists. They can exhibit varying degrees of selectivity. A glance at the accompanying illustration showing typical smallmouth bass prey clearly shows the wide variety of food they dine on.

TYPICAL SMALLMOUTH PREY

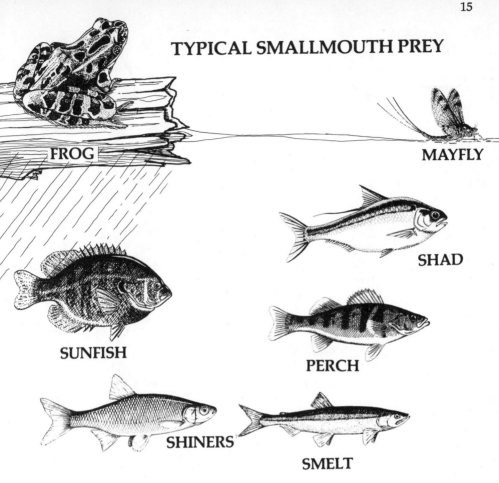

FROG

MAYFLY

SHAD

SUNFISH

PERCH

SHINERS

SMELT

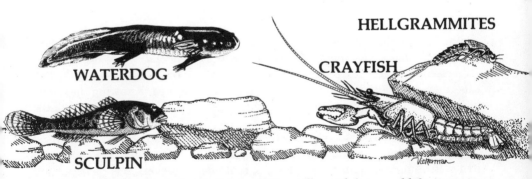

HELLGRAMMITES

WATERDOG

CRAYFISH

SCULPIN

Let's compare the basic food chains of (1) smallmouth bass and lake trout in a cold water lake, to (2) the food chain of smallmouth bass and walleyes in a cool water lake. As you may suspect, the smallmouth's food chain is interrelated with the food chains of the other predators.

The accompanying diagrams illustrate the essential members of the two, basic food chains. Note that the cool water lake contains a more complex food

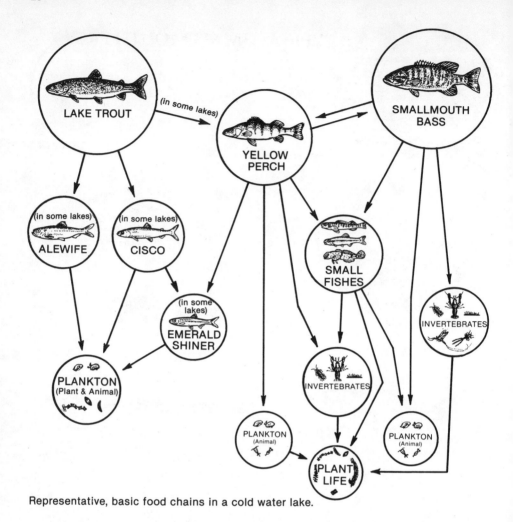

Representative, basic food chains in a cold water lake.

chain, in that the smallmouth bass and walleye may prey upon each other. Also, both share the same prey, so competition develops.

In essence, if you understand the dynamics of the food chain—what the fish eat—then a piece of the smallmouth puzzle can be solved. Knowing the habits of the smallmouth's prey, you can predict (to some extent) the behavior of the smallmouths.

Reservoirs and rivers each have their own distinct food chains. In a typical highland reservoir, shad, crayfish and panfish can be major seasonal prey items. In comparison, in a river, insects, sculpin and suckers may be important foods. It all depends on what the environment provides.

In the game of "who eats whom," here are a few helpful tips. Scientific studies have proven that predators (smallmouth bass for one) will attack a prey that is conspicuously different from other prey of the same kind. Therefore, an injured or crippled minnow will be eaten first. Remember this when using live bait and retrieving an artifical lure.

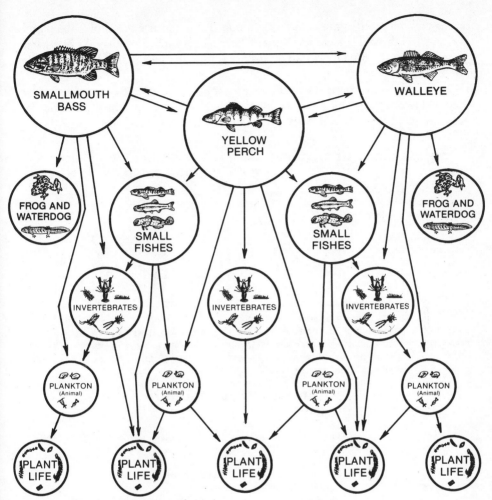

Representative, basic food chains in a cool water lake.

In any body of water, a smallmouth bass almost always has a *choice* of prey. If yesterday's prey is not available, the fish will eat something else. Smallmouths will not swim across the lake to find crayfish *if* another food source is locally available. Therefore, it is very important to locate the prime, multi-seasonal areas of a lake, river or reservoir with alternate prey available.

We stated earlier that smallmouths are usually not migratory fish. They'll use a limited area throughout the 10 calendar periods. Therefore, once you locate the prime areas, you'll have the fish nailed down all year long! Remember, catch and release—thank you!

Generally, there is a tendency for larger smallmouths to be attracted to larger prey—and smaller smallmouths to smaller prey. However, while adult smallmouth bass consume prey of different sizes, most anglers use smaller lures and baits. Certainly, these small presentations are effective and account for a majority of the smallmouths caught. However, don't neglect larger baits, too. At times, the big bait/big fish axiom is right-on! For instance, many monster smallmouths are caught each year in the tailrace areas of TVA dams using 4"-6" threadfin shad or skipjack herring for bait. Similarly, in northern natural lakes, 4"-6" shiners and chubs are topnotch bait for fall, trophy smallmouth bass.

Obviously, our example of the predator/prey relationship is greatly simplified. However, it should be obvious that a basic insight into what a smallmouth bass eats will help you catch and release more and bigger fish!

Average Lengths of Smallmouths vs. Age on Selected Waters

LOCATION	LENGTH (INCHES) AT END OF EACH YEAR							
	I	II	III	IV	V	VI	VII	VIII
Canadian Shield Lakes (Province of Ontario)	2.9	6.9	9.0	10.2	11.7	13.4	14.0	14.8
Lake Erie	1.7	4.0	7.7	9.1	11.1	12.2	13.4	14.5
Lake Cayuga, N.Y.	3.4	6.2	8.2	10.0	11.8	13.3	14.6	15.3
Grindstone Lake, Wis.	2.4	5.7	8.8	11.4	13.4	14.8	15.9	16.9
Mashapaug Lake, Conn.	4.1	7.2	9.6	11.5	13.1	14.6	15.9	16.9
Green Lake, Minn.	3.9	7.3	10.0	12.2	18.2	20.5	—	—
Acquackanonk Lake, N.J.	2.6	6.4	10.4	13.2	17.4	18.8	19.6	20.4
Norris Lake, Tenn.	3.1	8.9	13.3	15.8	17.4	18.0	18.6	20.9

Factors affecting growth of smallmouth bass are the length of growing season, water temperature, abundance of food in relation to population density, and absence or presence of pollutants. Since water temperatures may be favorable only five months out of the year in Canadian Shield lakes, adult smallmouth bass (four years or older) tend to grow at a slower rate than in other bodies of water.

Approximate Weight by Length

LENGTH	WEIGHT
12"	1¼ lbs.
14"	1¾ lbs.
16"	2½ lbs.
18"	3¾ lbs.
20"	5 lbs.

Note: These are only average estimates.

Male and female smallmouth bass grow at a similar rate. As with most fish, weight increases approximately to the cube of the length. Generally, maturity begins at ages 2-4 for males and 3-5 for females. The maximum age attained by the species is probably about 15 years.

Smallmouths in the Tennessee River impoundments grow approximately twice as fast as bass of the Great Lakes area. In Tennessee River impoundments, fish mature at 1-2 years of age and can weigh up to 6 pounds in 6 years!

TEMPERATURE PREFERENCE

Most bass anglers probably visualize smallmouths *preferring* relatively cool water temperatures (65°F-75°F), rocky-bottomed home areas, and crayfish for food. Yes, these are classic smallmouth patterns. However, this lifestyle is not always one of preference, but is often one of *necessity*!

As we said, smallmouths are often forced to compete with other predators. Smallies must frequently inhabit areas which other species, such as largemouths or walleyes, don't dominate. When other fish species stake their claim to prime spots, smallmouths often must make due with what's left—even if they're only second rate areas.

In many cases, competing predators force smallmouths out of warmer, food-rich, shallow areas, and they must take up residence in cooler, deeper water. Thus their use of such areas is not always by choice. Given a lack of competing predators, many smallies might prefer to remain in shallower water.

The "Circle of Errors" sequence on the following page demonstrates a classic case of misconception reinforcing misconception—a snowball effect. Once the snowball starts rolling downhill, it picks up speed and momentum. In this case, observations, quotes and re-quotes have perpetuated the cool water temperature myth.

The point of all this is, yes, smallmouths often inhabit cool (65°F-75°) water, *but,* given the opportunity, they can often function extremely well in warmer water! Thus, you can't always assume that they live only in deep, rocky areas. It's a logical starting point, but if you're fishin' and not catchin,' keep an open mind. Be prepared to fish other kinds of areas, even though they don't appear to be "classic" smallmouth areas. Some "oddball" areas may be more "classic" than you think!

CONCLUSION

In a nutshell, smallmouth bass have certain basic characteristics and requirements wherever they live. However, available habitat, food sources, competing predators, etc., all affect the way smallmouths live in that environment. As an "in between" species, smallies adapt as best they can.

Armed with this background knowledge, we'll move on to examine how Calendar Periods and different body of water types affect smallmouth bass behavior. It's a fascinating study of how living creatures adapt to their environment. More importantly, understanding these subtleties of nature will help you catch more fish!

A CIRCLE OF ERRORS!

Temperature myths have been maintained by the interaction of outdoor writers and writers of fisheries journals. In the early days of fisheries management, only a few biologists were on a typical agency staff. Fisheries science was in its infancy, and semi-professional fisheries workers routinely referenced popular fishing literature to fill in existing knowledge gaps. As a result, wildlife agencies often repeated in departmental brochures the temperature myths found in fishing magazines. These were, in turn, cited by angling writers, and a circle of errors was created.

Even today, fisheries biologists and outdoor writers who have not specifically reviewed the extensive scientific literature on temperature requirements and preferences of fish continue to perpetuate myths.

In the late 1940's and early 1950's, a major series of studies was made at Norris Reservoir, Tennessee. In that lake, largemouth, smallmouth and spotted bass competed for food and space. As usual, the largemouths won. In the summer season, largemouths dominated surface waters that exceeded 80°F. The adult smallmouths and spotted bass were predominantly found in the 65°F-78°F range.

However, subsequent lab tests have shown that these two species also prefer 80°F+ water. It may be, therefore, that these smaller-mouthed species were forced into the cooler areas by competition.

Nevertheless, smallmouths were taken from water of the same temperature as that reported in northern lakes, and this has reinforced the impression that smallmouths, and their cousin, the spotted bass, actually "prefer" cooler temperatures. Ironically, outdoor writers failed to emphasize that large-mouths in Norris Reservoir selected 80°F-86°F water. The Norris

studies were used to incorrectly assign a 68°F-74°F "preference" to smallmouths and spots, but were not used to correctly identify the preference of largemouths for 80°F+ water.

Much of the early research into bass habitat preferences was done in the North and Northeast. The black bass habitats in many of the lakes studied seldom warmed to the optimum range (78°F-86°F) for most northern bass strains, and the bass were often found in 65°F-78°F water—*the warmest water available.*

Moreover, in deep, clear, nutrition-poor lakes, bass populations are often forced to disperse into deeper and cooler water in order to find sufficient food. Thus, some studies have strengthened the idea that bass "prefer" temperatures in the lower 70°F's, because bass are often found in cool water in such lakes.

Why Temperature Myths Exist

Simple Answers?

Laymen, and even scientists at times, tend to seek simple solutions to complex problems. Sometimes investigators seek a single factor that "controls" bass and other fish, so that behavior can be consistently predicted. Too many times, this seems to have prevented a full consideration of other factors that influence bass to use waters with less-than-optimum temperatures.

The Norris studies provide an example. One researcher, J.S. Dendy, published the correct temperature ranges for the three bass species in a *Guide to Norris Lake Anglers*. But other researchers and many angling writers made the assumption that the Norris Lake conditions were universal. That's not so.

There are reservoirs similar to Norris in habitat, temperature profile, and species mix. In these waters, the three black bass species often echo the habitat selections seen at Norris. Thus, the assumptions made about temperature "preferences" based upon the Norris studies were occasionally reinforced elsewhere.

Of course, there are exceptions to the Norris pattern that give a better indication of the real temperature preference range of smallmouths and spotted bass. Observed in isolation from competitive largemouths and other predators, they appear to occupy the same 80°F+ temperature range selected in laboratory preference tests. Moreover, when competition is limited, these bass also often occupy the weedy, food-rich shallows that largemouths traditionally dominate in mixed bass populations. The cooler water/rocky habitat/crawfish food base is the alleged "preference" of smallmouth and spots, but may be a forced adaptation rather than a positive selection.

Chapter 3

Introduction to the CALENDAR PERIODS

The *IN-FISHERMAN* Calendar Periods divide the year into cycles of fish response. There are no such things as weeks or months—only seasonal periods. Depending on weather, periods which might last a few days one year could run a month the next. Since our Calendar Periods depend upon climate and water conditions from year-to-year, they are elastic in duration. Calendar Periods do not last a fixed number of days, nor do they occur on given dates each year.

In one region of the continent, a period (for example, the Spawn Period) might arrive months earlier than in another part of North America. And in areas of northern Canada, a Calendar Period like Summer might last a brief five weeks—while farther south in Tennessee it might be three or more months in duration. In fact, the timing of Calendar Periods is entirely different for the huge Great Lakes in comparison to Canadian lakes, or to typical U.S.

smallmouth rivers, even though they lie in the same region.

Further, some of our Calendar Periods relate primarily to the smallmouth's biological demands, such as Pre-spawn, Spawn and Post-spawn. Others, like the various summer and fall periods, relate more to water temperature and the environment. We have even divided the Cold Water Period into two separate phases to better describe the smallmouth's response to cold water. The subtleties will become more apparent as we discuss each Calendar Period in detail.

The Calendar Periods are not, as some think, simply the seasonal conditions of a body of water. A lake, river or reservoir may be in a seasonal time frame (spring, summer, fall or winter), but the smallmouth bass's response to that environment determines the Calendar Period. Different species of fish, as well as the different sizes of smallmouth bass in any given body of water, can be in different Calendar Periods at the same time.

There is another fine point you must understand to view the Calendar Periods in their proper perspective. You might assume that the "best" time to fish would be during a Calendar Period when the water temperature is at an optimum for the smallmouth's metabolism, causing it to feed the most. But it doesn't always work that way.

An adverse water temperature does not always mean fish are hard to catch. The available food supply, timing of feeding movements, overall population levels and competition, as well as the differing response by different sizes of smallmouths, all play an important role in angling success. These are the factors we took into account when the Calendar Periods were developed.

Once you learn to "read the signs," you'll have little difficulty identifying one period from another, and discerning when different species are in different Calendar Periods. The difference between the unsuccessful angler and the truly successful one often boils down to two things: recognizing (1) the seasonal movements and (2) probable response patterns of smallmouth bass.

DAILY FISH BEHAVIOR

Spring, summer, winter and fall are events common only to the temperate world. The tropics, on the other hand, display alternating cycles of rain and wind that signal to the various life forms that the earth's angle to the sun is changing. In the inhospitable polar world, spring, summer and fall are but a brief pause in an otherwise harsh, constant gloom and cold. Only the middle (temperate) zones experience the four separate and distinct seasons. Here the pendulum swings noticeably enough between periods of darkness and brightness that we can easily recognize definable patterns emerging within nature.

Beyond seasonal differences, there are many factors that affect fish activity on a daily basis. Weather is obviously a key factor. We also know that light (or length of daylight) plays a major role in the day-to-day feeding, movement and activities of smallmouths and other fish. Light seasonally controls or regulates migrations, and plays an important part in the spawning process.

A fish's movements, actions and attitudes are not arbitrary. There are valid reasons for each and every activity. The most obvious of the myriad forces that control the aquatic world is the intensity and duration of light. This is related to the earth's yearly orbit around the sun.

On land, the many seasonal changes are quite evident, but underwater it's difficult to see nature's forces at work. Consequently, aquatic seasonal cycles are a mystery and very confusing to some people. But it is in this mysterious and constantly changing environment that fish live. Thus, you must be in touch with the aquatic environment to catch smallmouths with any consistency.

IDENTIFYING PATTERNS

A vast number of good technical fishermen have mastered a variety of presentations, but still fail to understand how the predator/prey link relates to the Calendar Periods. So, they run into recurrent problems at various times of the year. Our experience shows that understanding baitfish movements, and patterns of other forms of prey, is another key to successful angling. Different lake conditions not only dictate different lure presentations and techniques, but gamefish demonstrate marked preferences for certain kinds of lures and baits throughout the various Calendar Periods.

In the final analysis, the only way to understand how the different Calendar Periods function on your particular body of water, or any other for that matter, is to spend enough time there to begin identifying these patterns. Comparing notes with other anglers will help you get a grasp of the Calendar Periods. Keeping a daily log of weather and water conditions, as well as fish feeding patterns, also helps considerably.

A review of last year's fishing log during a cold winter night often provides not only a glimmer of past fishing glories, but also an insight into seasonal fishing patterns you never noticed before. In this way, you can learn the seasonal circumstances that trigger fish response, and the locational patterns that result from them.

As we cover the Calendar Periods, we'll include clues on smallmouth bass behavior and activity. The activity mood levels are broken into three basic groups: negative, neutral and positive. These are defined as appetite moods, and are further described in our glossary.

Head-shaking, gill-rattling leaps are a smallmouth trademark!

THE TEN CALENDAR PERIODS

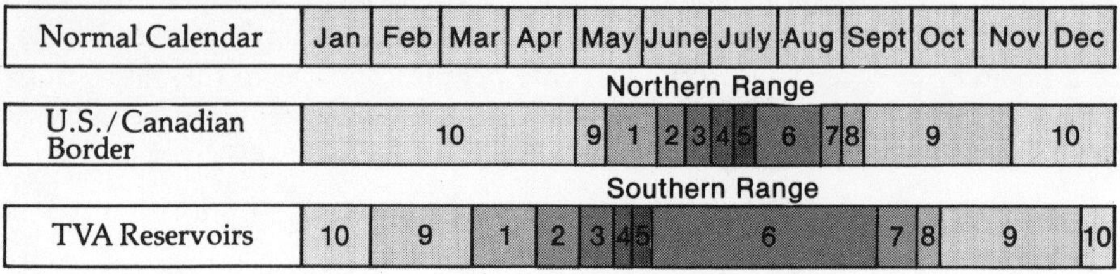

Normal Calendar	Jan	Feb	Mar	Apr	May	June	July	Aug	Sept	Oct	Nov	Dec
						Northern Range						
U.S./Canadian Border	10				9 1	2 3 4 5	6	7 8	9		10	
						Southern Range						
TVA Reservoirs	10	9	1	2	3 4 5	6		7 8	9			10

1. Pre-spawn
2. Spawn
3. Post-spawn
4. Pre-summer
5. Summer Peak

6. Summer
7. Post-summer
8. Fall Turnover
9. Cold Water
10. Frozen Water*

*Ice cover is actually a phase of cold water, but is used to differentiate conditions.

These are typical Calendar Periods in a "normal" year. Unusually warm or cool weather can obviously increase or decrease the overall length of the periods. The periods are somewhat elastic; they're not carved in stone. The key concept is how the timing of the Calendar Periods varies for the different areas of the country.

The TVA reservoirs of the South have a long growing season due to the overall warm climate. As you would expect, the Cold Water and Frozen Water Periods (coldest water) are very short in duration. In contrast, the lakes along the U.S./Canadian border typically have very long Cold Water and Frozen Water Periods. Here, the spring and summer growing seasons are squeezed into a couple of short months. Smallmouths might be spawning in Tennessee just as the ice is "going out" in Minnesota.

Obviously, lakes located between these areas experience Calendar Periods that lie somewhere in between these two extreme examples. Using the information presented in this book, you should be able to create a smallmouth bass Calendar for your locality.

Chapter 4

THE CALENDAR PERIODS

THE COLD WATER PERIOD (SPRING)

A Time of Preparation

Generalized Environmental Conditions
Surface Water Temperature Range: Mid 30°F's to Mid 40°F's
General Fish Mood: Neutral to Positive

The Spring Cold Water Period is characterized as a time of preparation—a prelude to the annual spawning ritual. The aquatic environment goes through numerous alterations during this period. Some lakes have been ice-bound for months. Now the ice slowly begins to melt, and eventually the lakes become ice free. The increasing amount of daylight intensifies the warming effect of the sun. As the water warms, the spawning progression of the various fish species takes place. The smallmouth bass (as do all fish) responds to these changes.

The Spring Cold Water Period can be subdivided into two temperature-related phases—the Early Cold Water Period and the Late Cold Water Period.

The fish's location and attitude are different in each; there are subtle, but important changes taking place.

During this period, the water temperature and length of daylight appear to be two of the key factors affecting smallmouth (and other species) behavior. In addition, hormone levels may trigger the initial spawning urges as the eggs and milt continue to develop in the fish.

In natural lakes, the Early Spring Cold Water phase is characterized by the approximate water temperature range from the low 30°F's to the low 40°F's. Initially, smallmouth bass are located in harder bottom, sharp-breaking, deep water wintering areas. They'll relate to the base areas of various structural elements. Pay careful attention to the deep areas where the transition from harder to softer bottom occurs. For example, any bottom content transition from (1) rock to gravel or clay, (2) rock to muck, or (3) clay to muck all qualify as potential fish concentration areas. Odds are the fish are lying right on the edge, inactive but still catchable. The best choices for this condition are a live bait rig or a jig, because both give you precise depth control and can be worked ultra-slow.

In a typical highland reservoir situation, smallmouths will be located in or near a deep water channel wintering area. The prime wintering areas are in the vicinity of both a spawning and a summer habitat area. At this time, most fish movement will be of an unpredictable, short duration, normally toward the deep, sharp drop-off features of the bottom near the river channel.

Various fish and crayfish are the major food items at this time. Fish can be caught on jigs, spoons, tail spinners and live bait—all fished slowly.

The Late Spring Cold Water phase begins as the water temperature rises into the mid 40°F's, and a locational change begins to take place. Smallmouths continue to remain in deep water; however, they'll move closer toward the shallows; not shallower, but *toward* the shallows. At this stage, smallmouths begin to vacate the wintering/Early Cold Water home area and move closer to the shoreline spawning areas. Fish might be found in 20-40 feet of water; however, they could be a bit more aggressive than they were earlier.

Smallmouth bass display a marked tendency to move up the edges of bar formations, rather than right over the top of them, as they filter toward shallow spawning areas. Interestingly, there appears to be a natural tendency for hard bottom to be found at the inside corners of shoreline projections.

A live bait rig or jig are still good choices for locating and catching these fish. Since cold water fish concentrations can be massive, quite a few nice fish can be caught by casting. During periods of warm weather when the water temperature increases, the fish's mood can be positive, and they will feed actively.

In a highland reservoir, numbers of smallmouths begin moving toward the bay and cove spawning areas. This activity can be stimulated by an early spring rain and warming trend, plus other factors. The rain increases water temperature and puts a little color into the water, which may help trigger smallmouths to move shallower.

Smallmouths will use well-defined, shallower protruding points, bars and humps. The bottom content of these structures can be rock, gravel, rubble, or clay; when present, wood (fallen timber or logs) can be a prime smallmouth attractor—especially for big fish! Many times, the smallmouths will concentrate at various depth levels on the inside turn of the upstream, sharper-breaking portion of the bar. Here, under ideal conditions the fish can make short, vertical movements into the shallows, and yet have access to deeper water when weather conditions push them out.

In addition, some fish may move to the mouths of the shoreline coves where the warmer, feeder creek water may accelerate the entire pre-spawn process. Usually, the larger creek arms provide the optimum habitat areas. Small crankbaits, jigs, spinnerbaits and live bait presentations are effective on these fish.

As the actual Pre-spawn Period approaches, most smallmouths will have moved from the deeper water area into a pre-spawn staging area. The fish will be in deeper water adjacent to spawning areas like bays, coves, bars, etc. This sets the stage for smallmouths to begin actual, pre-spawn activity.

The Cold Water Period is a time of preparation, and smallmouth bass undergo locational and physiological changes as a prelude to the Pre-spawn Period.

THE PRE-SPAWN PERIOD
A Time of Anticipation
Generalized Environmental Conditions
Surface Water Temperature Range: 46°F to 55°F
General Fish Mood: Neutral to Positive

The smallmouth bass Pre-spawn Period can be subdivided into three separate phases. These phases are not etched in stone, but are approximate temperature levels for spawning-related activities. The Pre-spawn Period is composed of:

1) Early Pre-spawn—46°F-47°F
2) Mid-Pre-spawn—48°F-52°F
3) Late Pre-spawn—53°F-55°F

Each phase is temperature dependent, and the smallmouth's location and behavior is different in each. Let's take a closer look.

The Early Pre-spawn phase is a transition stage for smallmouth bass. The fish begin to vacate their deep water staging areas and start filtering up into the shallows. A spell of warm, stable weather with bright skies will cause some fish to move up from the depths to begin cruising shallow water. The purpose of these initial movements may be to seek potential spawning sites, search for prey (crayfish are spawning in the shallows at this time), or simply be activity stimulated by the warmth of the sun. While the fish are not chiefly interested in prey during the staging process, they will feed actively, especially during a warming trend. Male and female fish are both catchable at this time.

As the water temperature nudges up to 50°F, smallmouths are generally in a full-fledged, mid pre-spawn movement. The bulk of the fish should be in the shallows. Rocks, reeds, docks, fallen trees or other cover may all draw fish. Male and female fish are shallow; they're feeding, moving, scouting, and very aggressive. Prime areas that concentrate fish will be well protected from excessive wave action and usually have a harder bottom content such as sand, gravel, broken rock or rubble. However, smallmouths will use other bottom types depending on habitat availability.

One essential feature appears to be the protected area! Interestingly, studies have hinted that smallmouths will seek the *most* protected waters. For example, the back portion of a shallow bay may be used for spawning. Here, the water will warm rapidly, even though many times only second-rate bottom content is available. To all appearances, this area seems similar to largemouth bass spawning territory.

In some protected bays, reeds can be a major fish attractor. It all depends on what options are available to the fish. Once the preferred areas are determined, you can locate similar spots on the lake. Remember, the fish didn't read the book; they're only reacting to the environment. If the fish aren't using the prime territory, try searching for a secondary area.

At this time, reservoir smallmouths typically begin moving closer and closer to the actual spawning areas. For example, some fish may move to the back of a cove, while others may move up onto the flat sections of a protruding bar or point. Additionally, some fish may seek out small, shallow shoreline pockets. While some fish will spawn on rocky areas, the preferred bottom content appears to be sand, gravel, or clay—usually on bars and points in the coves. Deep, submerged willows with hard bottom can also be excellent smallmouth areas.

While a warmer water creek can speed up the pre-spawn/spawning process by raising the temperature, too much rain can present water level and siltation problems if flood conditions exist. Stable conditions are far more conducive to good pre-spawn fishing.

Since large numbers of big smallmouth bass are available and easy to catch at this time, catch and release practices should be observed. Scientific studies have indicated that unexploited fish populations are fragile, so take a few to eat, and release the rest.

The Late Pre-spawn phase is characterized by a significant change in the smallmouth's behavior. Early in the phase, fish are normally active and spend a majority of their time in the vicinity of the spawning area. Later, as the water warms steadily into the mid-50°F's, the aggressive behavior wanes. The fish begin to exhibit spawning behavior and become uninterested in feeding.

Late in this phase a segregation of the sexes appears to occur, too. The male fish scatter, and actively seek spawning sites in the preferred areas. Many times the male fish sweep out a nest near a prominent bottom feature like a large rock, dock piling, fallen tree or a large concrete boat mooring.

Water clarity is a factor that is vital to locating the males at this time. Smallmouths tend to build nests at a precise depth level, particularly on dark or stained lakes. The particular depth this occurs depends largely on the water color and the resulting sunlight penetration. The sun provides the necessary warmth to incubate the eggs. Scientific studies have reported that smallmouths will nest in water from 18 inches to 20 feet deep! However, bass nests are usually found in 2-5 feet of water, near cover, on a gravel or rubble bottom. Remember, whatever the depth, a vast majority of the nests are often built at the same level.

Late pre-spawn female fish, meanwhile, are noticeably absent from the extreme shallows. So where did they go? After the initial mid pre-spawn activity, the females appear to vacate the extreme shallows and drop back a little deeper. They may relate to small rocky fingers or other bottom cover and wait for their eggs to ripen, and for the males to build the nests. Later, when they're ready to spawn, the females will move back into the extreme shallows. This is *not* a major locational change; however, the females are deeper than the males, and are still in the direct proximity of the nesting area.

THE SPAWN PERIOD
A Time of Tension
Generalized Environmental Conditions
Surface Water Temperature Range: 56°F to 65°F
General Fish Mood: Negative

This is a brief and variable period usually lasting from one to three days for the female smallmouth and a little bit longer for the male. The Spawn Period includes the peak spawning temperature range for smallmouth bass (approximately 56°F-64°F). The fish may begin spawning at temperatures as low as 55°F, and have been recorded spawning up to temperatures in the low 70°F's. However, most eggs will be deposited between 61°F-65°F. Water temperature is not the only factor inducing spawning, as other environmental conditions such as weather, degree of light intensity and moon phase all appear to have an effect.

While a fish that has not spawned is still technically in the Pre-spawn Period, in reality, the closer the fish comes to actually spawning, the less likely it is to strike a bait or exhibit other pre-spawn traits. Feeding activity during actual spawning is practically nonexistent. However, cantankerous ripe males will make reflex strikes at baits, lures or other intruders in the nesting area, but not during the actual spawn. Yes, it is a notoriously poor time for smallmouth fishing.

While actual spawning is taking place in one area, there can be aggregations of smallmouths waiting to spawn in different areas, and groups which have completed the spawning ritual in still others. The Spawn Period must therefore be considered a local activity. On most bodies of water, the great majority of the smallmouth bass population will usually spawn within a two-week period. In huge bodies of water like giant reservoirs or the Great Lakes, however, it can last from two to four weeks.

In a highland reservoir, the majority of the smallmouths spawn in coves, on bars or in shallow shoreline pockets with the proper bottom content. The warmer cove areas may see the first spawning activity, while cooler main lake areas will be last. All fish do not spawn at the same time, especially on these huge, complex bodies of water! Angler observations indicate that the largest female fish seem to spawn earliest, and they spawn in the prime areas.

The actual length of the spawn depends on environmental conditions. In essence, stable conditions optimize spawning success. On the other hand, studies indicate that nesting stops if the water temperature drops below 60°F.

So, unstable weather with accompanying cool winds can have an adverse effect on the fish. However, a second spawning can occur when the conditions stabilize, which could extend the Spawn Period for a month or more.

Just prior to spawning, the females filter into the extreme shallows. They are very spooky and usually move up at night. Under normal conditions, the height of the spawning activity appears to occur in early afternoon. In fact, still, calm, sunny days seem to be the most advantageous mating time.

In preparation for the actual spawn, the male chooses a ripe female and lures or forces her onto the nest. The male and female swim about the nest, and eventually come to rest on the bottom with their vents nearly touching. As the eggs are released from the female, they are fertilized by the male. While reports vary, the average number of eggs range from 2,000 to 20,000, depending on the size of the female. The eggs are adhesive and attach to the stones in the nest.

The actual spawning act takes about 2 hours. However, spawning usually requires several days and is resumed as more eggs and milt ripen in the fish. Most females will deposit their eggs in 24-48 hours under stable conditions. The female leaves the nest after spawning, but may spawn again with another male. The male guards the nest and gently fans the eggs. Sometimes, the male may spawn again with another female.

As the Spawn Period draws to a close, we find the males aggressively guarding the nest and the females filtering away from the nesting area. All in all, this period is a time of tension—a period when smallmouths are subjected to a great deal of stress.

THE POST-SPAWN PERIOD

A Time of Recuperation

Generalized Environmental Conditions
Surface Water Temperature Range: 65°F+
General Fish Mood: Negative to Neutral

Any characterization of the Post-spawn Period in specific terms is misleading. It is a complex period with numerous variables, and is difficult to explain in simple, absolute terms. The Post-spawn Period remains a somewhat mysterious period, largely because of the lack of concentrated smallmouths (especially female fish) and our limited knowledge of exactly what they are doing.

For example, we can generalize that the water temperature will usually be in the mid 60°F's (65°F+), but water temperature is not the only factor influencing this period. Since it is a recuperation period, time is also of the essence. Logically, the time required for an individual smallmouth, and ultimately the entire population, to recover from this "time of tension" can vary. So, it is vitally important to keep both time and temperature in mind when considering the Post-spawn Period. Depending on the body of water and local weather patterns, it may require 2-4 weeks for the fish to recuperate from the rigors of spawning.

The behavior of male and female smallmouth bass is vastly different during this period. Studies show that, after spawning, the male aggressively guards the nest against predation. In addition, the male may fan the nest to provide oxygen, remove wastes and prevent siltation. The usual developmental period required for the eggs to hatch ranges from approximately 2-10 days, depending on water temperature. Patiently, the male remains on guard until the black fry disperse from the nest—often a period of a month or more.

During this entire time frame, the male is extremely vulnerable to fishing pressure. Once you locate a spawning area, it's like fishing-in-a-barrel for these aggressive, protective males. However, do not remove the fish, or better yet, do not fish at this time. Removal of the male bass from the nest simply allows the eggs or fry to be eaten by other predators. Obviously, this type of nest destruction can be prevented. Various scientific studies indicate that the presence of the male bass is necessary for successful hatches—so leave them to their parental chores!

Where are the big females? Good question, and a tough one to answer! Apparently, after a female deposits all of her eggs, she filters out of the extreme shallows into deeper water areas to rest. Remember, the smallmouth is a homebody, and consequently these deeper water haunts will be adjacent to the spawning area. Early in the period, the fish will be scattered; later, the fish will begin grouping.

While big, post-spawn females usually have terminal "lockjaw," a few are occasionally caught. During this time, some females may seek deep water, others may opt to relate to weed/rock areas, and still others may choose heavy cover such as timber, logs or boulders.

Just as there is a pre-spawn assembly of smallmouths, there is also a post-spawn dispersal. How rapidly this occurs depends on a number of factors. Experience shows that a body of water's physical make-up affects smallmouth dispersal patterns. In lakes, rivers and reservoirs, the smallmouths have different options available to them, and will react differently in each.

Logs, brush and timber are prime cover for post-spawn female smallmouths in some waters.

After spawning, female reservoir smallmouths vacate the immediate spawning area and relocate adjacent to it. For example, a female smallmouth may move to the deeper water area near the mouth of a cove, drop into deeper water near the bar or point she spawned on, or simply seek out a shallow rock/wood area to rest. The male fish will remain on the nest until the fry disperse, and then move into a summer habitat area.

Forage can also influence post-spawn smallmouth behavior. At some point during the recuperation process, the fish's basic needs return to normal. The fish become interested in food and comfort. If there is forage on or near a spawning area, some smallmouths have the option to feed on targets of opportunity.

As the surface water temperature in the spawning area reaches the upper 60°F's, it often triggers the resumption of active feeding. This signals the end of the Post-spawn Period. Basically, this period is a time of recuperation when the fish's hormone levels change. The smallmouth's biological emphasis switches from reproduction to satisfying basic needs.

THE PRE-SUMMER PERIOD
A Time of Transition

Generalized Environmental Conditions
Surface Water Temperature Range: Upper 60°F's to 70°F's
General Fish Mood: Neutral to Positive

While the Post-spawn Period is characterized as a resting stage when fish scatter and feed only sporadically, a change in behavior is imminent. The smallmouths' bodies require nourishment, and the resumption of regular feeding activities indicates the beginning of a new pattern we call the Pre-summer Period. This period can be one of the fish's prime growth times of the entire year. During this and the Summer Peak Period which follows, the bass can grow the most in length, though not necessarily in weight.

The abundance and type of forage available has a direct correlation to the fish's growth. Other factors affecting growth of smallmouth bass are genetics, sex, length of growing season, water temperature, population density and pollutants. In general, growth rates of smallmouth bass are comparable in waters of the same latitude.

During the Post-spawn recuperation period, smallmouths change from being primarily preoccupied with the reproduction ritual (and its various aftereffects) to becoming primarily interested in satisfying their everyday needs of food and comfort. While no absolute temperature level indicates when the fish enter the Pre-summer stage, the surface waters will have warmed to a point where the smallmouths' metabolism demands more food to sustain their energy levels. When the surface water temperature reaches 70°F, you can assume that the smallmouths are "back on the bite."

Pre-summer is a time of emerging weedgrowth and a developing food chain. Generally, surface water temperatures vary less from section to section of a lake compared to the earlier spring periods. Rivers and streams usually exhibit more constant temperature levels, although certain sections of lakes and reservoirs can be warmer than others.

Prior to this and depending upon the area of the lake, different groups of smallmouths could have been in a pre-spawn, spawn or post-spawn attitude within the same broad time frame. But during the Pre-summer Period, most of the smallmouth bass population will have completed the spawning ritual and the after-effects phase. Inclement weather and the resulting temperature instability, however, may cause some stragglers to still be in a spawning attitude. In addition, Great Lakes fish may likewise experience a time variation due to the huge, cool water environment. Basically, however, the majority of the fish begin displaying the same feeding attitudes.

Female fish which returned to deeper water areas during the post-spawn dispersal will begin to feed more regularly. Depending on the available habitat, some males may filter onto the flats, while still others may temporarily remain in the shallows. The fish are scattered, but a movement from shallow to deeper water is evident.

Pre-summer is characterized by a variety of fishing patterns. You may catch several smallmouths by rigging live bait in deep water, a couple more fish crankbaiting the mid-depth flats, and you may even find a few fish in extremely shallow water.

In general, then, there is a locational transition from the spawning area to the smallmouth's summer territory—generally a movement from shallower to deeper water. In Pre-summer a body of water itself offers the most siginificant clues to smallmouth behavior. Pre-summer is a time when fish are difficult to pinpoint.

Slowly, as the surface water temperature continues climbing upwards, smallmouths move into the habitat area they will occupy for the next Calendar Period. In addition, there is a gradual tendency for smallmouths to start keying in on more specific food sources. Smallmouths are feeding generalists, and the fish utilize the most available food source within their environment.

Typical smallmouth bass prey could be any of the following, depending on the body of water and available prey: shad, alewives, smelt, crayfish, sculpin, shiners, various insects (larvae and adults), frogs, or other food items. Food habits appear to be directly related to forage abundance, and are reflected in seasonal preference differences.

Basically, Pre-summer is a time of transition when a body of water transforms from the cooler water environment of spring to the warmer environment of summer. Fish begin to regroup, and classic patterns start to emerge.

THE SUMMER PEAK PERIOD
A Time of Fulfillment

Surface Water Temperature Range: Low 70°F's
General Fish Mood: Positive to Neutral

As early summer progresses, the Pre-summer Period develops into what we term the Summer Peak—a short period of fast-action fishing. At this time it is impossible to walk in the woods, along a beach, or down a country road and not feel nature's increased rhythm. Nature is alive, conscious and moving.

The final trigger that pushes the fish from the Pre-summer Period into the short-lived period of feeding we term the Summer Peak always appears to be the same: namely, a span of relatively calm, very warm weather. In many cases this is the first really hot, summer weather of the season—and more importantly, the first hot nights of early summer.

Most of a lake's ecosystem reaches its maximum fruition during this cycle. All the cool and warm water species (in most cases) will have spawned. The transformation from a colder to a cooler to a warmer water environment is complete. Insect hatches explode. Most major rooted weedgrowth begins to mature. Most distinct weedlines and edges are perceptible, and plankton are multiplying. Nearly everything is reaching its peak of production. Fishing is generally excellent for cool and warm water fish like walleyes and largemouth bass.

Here are some basic rules of thumb to go by for recognizing the onset of the Summer Peak. First, the surface temperature of meso (middle-aged) lakes usually hovers around 72°F-74°F. It may eventually climb into the upper 70°F's, or even low 80°F's, but this typically happens very slowly. Thus, the Summer Peak Period seems to begin with the end of the rapid, early-summer rise in water temperature. In cooler Canadian lakes the water temperature might only reach the mid-60°F's, yet the principle is the same.

While the Summer Peak can be one of the best times of the year for walleye fishing, it's not necessarily so with smallmouth bass. Apparently, the combination of environmental factors that stimulates a walleye's feeding binge does not have the same effect on smallmouths. They don't display the intense feeding activity demonstrated by other species. Possibly the larger smallmouths are still affected by the rigors of spawning, or might be selectively feeding on insects at this time. The period may simply be extremely short and difficult to pinpoint. It is, nonetheless, a good time of year to catch numbers of small to moderate-sized smallmouths, even though you might not encounter many lunkers.

Basically, then, a combination of environmental factors stimulates Summer Peak activity. These three seem the most important: (1) The fish are hungry, aggressive, and catchable. This is the period when much of their yearly growth occurs; (2) This is the first time since spawning that *big* female smallmouths begin grouping together. Their competitive group activity helps stimulate feeding activity, and you can catch lunkers—*if* you can find them; (3) There are plankton of all sorts and hordes of fish fry. The entire lake is blooming and brimming with food.

The Summer Peak is basically a time of fulfillment.

THE SUMMER PERIOD
A Time of Plenty
Generalized Environmental Conditions
Surface Water Temperature Range: Maximum Temperatures of the Year
General Fish Mood: Neutral to Positive

The Romans believed the dog star Sirius rose with the sun, giving the days of July and August a double measure of heat. Thus, the term "dog days" was thrust into angling. It's a misnomer that implies lethargy, but this is an illusion. More than at any other time of the year, nature is converting the sun's energy into living matter in full gear. We call this interval the Summer Period.

Abundant prey is available in the form of fry, fingerlings, insects, and crayfish. Lakes blossom with food, and fish become more selective in their choice of meals. Controlling factors like thermoclines, sunlight, increased metabolism and presence of prey all demand order. Plus, there are a host of other factors. Nature responds by regulating feeding times.

Smallmouth fishing during the summer can be a real challenge. The fish can be scattered over a large habitat area. Some fish may forage in the shallows, others may choose to feed on the flats, and still others may opt to feed in deeper water. Consequently, the fish are spread over a large area at different depths. As the groups of fish become less concentrated, you must cover more water in order to contact fish. Algae blooms, cold fronts, increased natural food supplies and many other factors can make this an unpredictable period.

In addition, feeding activity can be of short, intense duration. On many clear bodies of water, low light conditions seem to trigger smallmouth feeding activity. In fact, nocturnal feeding movements are common on clear water natural lakes and reservoirs. At night, smallmouths can be up on the flats foraging for insects, small fish, crustaceans and other targets of opportunity.

On Canadian Shield lakes, large sunken islands and lip areas composed of broken rock, gravel and rubble are good feeding areas for summer smallmouths. In addition, the presence of weeds like cabbage, coontail and/or sandgrass can make these prime fishing spots. On many northern natural lakes, summer smallmouths forage on rock-capped sunken islands and rock/gravel bars. Slow-tapering flats that contain sandgrass on the deeper edges can be overlooked smallmouth home areas.

Doug Stange carefully releases a nice smallmouth.

In reservoirs, the smallmouths can be scattered over a large habitat area during the summer. However, several areas tend to draw concentrations of fish. For example, groups of smallmouths may be located in various areas, such as: long points or rounded bluff points on the main reservoir; steep, rocky banks with isolated fallen trees; and deeper water humps or submerged islands. These areas can all provide cover and a variety of smallmouth prey. Typically, the fish's diet is composed of crayfish, various young-of-the-year fish and shad, plus other items.

Since most highland reservoirs have clear water, many fish will suspend near bluff points in deeper water during the day. However, some smallmouths will move at night to feed in the shallower, flatter areas that contain rocks and/or wood. These fish are aggressive and catchable. Also, later in the summer, look for surface feeding activity as smallmouths feed on the abundant shad forage.

Basically, the Summer Period is a time of plenty—plenty of food, plenty of cover, and plenty of distraction in terms of increased boat traffic, sun penetration, cold fronts and the like. This completes the warming trend for the year.

THE POST-SUMMER PERIOD

A Time of Impending Change

Water Temperature Range: The Water Begins Cooling Quite Rapidly from its Generalized Highest Temperature Range
General Fish Mood: Neutral to Positive

Post-summer, in effect, is the reversal of the Pre-summer process. It is a time when a body of water changes back from a warmer to a cooler water environment. This period takes place during the tail end of summer. Hot days with dead-calm periods, followed by cool nights, are typical. The days grow shorter, and this becomes the cosmic signal to the ecosystem that things are slowing down.

Most of the food in any lake, river or reservoir has already been produced for the year, and the summer (time of plenty) is slowly giving way to reduced food stocks. The density of the weeds, too, begins to noticeably diminish. Insect hatches dwindle, and, in some cases, water levels can be quite low. Last, but not least, baitfish start shifting position as they mature, are lessened in numbers by predators, or as cover diminishes. In fact, during Post-summer, everything slowly shifts as the water abruptly cools.

Early in the Post-summer Period, smallmouths can be scattered both deep and shallow in their summer habitat areas. Due to the natural reduction of the forage base, the fish tend to grow less specific in their feeding habits. In many cases, smallmouths begin to move about more while foraging, and they may linger in feeding periods longer. These, plus other factors, all add up to easier fishing, and sometimes fantastic action.

In Canadian Shield lakes, smallmouths can move extremely shallow under ideal warm, calm weather conditions. They'll move into 1-3 feet of water on large boulder/rock reefs and islands located in main lake summer areas. This movement can produce some excellent fishing—even fast and furious.

In natural (meso) lakes, fish can also be scattered in the summer habitat areas, both deep and shallow, feeding on available prey. In general, the more prime habitat and forage available, the more scattered the fish will be.

Where available, smallmouths can use reed beds to forage on minnows, etc. The best reeds will be located adjacent to a deep water drop-off with the bottom content a mixture of sand/gravel and/or rock. Under warm, stable conditions, smallmouths will move into the reeds to forage on minnows, etc. This can be an excellent time for fishing. While not a "classic" situation, the smallmouths are simply using an available environmental option.

The internal workings of the environment trigger changes in a pattern of operation. Summer fish, depending upon the kind of lake, river or reservoir, might have been restricted from doing a lot of things. But come Post-summer, many of these restrictive factors disappear.

For example, in certain mesotrophic lakes, thermoclines (which often limit oxygen in the depths) might have pushed fish out of the deep water during the summer months. Direct sunlight (for long periods of the day) might have further kept these shallow water fish buried in cover like weeds; they might only have fed for brief periods during low-light periods. But come Post-summer, the sunlight is less intense and the fish might wander out of the weeds for longer periods.

Since the food supply is less plentiful, it takes longer to fill their needs. So, in this case, we vividly see how the environment affects fish activity—and, of course, "catchability."

In some rivers, smallmouths which spent the summer scattered in shallow stretches might, with the low water levels so indicative of the Post-summer Period, begin regrouping with other fish and relating to deeper holes. Again, the change in environment makes for a change in fish operation.

Basically, Post-summer is a time of impending change, when a body of water (and the aquatic life in it) goes through the transition from a warmer to a cooler environment.

THE TURNOVER PERIOD

A Time of Turmoil

Generalized Environmental Conditions
Water Temperature Range: Variable
General Fish Mood: Very Negative

As a time of turmoil, the Turnover Period is relative. First, all bodies of water do not thermocline during summer, so they do not "turn over" as such. Most rivers are a case in point. Lakes and reservoirs, too, may or may not stratify. Usually, shallow bodies of water—which the wind periodically stirs up—or ones with a lot of current flowing through them, are fairly immune to the stratifying process. Consequently, the fish in these waters are not subjected to as much stress as fish in waters where the transition from a warm to a cold water environment is an explosive event. Nonetheless, the change from a warmer to a cooler to a colder water environment demands some adjustment.

The most classic (drastic) turnover situation occurs in bodies of water which set up (stratify) in distinct temperature layers during the summer. Since cold water is heavier than warm water, the warmer water stays on top and the colder water sinks and builds up on the bottom; in between lies the narrow band of rapid temperature change from warm to cold called the thermocline.

In these waters, a thermocline condition usually remains in effect throughout most of the Summer Peak, Summer and Post-summer Periods. But during the tail end of the Post-summer Period, as the sun grows less direct, seasonal hard, driving, cold winds and rain begin chilling the surface temperature of the water very quickly. As the heavier (colder) water begins sinking, it comes in contact with the warmer water below. This action forces the lighter, yet warmer, deeper water back to the surface. Eventually, the narrow thermocline layer ruptures, and a mixing or "turning over" process takes place. As the wind beats the water, the mixing action continues until it thoroughly homogenizes the water to a point where the whole body of water is the same temperature. This process also reoxygenates the deep water.

Turnover usually occurs after several days to a week of the first late-summer cold snap characterized by a succession of dark, cold, wind-driven rainy days. This is a signal that the Cold Water Period is about to arrive. At times, you can actually smell the stagnant bottom water as it rises to the surface. You might even see dead weeds, decomposed fish and other bottom debris floating on the surface or washed ashore.

The actual Turnover process itself takes place once the thermocline layer ruptures. But the turmoil that takes place usually adversely affects the fish for a period of time before and after this event actually occurs. Fishing doesn't pick up again until conditions stabilize. In general, once the water temperature drops to about 55°F and the water clears perceptibly, cold water fishing patterns emerge.

Fishing during the Turnover Period on bodies of water that actually thermocline is tough, to say the least. However, since all bodies of water do not turn over at the same time, it is usually best to switch to waters which have already turned over—or bodies of water which have not yet begun to—or to waters which don't actually thermocline and turn over so drastically.

Exactly what happens to fish, and smallmouth bass in particular during Turnover, has yet to be documented. In fact, anglers are some of the best sources of information about this turbulent time. Fish are stressed during unstable conditions, so the best fishing usually occurs in areas where the turnover is minimal. Shallow waters are usually best, or perhaps, the shallowest areas of a lake which are least affected by the main lake turnover.

If you're forced to fish a lake under these conditions, seek out the best available shallow water cover. While you probably won't get into numbers of fish, a few stragglers could save the day from being a complete waste. Areas of shallow, broken rock with weeds or wood present are good choices. If available, also check out any reed beds near deep water.

Basically, the Turnover Period is a time of turmoil when fish activity grinds to a halt, although action will pick up as conditions gradually stabilize.

THE COLD WATER PERIOD (FALL)
A Time of Stability

Generalized Environmental Conditions
Surface Water Temperature Range: 55°F and Down
to the Lowest Temperature of the Year
General Fish Mood: Neutral

The entire time span from the end of the Turnover to freeze-up (on bodies of water that freeze over) is termed the Cold Water Period. This period is characterized by a gradual slowing down and stabilization process of the entire ecosystem. The water temperature descends to the lowest of the year, and the smallmouth bass's metabolism slows in response to the changing environment.

As the days grow steadily shorter, weedgrowth, insect hatches and plankton blooms diminish. In addition, the chemical characteristics of the water can vary considerably with the changing season, and have multiple effects on the plant and fish life. During this time frame, smallmouth bass make both significant locational and behavioral changes in response to these seasonal environmental variations.

A key to understanding smallmouth bass during the Cold Water Period is realizing that the combination of falling water temperature and diminishing light levels (plus other factors) appears to stimulate the smallmouths to shift location into deeper water habitat areas. Remember, the Turnover has literally opened the door to the deeper areas which thermoclined during the summer. Since the depths have been reoxygenated, smallmouths are able to utilize deeper water.

In general, a majority of the smallmouths will vacate shallow flats and relocate in the deep water habitat area adjacent to them. Yet under stable, warm, sunny weather conditions, groups of smallmouths will move shallow, scatter across the flats and feed actively. After feeding, the fish will drop back into the deeper water home area. However, these feeding binges are very sporadic and difficult to pinpoint.

Under most conditions, the fish will not move shallow, but will remain in the deeper water and feed on available forage (minnows/crayfish) in the 25 to

40 foot levels. These prime fall drop-off areas are located as far from shore and as close to the lake basin as possible. For example, a long, shallow, multi-structured bar that extends far into the lake before dropping sharply into the lake basin could be a prime spot. This classic area can draw a "mega" concentration of smallmouths.

At this time, highland reservoir smallmouths tend to congregate near the steeper-dropping points and bluffs. The prime areas typically have cover in the form of boulders, rock, rubble and/or stumps, as well as a steep drop-off. In early fall, the bulk of the fish will remain in deeper water, but some fish can be caught in the 2-15 foot depths.

Night fishing can be good in shallows at this time. In addition, since shad are an abundant open water prey source, look for surface activity as schooling smallmouth bass feed on shad in early morning and late afternoon. Later, as the water temperature drops, smallmouths move to the ends of points in 25-40 feet of water. Here they feed on various fish, crayfish, and targets of opportunity.

This can be a great time for fishing for both numbers and lunkers. Small-mouths are concentrated and catchable. For numbers of smaller fish, try the shallower areas on the points, creek ledge areas or around cover such as logs, bushes, stick-ups, rock piles or other cover. Small crankbaits, spinnerbaits and jigs are all effective. For trophy fish, try the deeper areas in the 25-40 foot depths using a jig'n pig, jig and grub or a tail spinner. Billy Westmorland, noted smallmouth expert, recommends retrieving your lure *up* the contour, as opposed to moving down it.

General activity levels of the fish vary throughout the Cold Water Period. Actually, it is best to view the "slowing down" process as a series of activity levels the fish pass through. These activity levels are not absolute values; rather, the levels reflect an overall behavioral modification.

During the Cold Water Period, the smallmouth bass's activity levels may be anywhere on the active/neutral/negative feeding attitude range. As a rule of thumb, when the water cools, the lower temperatures slow down the metabolic processes and decrease fish activity. Consequently, you must be versatile in order to contact and catch fish consistently.

Early in the Cold Water Period, smallmouths can be active and will strike a moving crankbait with vigor. Conversely, by the end of the period, the fish seem to prefer a very slow live bait or vertical jigging presentation. Interestingly, some of the most productive fishing periods are the early hours, so get out early.

In summary, during the fall re-staging process, the fish will be tightly grouped in drop-off areas at the end of a bar, as far from shore as possible, and close to the lake basin. Additionally, seek out transition areas of harder to softer bottom, such as on the edges of rock-capped sunken islands and hard bottom humps. A forage base near these areas is an essential ingredient for smallmouths. As the water cools, slow down your presentation.

Understanding the entire Cold Water Period is important, because this period can offer some of the finest smallmouth bass fishing of the year—if you understand fish location and behavior.

The Cold Water Period, however, is a time of stability. Though smallmouth bass may bite, everything seems to move at a slower pace. In general, the more stable the environment, the better the fishing. The combination of stability, tightly-grouped fish and a limited forage base make this a prime time for trophy smallmouths.

Caution: Catch and release practices are strongly recommended, because a group of fish can be depleted by the knowledgeable, but unthinking, angler!

THE FROZEN WATER PERIOD

A Time of Rest

Generalized Environmental Conditions
Surface Water Temperature Range: When a Body of Water
is at its Coldest for an Extended Period of Time
General Fish Mood: Neutral

The Frozen Water Period is defined as the longest period of the coldest water of the year. Ice cover is common in the northern areas of the smallmouth bass's distribution. In fact, this period can last up to 5 months or more in some areas. However, in some southern reservoirs, ice cover may only briefly occur in coves and wind-protected bays, while the main lake never freezes. Similarly, rivers may or may not experience ice-up, depending on their geographical location. The point is, the Frozen Water Period occurs when a body of water remains at its coldest range for an extended period.

Despite its stable winter water temperature and outwardly tranquil appearance, a lake is constantly in a state of change—though unseen. Oxygen depletion, pH changes, and a host of other environmental factors all affect the fish. A body of water is never a static entity; changes in the environment are commonplace. During this time span, the fish's metabolism slows.

Surprisingly, there is little documented information available on smallmouth bass during this period. The bits and pieces of scientific and angler observation information gathered indicate that smallmouth bass remain in their late fall, deep water areas. Angler observations suggest that smallmouth bass may make limited movements, both early and again late in the Frozen Water Period. However, during the middle of the period, the fish appear to be inactive.

Obviously, due to biological necessity, the fish must feed. Female fish must feed to maintain their eggs and bodies, while the male fish feed to sustain life. However, these feeding periods appear to be sporadic and very difficult to nail down.

Locationally, the fish seem to be grouped in the late Cold Water Period, steep drop-off areas. Look for the fish to relate to the base of a rock reef, bar or sunken island. Typically, in many natural lakes, these are at 25 to 40 foot depths. In some lakes, a hard bottom rise on a deep water area could hold the major concentration of wintering smallmouths.

Since these fish seem to be finicky feeders, proper presentation is vital to success. In addition, smallmouths appear to prefer smaller food items, and become very specific in their feeding habits. At this time, a $\frac{1}{32}$ to $\frac{1}{64}$ oz. jig or ice fishing spoon, dressed with a wax worm or similar morsel, is the ticket. Jig this combo with frequent pauses, because too much movement can spook the fish.

The majority of large reservoir smallmouths will be located in the same deeper water areas on steep points, bluffs, and submerged islands which they used in the Cold Water Period. Fish and crayfish are major food items. Smallmouth feeding patterns will be sporadic; fish can be caught, however, if located. Try late cold water areas using jigs, spoons or live bait.

All in all, the Frozen Water Period is a time of rest. Activity doesn't cease completely; however, the ecosystem moves at a slower pace than during other Calendar Periods.

Calendar Summary
A VEST POCKET GUIDE TO THE CALENDAR PERIODS

Period	Description	Key Factors
Cold Water (Spring)	Locational change from deep water wintering areas near the lake basin toward the shallows (not shallower). Hard bottom areas on the inside corners of bar formations may concentrate fish. Fishing can be good.	Water temperature. Length of daylight. Hormone level.
Pre-spawn	Length dependent on seasonal weather conditions and will vary between lakes, rivers or reservoirs. Fish activity keyed to warming trends and stable weather. Groups of fish migrate into rock/gravel/rubble areas or other available habitat in shallows. Super fishing—numbers and size.	Water temperature. Length of daylight. Hormone level. Bottom content.
Spawn	Timewise a very short period. However, not all smallmouths spawn at the same time. Do not disturb spawning fish. Fishing poor.	Water temperature. Hormone level. Bottom content. Moon phase.
Post-spawn	Recuperation period for females who filter back toward deeper water. Males are aggressive and guard the nest. Fishing is usually slow. Do not disturb.	Water temperature.
Pre-summer	Movement from spawning area to summer locations. Fish begin to regroup. Fishing fair to good with several patterns available.	Water temperature. Food chain.

Summer Peak	Fish are active and classic vertical movements begin. Low food supply due to undeveloped food chain can mean very good fishing.	Water temperature. Food chain. Weedgrowth.
Summer	The bulk of the fishing season for most anglers. Natural food chain has peaked. Fish active and patterns identifiable. However, fish are spread out over good habitat areas at various depths. Presentation becomes the key.	Food chain. Weedgrowth. Water temperature. Weather patterns.
Post-summer	Rapid cooling of water to low 60°F's. Food chain slows down. Fish scattered both deep and shallow. A variety of fishing patterns exist.	Food chain. Water temperature.
Fall Turnover	Cold nights cause top layer of water to sink and a general mixing of the water to occur. Fish are disoriented and generally move into deeper water. Fishing is slow until environmental conditions stabilize.	Weather—wind. Mixing water. Temperature. Re-oxygenation of depths.
Cold Water (Fall)	Lunker time! Fish are tightly grouped in deep water areas far from shore and near lake basin. Try early AM hours. Presentation is critical. Fishing can be super.	Water temperature. Location of prey. Bottom content. Length of daylight.
Frozen Water	Sporadic feeding occurs. A few fish can be caught in deeper water areas the fish used in late fall.	Location of prey.

Chapter 5

UNDERSTANDING SMALLMOUTH BASS WATERS

Why do some lakes, rivers and reservoirs support healthy populations of smallmouth bass, yet other similar waters, even in the same geographical area, do not? Obviously this is a loaded question which requires a lengthy, complex answer. However, basically, the total environment of a particular body of water must have all the key ingredients necessary for smallmouth bass survival.

These are not "magical" key ingredients that are etched in stone; in fact, they may vary considerably in lakes, rivers and reservoirs. In essence, each body of water must provide suitable habitat, forage, water temperature and other factors for each of the smallmouth bass's developmental stages, from egg through adult, during the ten Calendar Periods.

A glance at the map showing smallmouth bass distribution (page 12) graphically emphasizes the wide geographical area that the fish inhabits. The point is, with this geographical dispersion, there is an inevitable variation in the available habitat. Mr. Smallmouth, being a very versatile critter, simply adapts to each environment as best he can.

This adaptation process makes it essential that we generalize about smallmouth behavior; there are few absolutes. The fish will adjust their behavior according to their needs in each body of water. In other words, it's what is available for the fish to utilize, and what the fish have to adapt to, that's important.

For example, in the gin-clear, rocky lakes of the Canadian Shield, smallmouths make extensive use of the shallower waters, such as rock-capped sunken islands and broken rock, extended lip areas. Contrast this environment to an upper Midwest natural lake which may have stained water, limited rocky areas and weeds. In this lake, smallmouths could relate to the rocks and/or weed edges. Smallmouths and weeds? You bet! Resevoirs, on the other hand, may see smallmouths utilizing stump flats near deep water! You see, it depends on what options the environment provides.

In order to fully understand smallmouth location in any body of water, you must first determine the type of lake, river or reservoir you are fishing. The *IN-FISHERMAN* has classified each. The following chapters identify those waters which can support viable smallmouth bass populations. We'll examine the prime types of lakes, rivers and reservoirs that house smallmouth bass, and explain how to identify each of them.

We'll begin with our Natural Lake Classification System. Then we will analyze the various river categories, and lastly, investigate the different kinds of reservoirs. Each type of lake, river or reservoir is more or less inviting to smallmouths, and you will learn how to recognize one from the other.

Before we zero in on any of these in particular, it is important to understand how we categorize bodies of water. They are broken into "age stages" that start at the youngest stage (which primarily provides cold water environments), advance to the middle-aged stage (which are primarily cold water environments), and finally proceed to the oldest stage (which primarily offers warm water environments). In between these major categories lie a number of lakes in *transition* stages; for instance, from a stable, cold water environment to a less stable, cold/cool water environment. Thus there are many different lake types, and each category often has a distinct bearing on smallmouth bass location and behavior. This is true for rivers and reservoirs as well.

Chapter 6

CLASSIFICATION OF NATURAL LAKES

The first step in becoming a proficient smallmouth bass angler is acquiring a basic knowledge of natural lakes. Yes, you must understand the differences between lake types. Quite simply, lake type has a direct bearing on the resulting fishery, and thus your fishing approach.

In essence, each lake type provides a different set of environmental conditions, and, consequently, different fish population dynamics. For example, a lake that provides the proper environment can support lake trout and smallmouth bass, while another lake with a different set of environmental conditions could only support carp and bullheads.

Biologists classify bodies of water according to their ability to produce and sustain aquatic life. How much plant life a body of water is able to produce determines, in part, how large a fish population it can support. But there's much more to it than simply plant life. The overall water chemistry (the amount of mineral richness of the water) is another of the many factors. Ultimately, a lake's productivity is determined by its total make-up.

The *IN-FISHERMAN'S* classification of natural lake types contains three very broad, but basic categories:

1. Oligotrophic (infertile).
2. Mesotrophic (fertile).
3. Eutrophic (very fertile).

Each of these categories is characterized by its ability to produce and sustain varying amounts, as well as different kinds, of aquatic plant and animal life.

When you visualize a particular lake, remember that these categories are points of reference. We can think of many exceptions. For instance, mesotrophic, or "meso," is simply a convenient classification that fits between the two most extreme categories. For our purposes, then, a lake may either be infertile (have few fish); fertile (be a pretty good producer of fish); or very fertile (contain lots of fish per acre).

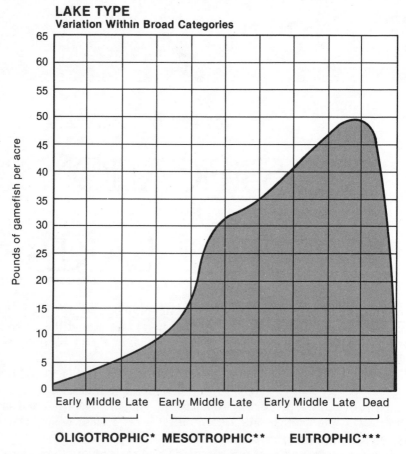

LAKE TYPE
Variation Within Broad Categories

Pounds of gamefish per acre

Early Middle Late Early Middle Late Early Middle Late Dead

OLIGOTROPHIC* MESOTROPHIC** EUTROPHIC***

*Deep water contains dissolved oxygen during summer.
**Deep water contains little or no dissolved oxygen during summer.
***Oxygen either evenly distributed during summer or, in deeper
lakes, oxygen is depleted in deep water during summer.

LAKE TYPE VS. GAMEFISH POPULATION

The accompanying chart tells part of the story. It shows what you might expect to find in *gamefish populations* only. Oligotrophic (infertile) lakes have low gamefish populations, while eutrophic (very fertile) lakes have extremely high populations. Some eutrophic lakes—if you count panfish and rough fish—can produce hundreds of pounds of fish per acre, and some oligotrophic lakes—if you count whitefish—can produce much higher totals than indicated.

At first glance, you might say that eutrophic lakes are "best for fishing," because they have the most pounds of gamefish per acre. But, generally, oligotrophic lakes produce lake trout, smallmouths and walleyes; mesotrophic lakes produce walleyes, smallmouths and largemouths; and eutrophic lakes produce largemouths.

Let's take a look at the life cycle of a lake. Historically, during the last ice age, the retreating glaciers created the vast majority of our natural lakes. As

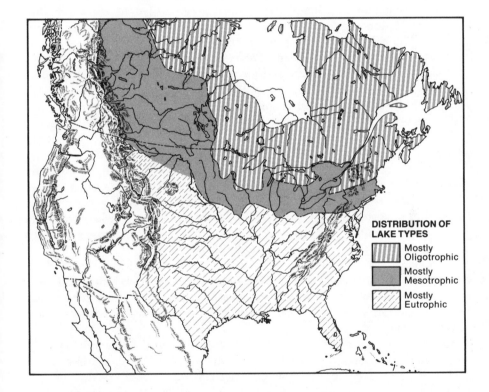

DISTRIBUTION OF
LAKE TYPES

Mostly Oligotrophic

Mostly Mesotrophic

Mostly Eutrophic

the ice masses receded, the multitude of holes in the landscape filled with meltwater, forming lakes.

The accompanying map shows how far southward glaciers advanced during the last Ice Age. At the turn of the century, all inland fishing—except in Florida and a few other isolated regions—was restricted to either lakes in the areas formerly covered by glaciers, or in rivers, streams, ponds and backwaters.

"AGING"

Nothing stands entirely alone in nature. Everything is affected in some way by something else in the environment.

Any body of water, whether it is a lake, river, or pond, can be regarded as a "living organism" composed of numerous elements such as water chemistry, bottom content, aquatic life, and so on.

No matter where your favorite lake is situated, that body of water is constantly changing. In some remote areas, the change can be so slight that it passes unnoticed, and might take a century or more to show a visible change. In other waters, this might occur in 10, 5, or even fewer years.

This is the natural aging process called eutrophication that all lakes pass through. The initial stages can take thousands of years, but the final ones may happen quickly—especially with the addition of man-made causes. Throughout this process, the total environment of a lake—its structural condition, food chains, vegetation levels and dominant fish species—change considerably. Man-caused eutrophication, or aging, is due to the expanding human population and disposal of waste products. These have caused changes in lakes so quickly that man has accomplished in a generation what it would have taken nature hundreds or thousands of years to do.

Consequently, we view and classify natural lakes according to their condition, and not necessarily their chronological age. A lake is basically either young, middle-aged or old. Since some lakes are in between these broad types and almost defy classification, our classifications should not be taken as absolutes. Instead, each category is meant to be a convenient point of reference—a definition we can start to learn from.

As lakes "age," their character changes. Generally speaking, geologically "young" lakes are deep and clean; older ones are shallow and murky.

The natural order is such that on one end of the aging scale we find young lakes (with oxygen-rich deep water) which can support fish like lake trout and whitefish. At the other end, we find lakes with another kind of makeup which can only support fish such as carp and bullheads.

Obviously, a lake trout cannot live in a shallow, murky, weedy, low-oxygen lake of the midwestern prairies. And carp have a tough time making it in the rocky, ice-cold, weedless environment of a trout lake. But between these two extremes fall lakes of all sorts—each of which are more or less hospitable to certain species of fish.

Smallmouths, for example, have a lot of latitude in their genetic makeup, and can at least exist to varying degrees, in all but very young or extremely old bodies of water. Sometimes this aging is determined by fertility—the youngest lakes being infertile while the oldest are very fertile. We categorize natural lakes in the following nine states:

THE STABLE, YOUNG, INFERTILE, COLD WATER ENVIRONMENT STATES
1. Early stage oligotrophic
2. Mid-stage oligotrophic

THE TRANSITION FROM COLD TO COOL WATER ENVIRONMENT STATES
3. Late stage oligotrophic

4. Early stage mesotrophic

THE STABLE, MIDDLE-AGED, MODERATELY FERTILE, COOL WATER ENVIRONMENT STATE

5. Mid-stage mesotrophic

THE TRANSITION FROM COOL TO WARM WATER ENVIRONMENT STATES

6. Late stage mesotrophic

7. Early stage eutrophic

THE STABLE, OLD, FERTILE, WARM WATER ENVIRONMENT STATE

8. Mid-stage eutrophic

THE TRANSITION FROM WARM TO VERY WARM WATER ENVIRONMENT STATE

9. Late stage eutrophic

Roland Martin hefts a Canadian shield lake lunker.
Is it a five pounder?

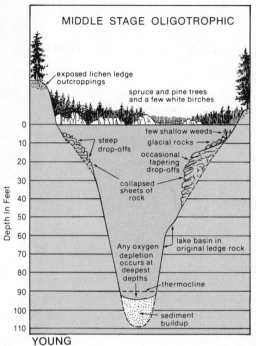

MIDDLE STAGE OLIGOTROPHIC

exposed lichen ledge outcroppings

spruce and pine trees and a few white birches

steep drop-offs

few shallow weeds

glacial rocks

occasional tapering drop-offs

collapsed sheets of rock

Any oxygen depletion occurs at deepest depths

lake basin in original ledge rock

thermocline

sediment buildup

Depth In Feet

0, 10, 20, 30, 40, 50, 60, 70, 80, 90, 100, 110

YOUNG

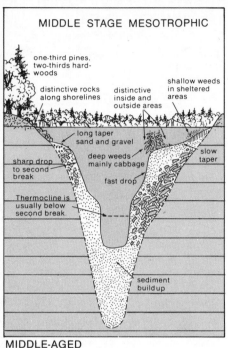

MIDDLE STAGE MESOTROPHIC

one-third pines, two-thirds hardwoods

distinctive rocks along shorelines

distinctive inside and outside areas

shallow weeds in sheltered areas

long taper sand and gravel

sharp drop to second break

deep weeds mainly cabbage

slow taper

fast drop

Thermocline is usually below second break.

sediment buildup

MIDDLE-AGED

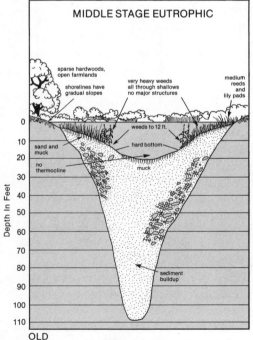

MIDDLE STAGE EUTROPHIC

sparse hardwoods, open farmlands

very heavy weeds all through shallows no major structures

medium reeds and lily pads

shorelines have gradual slopes

weeds to 12 ft.

sand and muck

hard bottom

no thermocline

muck

sediment buildup

Depth In Feet

0, 10, 20, 30, 40, 50, 60, 70, 80, 90, 100, 110

OLD

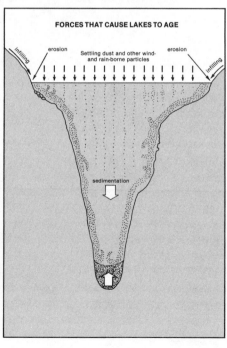

FORCES THAT CAUSE LAKES TO AGE

infilling

erosion

Settling dust and other wind- and rain-borne particles

erosion

infilling

sedimentation

NATURAL LAKE TYPES								
OLIGOTROPHIC			MESOTROPHIC			EUTROPHIC		
EARLY	MIDDLE	LATE	EARLY	MIDDLE	LATE	EARLY	MIDDLE	LATE
CONDITIONS OF ENVIRONMENT								
COLD WATER		TRANSITION STAGES		COOL WATER	TRANSITION STAGES		WARM WATER	

Key: ——————— strongest populations
     - - - - - - - - - weaker populations

This chart roughly depicts how the species relationships change as a lake ages. Oligotrophic lakes are the youngest, and eutrophic lakes the oldest, geologically. In between these two extremes lie mesotrophic lakes.

Smallmouths appear in mid-late "oli" lakes where they inhabit shallower water areas. In early-mid "meso" lakes, smallmouths can become very prolific if proper conditions exist. Eutrophic lakes are usually not prime smallmouth waters due to diminishing habitat and inter-species competition.

When you analyze a particular lake, remember that these categories are simply points of reference to work from. However, as you become familiar with the system, you will be able to easily recognize a lake as being early stage eutrophic—instead of late stage meso.

The youngest type of lakes—oligotrophic—typically have rock basins and are found almost exclusively in the upper portions of the North American Continent. They usually have steep, sharp drop-offs, few weeds, pine-studded shorelines, and a fish population composed of cold water fish like lake trout and members of the whitefish family. The nutrient level of the water is usually low, and oxygen is available in deep water at all times. Thus, the lake is termed infertile.

As this type of lake ages, the shorelines become less gorge-like, and the drop-offs less abrupt and steep. Big boulders turn to smaller rock, and more sand and gravel becomes apparent. Weedgrowth develops. The trees that bound the lake also tend to change. Since the surrounding terrain changes, the water quality takes on a new character (more nutrients). These are the first signs of the transitory process between the oligotrophic and mesotrophic categories.

Little by little, the lake changes and eventually develops characteristics typical of a middle-aged, mesotrophic lake. When a lake reaches its mid-mesotrophic stage, much of the exposed rock, except right along the shoreline, is gone. Sand and some gravel now prevails in the lake's basin. The shoreline-tapers become more gradual, more weeds appear in the shallows, and the trees that surround the lake begin changing from evergreens to hardwoods. A distinct thermocline and oxycline usually form.

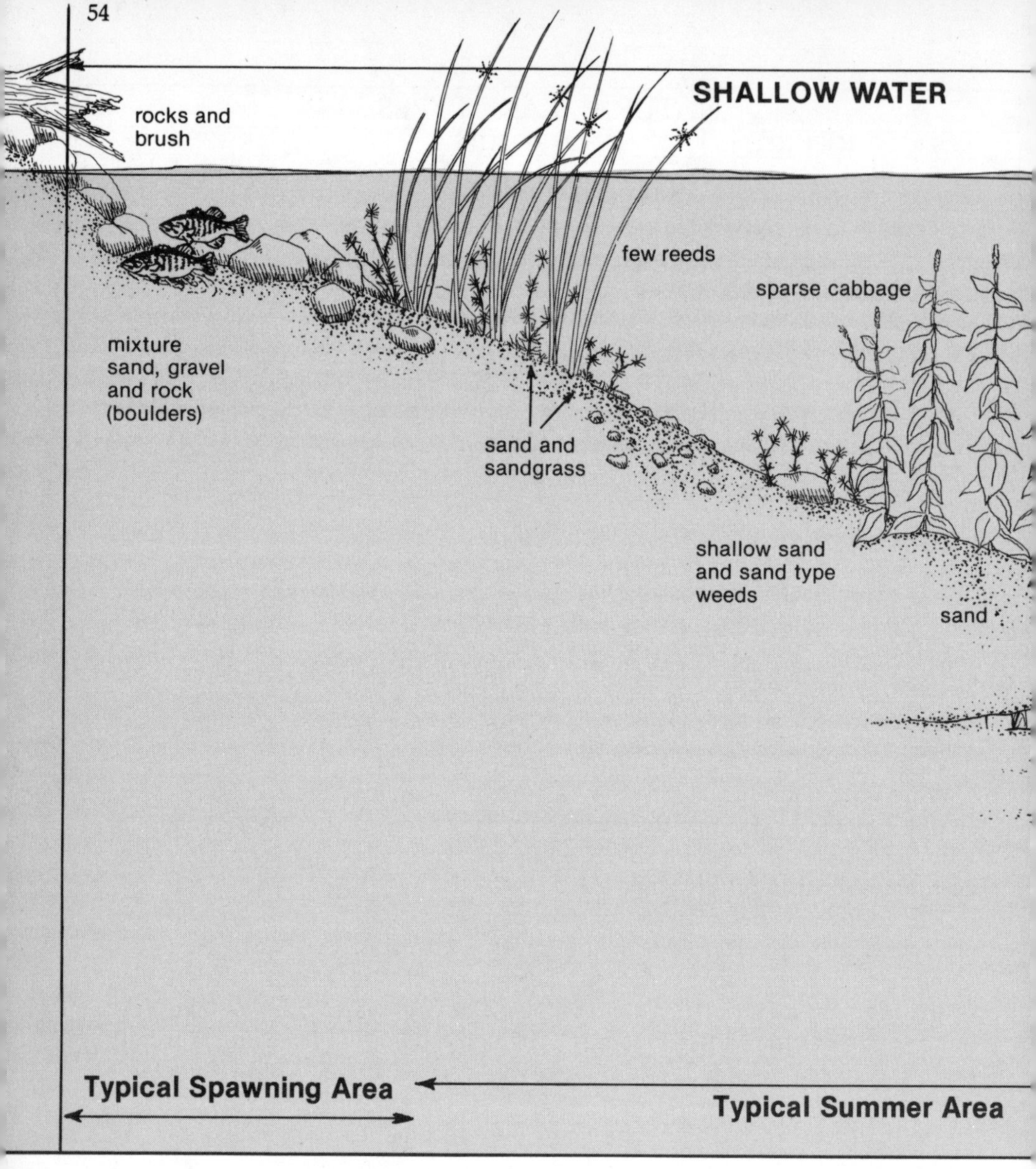

SHALLOW WATER

rocks and
brush

few reeds

sparse cabbage

mixture
sand, gravel
and rock
(boulders)

sand and
sandgrass

shallow sand
and sand type
weeds

sand

Typical Spawning Area ←

Typical Summer Area

The Elements of Structure

The cross-section on these two pages shows the various structural elements that could be found in many—but not all—natural lakes. The depths are relative. The edge of the weedline, for example, could occur at 8 feet or 18 feet, depending on water clarity. Some lakes might have extensive weedgrowth on the flats, and others very little. Reeds might be present or not. Some lakes have only one breakline, or drop-off; others may have two. The shallow water food shelf might be extensive or very short. There might be exposed rock or a limestone ridge, or there might be none. It all depends on the LAKE CLASSIFICATION TYPE.

Nevertheless, the terminology holds. The shoreline is always the shoreline. The edge of the weeds is always a point of reference. Familiarize yourself with these terms. They will be used constantly.

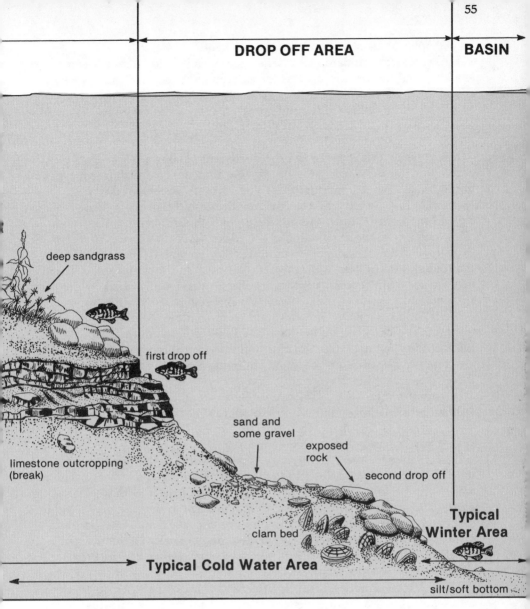

DROP OFF AREA **BASIN**

deep sandgrass

first drop off

limestone outcropping
(break)

sand and
some gravel

exposed
rock

second drop off

clam bed

**Typical
Winter Area**

Typical Cold Water Area

silt/soft bottom

By the time the next transition (mesotrophic to eutrophic) stage occurs, a lake, by geological aging standards, is getting old. First, it is getting shallower. Sand begins turning to muck or clay in certain sections, and the erosion process results in less extensive shoreline tapers than in the mid-meso classification. Secondary drop-offs in deep water are obliterated or less defined.

Marshy areas usually dot certain adjacent sections. Hardwood trees and flat shorelines, rather than steep cliffs or high hills rim the lakeshore. The lake is changing from a cool to a warm water environment.

When a lake moves into its mid-eutrophic stage, it becomes a true warm water environment. In its oligotrophic stage this body of water was a cold water environment; in its "meso" stage a cool water environment; and now in its eutrophic stage a warm water environment.

By geological standards, this lake is now quite old. It has become very shallow, and the erosion process is near completion. Farmlands usually surround these waters. Thermoclines generally don't develop or last a long time. Shallow weedgrowth is thick, and sandy areas become quite soft. Water color becomes darker, so weeds grow to lesser depths, and the shoreline just sort of blends into the basin of the lake.

In a nutshell, this is the aging process all natural lakes go through. Study the accompanying drawings carefully, so you understand the different types of natural lakes. Most importantly, as you learn to recognize lake types, you'll learn what to expect in terms of smallmouth size and probably population density. In the final analysis, this will help you fish smarter—not harder!

As a lake ages, the distribution of the various gamefish species also changes. In geological time, the oligotrophic lake is the "youngest"; the eutrophic lake is the "oldest." In between is the mesotrophic lake. In the oligotrophic (infertile) lake, species must complement each other to survive. Since lake trout often suspend and run in deep, open water, their prey must be within range.

In fertile lakes, plants will root and form shallow weedbeds. Most oligotrophic lakes, however, do not have the proper conditions for such weedbeds. Instead, the plant life is free-floating, and suspends at levels where species such as whitefish can graze on them and still remain within range of the trout. In these lakes, plant life is more abundant in deeper water than in the shallows.

In mesotrophic (fertile) lakes, walleyes are the dominant species, and smallmouths and largemouths begin to appear. These fish tend to use different levels. Bass use the shallower areas; walleyes, the deeper ones. Here, the yellow perch is usually the dominant forage.

In the eutrophic (very fertile) lake, shallow-rooted plant life provides both food and cover for all fish. Walleyes, smallmouths and other "semi-open water" fish begin to disappear, and the species associated with weeds, such as bluegills and largemouths, become dominant. The plant and animal life that sustained an open-water fishery in a mesotrophic lake diminishes sharply. This change continues, until the lake ultimately degenerates to a point where only rough fish can survive. Northern pike and muskellunge can be present, but rarely constitute a dominant species.

Therefore, by simply generalizing the natural lake type based on the classification guidelines, an astute angler can predict many potential situations. For example, you can make educated guesses as to the species present, predator/prey relationships, water clarity, structural conditions and weedgrowth.

In summary, this information, coupled with a few simple questions to the proper individuals (fisheries personnel or bait shop owners), is the basis for evaluating a lake's potential. Basically, this is how our staff evaluates many waters. Of course, there's no better way to check out a lake than to fish it; however, this is a good procedure for narrowing down several possible lakes to a couple logical choices.

Besides a lake's classification (which may not always fit into a neat little pigeon-hole), another key element to understanding smallmouth bass is the available structural conditions. These conditions are extremely important in understanding a smallmouth's response to the total environment. Some of the key items are: bottom configuration, bottom content, vegetation and water characteristics. In other words, what's the shape of the lake, and how deep is it? What's the bottom composition—sand, gravel, rock or muck? What types of weeds are present, and what depth is the weedline? What are the water clarity and oxygen level? All these features are important, and play an important role in determining where the smallmouth bass can be.

Obviously, no two lakes are the same; however, the structural conditions on many are similar. This similarity allows the comparison of lakes, and aids in generalizing smallmouth bass location within a lake. Review the elements of structure and familiarize yourself with the terminology, because a thorough understanding of the principles will help you visualize what's beneath the surface of a lake.

Our information on smallmouth bass behavior, coupled with an understanding of a lake's structural conditions, are two of the key ingredients for success.

NATURAL LAKE CLASSIFICATION SUMMARY

MID TO LATE STAGE OLIGOTROPHIC
EARLY TO MID STAGE MESOTROPHIC

In order to produce numbers of good-sized smallmouth bass, a lake must provide the proper environment on a seasonal basis. Remember, the smallmouth is basically a non-migratory fish, and appears to do best in waters that offer the proper habitats in a limited area. These lake types offer the proper spawning, rearing and living areas for the various stages of the smallmouth's life. In addition, the absence of a competing gamefish species in large numbers appears essential for the smallmouth bass to flourish. Another often overlooked factor is the amount of intelligent fishing pressure a lake receives.

In order for a lake to have a viable smallmouth population, it must have the proper prey available for the fish at each level of growth. Smallmouths are feeding "generalists" and will feed on targets of opportunity. For example, smallmouths may seasonally feed on insects, minnows, small fish, crayfish, plus other prey. Lakes that offer a high protein species like ciscoes or smelt also have the potential of producing real monsters. Bays of the Great Lakes, and some sections of the Great Lakes themselves, offer this situation. Because of their unique status, we'll discuss in a separate chapter the Great Lakes' oftentimes-untapped, yet phenomenal, smallmouth bass potential.

Chapter 7

CLASSIFICATION OF RIVERS

Why do some rivers contain trout, others smallmouths and walleyes, and still others mostly catfish and carp? This chapter answers this interesting question, and identifies the types of rivers a smallmouth bass can inhabit. In addition, the basics of current and its effects on fish will be explained. You'll be well on your way to becoming a river-rat after reading and applying the following information.

Rivers! There are mountain rivers, agricultural rivers, tidal rivers, swamp rivers and more; all are different in character. Some are warm, slow-moving, murky bodies of water, while others are fast, cool and quite clear. These different river personalities provide different aquatic environments and, as we have demonstrated, some environments are more hospitable to smallmouth bass than others.

Due to the incredible variety and changing character of rivers, a *general* classification system is necessary. Classifying a river can help determine the probable species present, water quality, key identification features, bottom content, plus other important factors. Let's take a look at how to classify a river.

Like people, rivers submit to the bane of the aging process. Not in the same manner, of course, but the principle is similar—a natural progression from young to old. Therein lies the clue to our classification system.

"Young," "middle-aged" and "old" are terms geologists use in referring to rivers. These terms describe the condition of the landscape carved by the river, more than the actual age of the river, or its primary environmental condition. Therefore, the surrounding geography and general shape of the riverbed are the main clues to a stream's age.

For example, in its flow, a young river plunges rapidly downhill, flowing over and cutting through solid rock. As a river matures, it flows downhill

Three Stages of a River

Photo #1 shows the very young class. Here the stream runs fast and cool through a rocky gorge. Fish like carp and white bass would find life difficult if not impossible, yet fish like brook trout and grayling would thrive in this type of environment.

Photo #2 shows a group of anglers working the White River of Arkansas. Here trout (stocked) and smallmouth bass both inhabit a mature stream that is a little older geologically than the solid rock streams. Boulders, broken rock and gravel become more prominent.

Photo #3 shows a wide, slow, middle-aged river. Walleyes and saugers, along with a whole host of other non-game fish species, are present.

more slowly, and begins to meander gently through broad valleys with sandy subsoil, bounded by smoothly-rounded hills. Finally, in "old age," a river curves widely across level or mud-bottomed flood plains, surrounded by eroded hills.

For a stream, the major catalyst to aging is erosion. In general, the longer a stream extends in length, the more aging occurs in the form of erosion. The process of erosion actually carries the aging process upstream. So, as time goes on, older geological conditions which form at a river's delta continue to move further and further upstream.

Since there are variations in the aging progression along the sections of a stream, as well as some overlap between the abundance and presence of the cold, cool, and warm water fish species, the only way to view a stream is by stretches. In this sense, a particular stretch can be young, old, or somewhere in between in terms of geological makeup.

For instance, a stream might be quite shallow, have a slow taper for several miles, and possess a number of backwater areas with soft bottom and aquatic weedgrowth. Here, largemouth bass and/or northern pike might find adequate habitat. But all of a sudden, this same stream might break into a sharp gradient as it shoots through a rocky, cliff-like area, creating a rapids, and finally pouring into a boulder-based pool. This younger stretch, although further downstream, could house smallmouth bass and possibly stocked rainbow trout.

Distribution of Species by River Aging Category

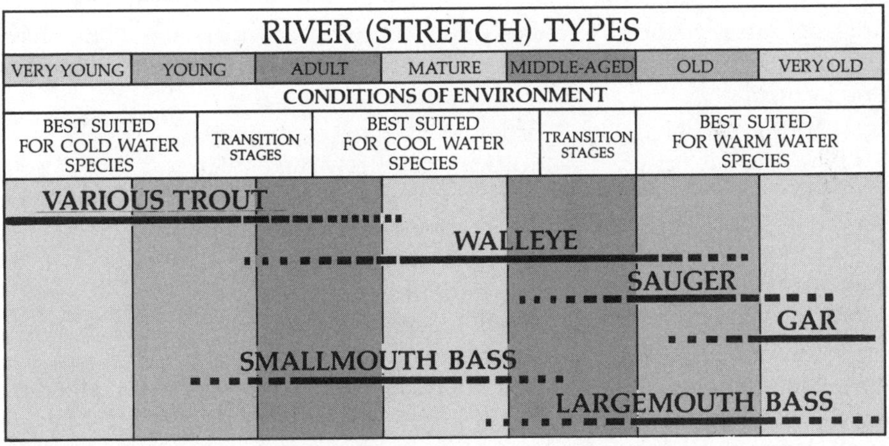

RIVER (STRETCH) TYPES						
VERY YOUNG	YOUNG	ADULT	MATURE	MIDDLE-AGED	OLD	VERY OLD
CONDITIONS OF ENVIRONMENT						
BEST SUITED FOR COLD WATER SPECIES	TRANSITION STAGES	BEST SUITED FOR COOL WATER SPECIES		TRANSITION STAGES	BEST SUITED FOR WARM WATER SPECIES	

VARIOUS TROUT

WALLEYE

SAUGER

GAR

SMALLMOUTH BASS

LARGEMOUTH BASS

Key: _____ strongest populations

- - - - - - - - - weaker populations

This chart shows the species present in each river category. Notice how a particular fish's numbers "peak" and then gradually fade out as the river evolves. It does not take into account seasonal spawning runs of northern pike, walleyes or steelhead. Pollution, too, can affect species' distribution by disturbing the natural water quality. Some streams which could house trout are thrown out of balance ecologically by heated power plant discharge or excess nutrients from agricultural run-off. Note that each of the aging stages tends to favor certain varieties of cold, cool, or warm water species.

Young, picturesque trout streams found in the mountains are usually unpolluted and unaffected by the hands of man. Despite their beauty, these streams are quite infertile since they run over rock beds and gain few nutrients from the land. For this reason, very-young and young streams cannot support a large fish population. They are limited to a few types of fish by this relatively sterile environment.

Cold water species, such as trout, disappear in the adult stage of aging. In these sections, with less gradient and a warm climate, the water flows slower and warms to a higher temperature where trout cannot survive. The environment now favors cool water fish like smallmouth bass. In the mature stage, other cool water fish like walleyes, saugers, northern pike, and muskies enter the picture. Then, as a river gets older, the cool water species begin to fade. Warm water fish like largemouth bass and catfish become dominant, and rough fish like carp become more populous.

Different stretches of the same stream can have different personalities and different fish species. Rarely is a stream the same from beginning to end, because few regions are geographically consistent.

Because of these limitless variations, we devised the following method of classifying streams. With these categories, we can identify and recognize most river stretches found in North America. Of course, there will be exceptions; those parts in transition between types are much like a natural lake that has eutrophic bays, while the main body of the lake is mesotrophic in character.

These classes are best viewed as guidelines to better understanding the rivers you fish, and the quantity and types of predominant fish you could expect to find in them.

(1) VERY YOUNG	—Brook trout and/or grayling
(2) YOUNG	—Stocked trout, few smallmouths
(3) ADULT	—Appearance of cool water fish (smallmouths)
(4) MATURE	—Good populations of smallmouths
(5) MIDDLE-AGED	—Walleyes, saugers, some smallmouths
(6) OLD	—Largemouth bass
(7) VERY OLD	—Mostly rough fish
(8) TIDAL	—Backwaters of the ocean

Within this context, we can isolate stretches which best support smallmouth bass. These conditions usually occur in river stretches we term Adult, Mature, and to some degree, Middle-Aged. There are several reasons why these river sections produce the best smallmouth fishing.

These tend to be "in between" river sections. They have mild current, moderate depth and few weeds. Slower, shallow rivers, by contrast, have more slack water, greater weedgrowth, and are better suited to largemouths and northern pike. Deeper rivers tend to favor fish like walleyes and saugers. However, river sections which are not *ideal* for bass and pike, or walleyes and saugers, often offer conditions that are ripe for smallmouth bass.

The accompanying charts give us the generalized makeup of the key river types.

	ADULT	MATURE	MIDDLE-AGED
SHAPE OF CROSS-SECTION	Prominent Shoreline Vegetation Gravel Deposits Begin to Build Erosion Really Flattens Out the Stream Bed	Flood Plain Sand and Gravel Deposits	Broadened Flood Plain Channel Bottom is Completely Smooth Sand and Mud Deposits
SOURCE AND GEOGRAPHICAL DRAINAGE AREA	This stretch can be of highland or pastoral origin and will drain an expansive area, like marginal hardwood forests that contain mixed pine, and fringe agricultural areas. At this stage, the river has its maximum number of tributaries and will drain generally infertile, sparse areas. The source is usually a young river, but could be a lake or spring in the lower foothills or in a sand or gravel locale. Sometimes adult streams drain "meso" lakes or highland reservoirs. There are almost no intermittent streams acting as feeders.	This stretch may either emerge from or cut through a pastoral landscape, usually composed of sandstone and other soil types. The drainage area can include farmland as well as major urban and industrial areas, which can have a major impact on pollution levels. The number of tributaries start to decrease at this stage.	This stage often has a farmland origin. The drainage area is very large and fertile due to adjacent agricultural areas. Tributaries consist mainly of adult rivers.
WATER QUALITY	The water is semi-clear but can become very murky during heavy rains, particularly in farm areas or small urban areas. Premature aging may occur in areas of intense agricultural activity when nutrient levels are high or where pollution is substantial.	The water will be semi-clear to semi-murky. During high water periods, it will be very turbid, especially around agricultural areas, usually taking four to five days to clear up after a rain. Slower-running water will make the temperature higher. Aging will accelerate because of agricultural and industrial pollutants.	The water is murky to quite turbid most of the time due to the suspended mineral and soil particles and increased organic nutrients. Turbidity is a constant factor because of the large size of the watershed, a situation that makes angling difficult. Where this river broadens into a large lake, settling will occur and water quality will temporarily improve.

	ADULT	MATURE	MIDDLE-AGED
PROBABLE SPECIES PRESENT	Generally cool water fish such as smallmouth bass, northern pike, some walleyes, maybe some carp, and possibly a few muskies.	Walleyes, sauger, some smallmouths, northern pike, muskies, catfish, white bass, sturgeon, a few largemouths, perch, crappies, carp, suckers, buffalo, and rock bass.	Northerns, saugers, walleyes, some smallmouths, a few muskies, silver bass, good largemouths, and catfish. Certain sections of a middle-aged stretch will be more hospitable to one species because of structural make-up, even though they cut through the same terrain.
TYPICAL ILLUSTRATIONS	These stretches are found in western Pennsylvania (in the Appalachians), Arkansas (the Buffalo), the St. Croix in Minnesota, the upper stretches of the Mississippi, the upper Potomac River and stretches of the Shenandoah.	These stretches can be found in major drainage areas in any part of the country. For example, large stretches of the Mississippi and the lower Allegheny River in Pennsylvania.	The St. Lawrence River bordering the U.S. and Canada has middle-aged stretches, as does the Detroit River, and, of course, a good part of the Mississippi and Ohio Rivers.
KEY I.D. FEATURE	Trout can no longer survive or reproduce naturally. The appearance of coolwater fish. (walleyes, smallmouths)	The ability to produce quantities of preferred game species such as walleyes, smallmouths, sauger, and northern pike. Deep pools provide refuge, and sand/gravel banks provide smallmouth spawning grounds. A mature stream can produce good populations of several kinds of gamefish; sandy, rocky sections with fast water will hold smallmouths while the deeper, slower sections or pools will contain walleyes.	The presence of naturally-reproducing walleyes and saugers mixed with fair levels of largemouth bass, plus some smallmouths and northern pike. There is a diversity of habitat for just about any kind of fish. This is the last stage for quantities of naturally-reproducing coolwater fish (smallmouths).
GRADIENT AND DEPTH	Gradient: Two to three foot drop per mile. Depth: Six to ten feet average with intermittent deep and shallow stretches based on the amount	Gradient: 1.5 to two foot drop per mile. Depth: Depth will vary. Some stretches will be four to five feet deep, while deeper holes can be fifteen to	Gradient: One to 1.5 foot drop per mile. Depth: Depth will vary from shallow, one foot deep weedy backwater pockets to forty foot pools. Runs of twelve

	ADULT	MATURE	MIDDLE-AGED
GRADIENT AND DEPTH	of sand and gravel present. Most pools following rapids are eight to ten feet with occasional isolated holes of fifteen to twenty feet.	twenty feet. There is a lot of eight to ten foot water.	feet are common. Under dams, gouges of fifty feet can occur.
GEOGRAPHICAL MAKE-UP AND BOTTOM CONTENT	The stream bed is alternating sections of gravel, sand, and fist-sized rocks with sporadic boulders and no silt. There will be shallower sections and some rocks dressed with moss. Weedgrowth is sparse. Shoreline banks composed of fist-sized rocks, trees, and brush. Occasional wing dams will be present.	The main channel is composed mostly of sand. Siltation is now a significant factor; wing dams are sometimes constructed to control this. There are some rock outcroppings. Aquatic growth is common, along with a higher nutrient level.	Flows mostly through soft sedimentary rock and sandy subsoils. Sand is the dominant riverbed material. Time and erosion have pulverized the rocks and gravel. There will be a few rock outcrops along the banks of the river. This stage will exhibit well-developed flood plains; flooding is common.
COMMON TRAITS	This stretch contains a higher nutrient level, and warmer and slower moving water than the very young or young stretches. Typical of this stretch are alternating "riffle" or "slick" sections. Gone are the roaring, cascading rapids— replaced by mini-rapids that are not dangerous. There is increased fertilizer runoff and sewage input. Damming is more frequent, and occasional islands will be found. Sand and gravel bars have become a prominent feature.	Rapids nonexistent; at best a few shallow "riffles" will occur. Mature rivers can and do overflow. They will begin to meander and develop flood plains. On this river stage, dams actually create miniature impoundments. Although they are called "pools," they function much like reservoirs. At certain times of the year, usually spring or fall, all the gamefish species could be stacked up against the dam! This stream is an *IN-FISHERMAN* paradise and is the first stage that produces multiple quantities of preferred gamefish.	This stretch usually flows by river towns and metropolitan areas where pollution can be a severe problem. It is at this stage that the river really starts to show the buildup of nutrients, erosion, and pollution. Except for trout and salmon, just about any type of fish can survive. This stream will offer the most pounds of gamefish per acre provided it is unpolluted. Flood plains can create backwater sloughs or flat, high, fertile fields. A dredged, mid-ship channel is usually maintained for barges, and dams with locks are common.

River fishermen face more sudden, dramatic changes in water conditions than lake fishermen can ever imagine. Most lakes are "a piece of cake" when compared structurally with rivers. Water levels in natural lakes remain relatively stable over long periods of time. It usually takes a long-term drought or heavy rainfall to bring about severe high or low water levels in a lake. Yet river anglers are always fighting rising or falling water levels.

More than just contending with water level "flux," they must adjust to bottom structure that is here today and gone tomorrow. Sandbars come and go. Flow patterns can change in a subtle manner with a shift of the stream's course, or an increase in current speed.

Changing bottom conditions obviously also affect fish location. As rapidly as water levels rise or fall, a key fish-attracting current break, like an eddy near a deep washout hole, can suddenly appear or completely vanish, and affect fish location accordingly. Remember, the ability to read current is the key to successful river fishing. Take the time to learn how it functions with rising or falling water levels, creating or eliminating fish-holding areas in the process.

CURRENT

Unequivocally, rivers offer people some of the finest fishing anywhere! Yet, except for a few seasonal trips, a vast majority of anglers never really experience the total multi-season fishery that's available. Considering the numbers of fish and variety of fish species, rivers are almost totally unexploited. In fact, rivers have been called the last frontier of American angling.

What exactly is a river, and how do they differ from lakes? Rivers, as opposed to natural lakes, carry surplus water off the land back to the sea. They are the earth's drainage system. Thus, a river continuously receives new water and nourishment from the surrounding terrain. Obviously, rivers are not static environments. Eventually, all life forms which rivers develop work their way toward the sea, through the food chain and out of the ecosystem.

The key to understanding rivers, and how smallmouth bass adapt to the mobile environment, is to grasp the concept that a river is a moving body of water. It is important to understand that a clear difference exists between a lake and river. The life forms (even the same species) adapt differently, because they inhabit totally separate environments.

CROSS-SECTION OF A RIVER

rolled water strip

eddy

boils

land water line

boils

A
REVERSE CURRENT
eddy flows begins
to sweep back
upstream

B
SLACK WATER
very little
directional
flow

water appears
to bulge slightly

The major difference between a lake and a river is current. It's the most important element that a fish must adjust to in a river. Much like the wind on dry land, current is a mixture of many interacting natural phenomena. Current is a powerful force that has a continual effect on the entire river ecosystem.

In order to fish rivers effectively, you must understand a few basic principles of moving water. Essentially, current is a key to smallmouth bass movement and location in rivers. Therefore, let's take a closer look at some of the more important factors that will help you visualize specifically how current acts.

In lakes, smallmouths relate to structural breaks like weedlines, drop offs and bars. The best way for an angler to be aware of these elements is with the aid of a depth finder.

However, on rivers the presence of structural details is revealed by breaks in the current. To a river fish a current break can be just as important as the object that caused it. The key to becoming a successful river angler is learning to relate subtle current changes with the underwater structures that create them.

Objects on the bottom slow, stop, divert, or in some way break the flow of current. Unfortunately, these breaks are not always obvious to anglers. Most cannot be seen on a depth finder, nor are they marked on maps. However, the smallmouths know where these breaks are located! A knife-edged wall of fast flowing water bounded by slower moving or slack water is just as real to the fish as a sharp rock drop-off. Clearly, in order to fish a river intelligently, you must understand current.

OK, let's get into the nitty-gritty of rivers. Just how does an angler go about understanding rivers and "reading" the water? The answer is that many times a good river fisherman will rely more on his *eyes* (visual observations) than on a depth finder or graph! The surface waters of a river give the eagle-eyed angler clues to the bottom structure. This "signpost" of underwater terrain allows you to read the bottom shape, locate underwater objects and visualize current breaks.

For example, a submerged boulder which may hold smallmouths shows its presence visually in the form of a surface "boil" downstream from the rock. In addition, a midstream, flat stretch of sand bottom produces a slick or smooth surface condition. Review the accompanying illustrations carefully; they'll help you understand current and visualize bottom features.

If you were to cut a river crossways at a point where the main downstream current and a reverse eddy current "break," you would see a condition much like this.

Section "A" *shows the eddy current breaking to make a reverse, circular, upstream sweep.*

Section "B" *depicts the "slack" water that occurs between the two. This "slack" water shifts downstream quite slowly in relation to regular flow, creating a vacuum where fish can retreat to but still be in position to take advantage of passing food. Because of the amount of energy expended by river fish fighting current, they feed more and are stronger, but usually grow slower, than lake fish. They spend much more time hunting food from spots like these that are great for casual meals.*

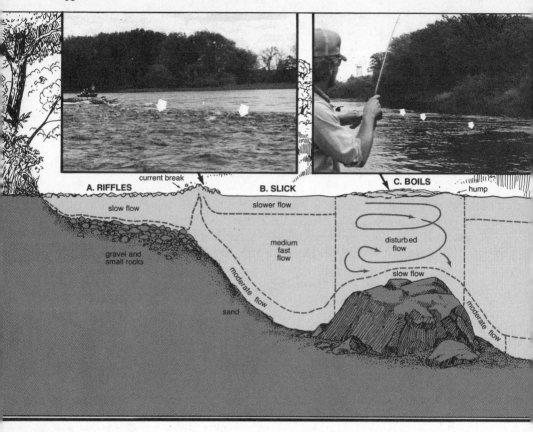

The Telltale Surface of a River

   The surface of a river will give you clues to its bottom structure. The accompanying illustration shows some of the more prominent surface features.
   Current velocity (speed) is not the same in all parts of a stream channel. Friction on the sides, around obstructions, and along the bottom produces different surface patterns. Note that surface riffles in condition A are produced by shallow water running over small rocks. But at the drop-off there is a current break which is revealed by a "bulge line." This happens when water of different speeds builds up and "breaks." A slick surface in condition B is produced when water runs over soft or smooth material like silt or sand. Here the turbulence is minimal and the flow smooth, so the upwelling of disturbed water doesn't happen. As soon as rock or similar object interrupts the water's flow, you will see "broken" water like condition D, or very disturbed water like the boils in condition C.

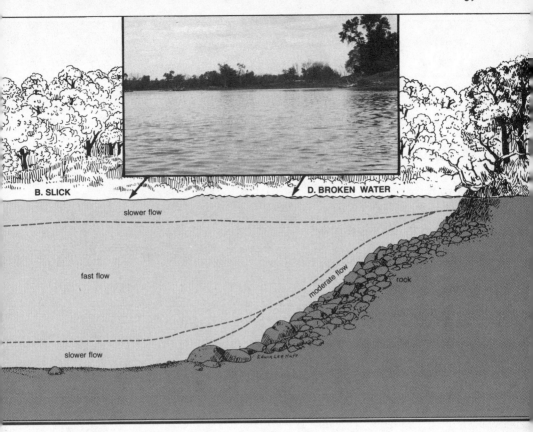

A list of some of the major structural elements found in streams would sure-ly include most of the following:
    (1) MAIN, FEEDER AND SIDE CHANNELS
    (2) POINT BARS ON THE INSIDE BENDS OF RIVER CURVES
    (3) MAN-MADE STRUCTURAL ELEMENTS
    (4) SLOUGHS OF DEAD WATER
    (5) NATURAL LEVEES OF HARD MATERIAL LEFT BY FLOODS
    (6) BACKWATER AREAS
    (7) SANDBARS
    (8) POOLS
    (9) RIFFLES
    (10) EDDIES
    (11) CURRENT BREAKS
    (12) THE INTERSECTION OF A TRIBUTARY STREAM
    (13) AREAS BELOW A DAM
Most streams contain these various components in differing combinations.

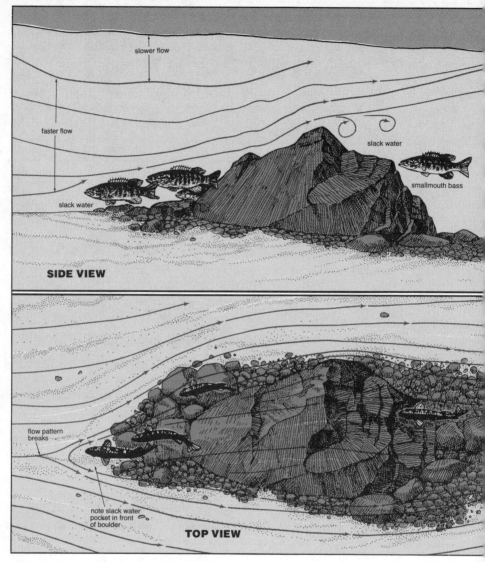

SIDE VIEW

slower flow

faster flow

slack water

slack water

smallmouth bass

TOP VIEW

flow pattern breaks

note slack water pocket in front of boulder

Current Flow—Boulders

This set of drawings demonstrates the reactions of current when it comes into contact with the bottom and underwater objects. They show an irregular boulder that is an excellent fish holding structure. The only clue an angler would have as to the presence of this rock is the downstream boils. *These boils are a key identification factor. Usually, the bigger and more turbulent the boil, the more slack water there is behind the obstruction. Note, too, that the blunt nose of this rock provides a slack water pocket in front of the rock—an excellent ambush point for a feeding smallmouth bass facing upstream. Smallmouth bass usually tend to hang tight to the rock itself, while walleyes will be strung out in the slack water pocket behind the rock at the knife edge of the fast and slow water (see top view). Many times a boil could occur 20, 30, or more feet downstream from the obstruction itself. The faster the current and the deeper the water over the rock, the further downstream the boils will first break the surface.*

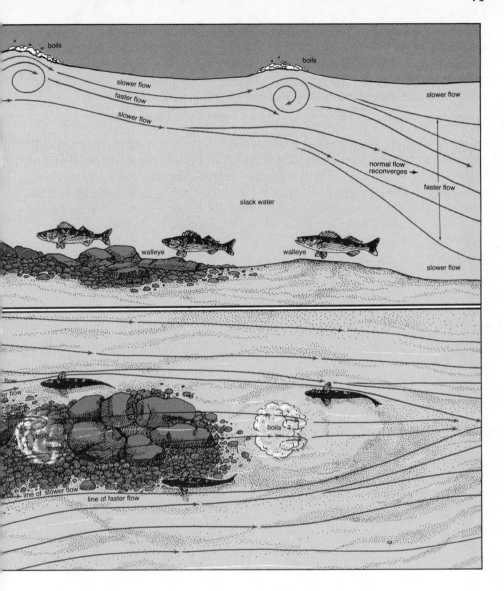

In addition to current, other key factors are turbidity and water level. Turbidity is the amount of suspended particulate (silt) matter in a river, which affects how muddy the water is. Typically, in rivers that have rock stream beds, the turbidity is usually minimal. On the other hand, in many plains' rivers, turbidity is at a maximum. In some river systems, high turbidity is permanent, while in others it's a seasonal, temporary condition. (Nonetheless, where highly turbid water exists for any length of time, the fish life will be affected.) Fishermen must realize that water turbidity will affect both light penetration and fish activity.

The water level will determine current velocity (speed of current flow.) This is also a very important factor in smallmouth bass location. For example, smallmouth bass tend to relate to the faster water areas, while walleyes prefer areas of slower current. The overall impact of current velocity cannot be over-emphasized.

In summary, current, turbidity and water level are all interrelated factors that affect the fish in varying degrees. To catch smallmouth bass consistently, you must understand these simple, yet important, concepts.

All in all, rivers offer an unexploited and diversified angling experience that can significantly increase your angling options. Many are "on their way back" as a result of clean-up efforts. Acre for acre, their potential is much greater than lakes. Fish in rivers must eat more because of the current they continually cope with, so they are more consistently active than lake fish. The fish are shallower and more localized, and are therefore more accessible (easier to catch). Bad weather conditions (cold fronts) do not seem to affect fish as much in rivers as they do in lakes. Given all this, wouldn't you like to explore America's last angling frontier?

Chapter 8

CLASSIFICATION OF RESERVOIRS

Some reservoirs can offer smallmouth bass—lots of them—plus big fish! In fact, the current world record smallmouth bass was caught in Dale Hollow Reservoir on the Tennessee/Kentucky border! However, all reservoirs are not created equal, and the differences between them are keys to determining the quality of the smallmouth fishery. This chapter investigates the fundamentals of reservoirs, how to classify them, and provides some guidelines for determining their smallmouth bass fishing potential.

Basically, a reservoir is an impounded body of water that is held back by a dam. The artificially-impounded water floods the natural landscape such as marshes, plains, hills, mountains, plateaus or canyons. This provides a clue to reservoir classification.

Reservoirs can be classified by their physical make-up and function, just as lakes and rivers are categorized. These classes are based on regional geography and geology of various landforms.

Taking a cross-section of North America, you'd see that some areas might be low, sort of swampy or marshy, or rather flat like an old flood-plain region. In other places, the terrain is hilly. Still others have mountains and highland ridges rising up to form foothills. These are usually low mountain ranges like the Boston or Ouachita ranges in Arkansas, the Appalachian chain in the East, the Cumberland highlands of Kentucky and Tennessee, or the low coastal ranges of the West Coast.

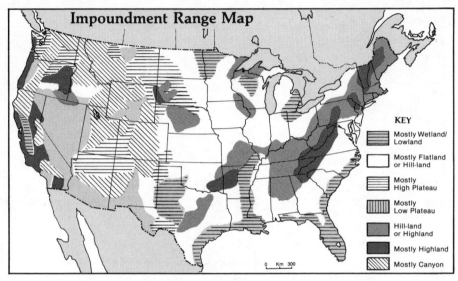

In the plains west of the Mississippi, you encounter what are termed "high plains." Just west of them is an immense plateau that lifts step-like up across the mid-section of the continent. This plateau area is adjacent to the rugged Rocky Mountains. Reservoirs built in the canyons of the mountains take on long, snake-like shapes, and their cross-sections have towering, sharp, almost vertical walls.

These changes in terrain provide a clear-cut basis to classify waters, since reservoirs lying within each of these landforms all have the same basic configuration. In other words, they have a similar cross-section and shape. For example, all canyon reservoirs are long and snake-like with towering, sharp, nearly vertical walls. On the other hand, waters impounded in flood plains tend to be wide, with expanses of shallow flats.

A mind-boggling array, isn't it? Yet it's not as awesome as it first appears, because fish within similar types of reservoirs respond in much the same manner. In short, reservoirs constructed in similar landforms—even if they're in different parts of the country—are enough alike that we can fit them, for identification purposes, into six basic groups. These groups are:

(1) CANYON

(2) HIGHLAND

(3) PLATEAU

(4) HILL-LAND

(5) FLATLAND

(6) WETLAND/LOWLAND

In addition to the general classification, each impoundment has its own "personality." The personality of an impoundment is more or less local, and consists of the bottom content, water characteristics, vegetation types, population density, availability of food, and competitive species. All of these may vary with the location of the reservoir, along with changes in the prevailing aquatic life.

The purpose for building a reservoir has a great deal to do with its personality. Was it built for flood control, irrigation, power supply, cooling or recreational purposes? Each of these is important in determining an impoundment's personality, but they do not necessarily affect its broad classification slot.

Some of the more important facets of personality are water level fluctuation, water color, fertility, temperature of a section or the entire reservoir, and the effects of wind. To better understand some of these traits, let's take a closer look at a few of them.

Fluctuation: Water level fluctuation—the amount of water level variation—is the curse of a reservoir's aquatic life. Few factors have more of an influence on the stability of a food chain than a constant raising or lowering of the water. Water level can fluctuate seasonally from 3 to 5 feet in a small reservoir, while in some very large, deep impoundments it could vary 20 to 200 feet! This kind of fluctuation can play havoc with the fishery. Dam construction (spillway vs. gates), type and size of feeder creeks, and drainage area all affect water level.

Water Color: Water color depends on the condition of the drainage area upstream and along the length of the reservoir. If black soil, red soil or clay deposits are characteristics of the landscape, then chances are that the amount of water being fed by the feeders will profoundly affect the water color, and the fishing as well. If the main river and creeks drain through rocky, gravel or sandy areas, the water will most likely remain relatively clear.

In very large reservoirs, the main body of the impoundment is usually affected much less by run-off than the headwaters and creek arms. Headwaters and creeks may be murky, but the main body of water or dam area can remain quite clear.

Fertility: This is a product of the chemistry of the water source, the soil composition of the lake basin and its surroundings, and the influence of man. A small, shallow reservoir, with a slow flow-through rate and many homes around its shoreline, could be very fertile due to surface run-off and leeching from septic tanks. This can have a bearing on how fast an impoundment ages.

Sedimentation, which ages a reservoir like eutrophication ages a natural lake, is a direct result of the water exchange rate and condition of the surrounding terrain.

Water temperature: Water temperature is determined by water color, depth, bottom type, wind, regional location, and last, but not least, man.

Water temperature is a complex subject. It would take several chapters to adequately touch most of the bases. Some reservoirs thermocline; others don't. Some get extremely warm in summer; others don't. Basically, however, water temperature largely dictates which fish and prey species the impoundment contains, as well as the length of the growing season.

Wind: Wind is a catalyst, rather than an actual personality trait. It can af-

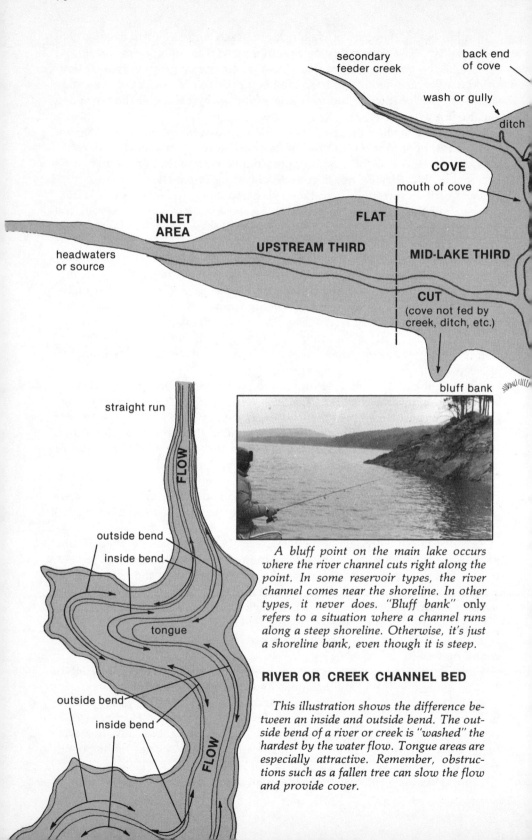

secondary
feeder creek

back end
of cove

wash or gully

ditch

COVE

mouth of cove

**INLET
AREA**

FLAT

headwaters
or source

UPSTREAM THIRD

MID-LAKE THIRD

CUT
(cove not fed by
creek, ditch, etc.)

bluff bank

straight run

FLOW

outside bend

inside bend

tongue

outside bend

inside bend

FLOW

A bluff point on the main lake occurs
where the river channel cuts right along the
point. In some reservoir types, the river
channel comes near the shoreline. In other
types, it never does. "Bluff bank" only
refers to a situation where a channel runs
along a steep shoreline. Otherwise, it's just
a shoreline bank, even though it is steep.

RIVER OR CREEK CHANNEL BED

This illustration shows the difference between an inside and outside bend. The outside bend of a river or creek is "washed" the
hardest by the water flow. Tongue areas are
especially attractive. Remember, obstructions such as a fallen tree can slow the flow
and provide cover.

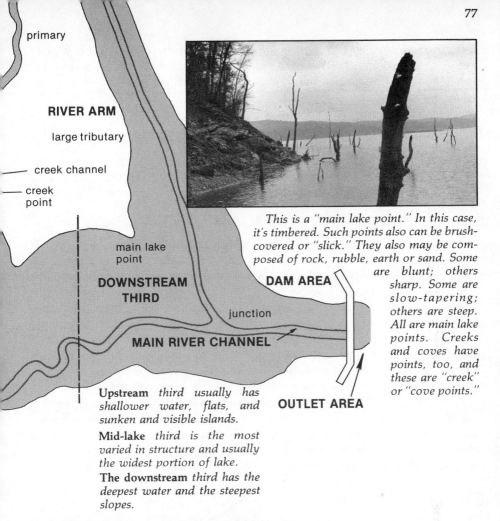

primary

RIVER ARM

large tributary

creek channel

creek point

main lake point

DOWNSTREAM THIRD

DAM AREA

junction

MAIN RIVER CHANNEL

OUTLET AREA

This is a "main lake point." In this case, it's timbered. Such points also can be brush-covered or "slick." They also may be composed of rock, rubble, earth or sand. Some are blunt; others sharp. Some are slow-tapering; others are steep. All are main lake points. Creeks and coves have points, too, and these are "creek" or "cove points."

Upstream *third usually has shallower water, flats, and sunken and visible islands.*

Mid-lake *third is the most varied in structure and usually the widest portion of lake.*

The downstream *third has the deepest water and the steepest slopes.*

Typical Impoundment Features

We've prepared the accompanying illustrations to show various impoundment features and our terms for them. There are so many regional variations that we were forced to adopt or coin words or phrases which we felt would be suitable nationally. For example, we dropped the word "bay" and become more specific by using the terms "cove" or "cut." The top view below is not meant to depict any specific type of impoundment. It is simply a composite. Also note that it is divided into three sections.

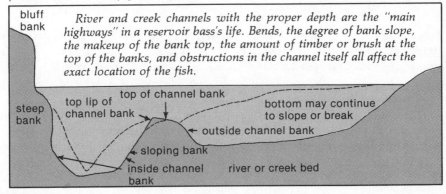

River and creek channels with the proper depth are the "main highways" in a reservoir bass's life. Bends, the degree of bank slope, the makeup of the bank top, the amount of timber or brush at the top of the banks, and obstructions in the channel itself all affect the exact location of the fish.

bluff bank

steep bank

top lip of channel bank

top of channel bank

bottom may continue to slope or break

outside channel bank

sloping bank

inside channel bank

river or creek bed

fect color, oxygen levels and temperature. These effects, however, are usually not great or prolonged. High winds mix the water and cool or warm the surface. Discoloration caused by wind is usually confined to sections of a lake where waves erode the shoreline or stir up shallow, flat areas. One of the more pronounced effects of wind action is the amount of available oxygen.

Of significant note is the effect of strong, prolonged winds that "push" the water level up at one end of the reservoir, creating a back flow across the bottom of the basin, or along the top of the thermocline, in the opposite direction of the waves. This action can cause currents along the reservoir bottom, and set up slight eddy effects around submerged humps and riverbeds.

PRIME SMALLMOUTH RESERVOIRS

In general, the environment of deep, clear, highland impoundments comes closest to being "ideal" for smallmouths. They're generally too steep and rocky to develop strong largemouth populations, and may lack substantial walleye populations. The lack of numbers of competing predators allows smallmouths to expand into the available habitat. Given suitable prey, favorable water temperature, good nesting sites, etc., smallmouths can grow extremely large.

The Tennessee River TVA impoundments offer the smallmouth bass a somewhat unique environment. These impoundments provide an "in between" set of conditions; they contain some reservoir and many river characteristics. Actually, these waters could be accurately classified as rivers!

Characteristically, these impoundments are relatively narrow and have a rapid water exchange (current) through them. In addition, the water is darker in color and warmer than most "typical" smallmouth bass reservoirs. All of the preceding factors, in combination with the plentiful prey (crayfish, shad, skipjack), produce a dynamite smallmouth fishery. Due to the overriding river

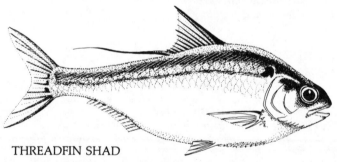

THREADFIN SHAD

personality traits of these impoundments, you can simply consider them as rivers, and fish them accordingly. In other words, current breaks (rocks, stumps, islands), current velocity, eddies, and channel areas are all important features to take into account. All in all, these Tennessee River impoundments yield smallmouth bass—and lots of them!

What about other reservoir types? That's a tough question. Hill-land impoundments may or may not have good smallmouth populations. It depends largely on the presence of other competing predators, but by and large, they're only fair smallmouth waters. They're usually more conducive to other species of fish.

Most canyon and plateau environments appear to be too deep and cold to favor smallmouths. They're better suited to walleyes, pike and trout. Northern flatland reservoirs, meanwhile, generally produce better walleyes, while southern weed or timber-filled impoundments usually host strong populations of largemouth bass. Shallow, weedy, lowland/wetland impoundments are normally largemouth/small pike/small walleye waters, depending on the area of the country they're in.

In short, highland impoundments, or impoundments with highland characteristics, come the closest to being ideal reservoir smallmouth waters. In addition, several of the unique TVA river/reservoir systems grow huge fish. These are your best bets for giant smallmouths. Granted, there are exceptions, but not many. If you're after smallmouths, play the odds and concentrate on these types of man-made lakes. Some host the largest smallmouths in the world!

TVA BUOY

TVA's Fish Attractor Program

Natural vegetation is sparse or almost totally lacking in many TVA reservoirs. This lack of vegetative "cover" for fish, together with other factors, results in the dispersion of fish populations. Recent experimentation with man-made "cover" in the form of artificial fish attractors has proven effective in concentrating fish in the area for food and shelter, and as a location for increased angling success.

A population study conducted on Barkley Lake indicated that brush fish attractors harbored 19 times the weight of crappies found in open water areas without attractors, as well as 13 times more largemouth bass.

In joint effort, TVA and Mississippi, Alabama, and Tennessee State Fisheries biologists began attractor installation in Tennessee Valley reservoirs in 1977, and to date have put over 12,000 individual structures in 18 reservoirs.

Fish attractors are especially helpful to fishermen unfamiliar with reservoir topography and conditions, and to those who don't have sophisticated gear for locating natural concentrations of fish. Fish attractors can increase catch rate, fisherman satisfaction, and achieve a better balance of sport fish harvest with the individual reservoir's ability to produce fish.

Fishing on Attractor Sites

Fish attractors are piles of brush anchored to the bottom of the lake. Fishermen can locate them by using a weighted line or depth recorder. The following suggestions should help you catch fish that take cover in the attractors:
1. *To avoid getting hung, use wire hooks which will bend and release your line.*
2. *If fishing directly over the attractors, put your anchors on either side of the brush pile to avoid scaring the fish. Slowly lower your bait or lure until you feel resistance, and then stop. (Count the turns of the reel so you can return to the same depth.) Hold a live bait steady in one place, but move a lure up and down. Both can be fished above the attractors with a float.*
3. *If you are casting, stay to one side of the attractors and work your lure over the top or through the brush pile.*
4. *Trollers do well around attractors in coves and around elongated deep-water sites. Troll parallel to the strung-out brush piles, around the end, and down the other side.*

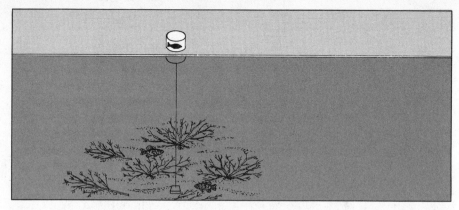

Deep-water attractors are of two types and are marked by white buoys with an orange design depicting a fish. A single buoy indicates the center of a one-half-acre brush pile. Two buoys indicate either end of a long brush pile.

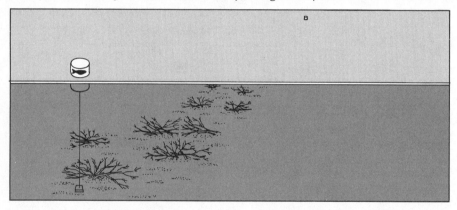

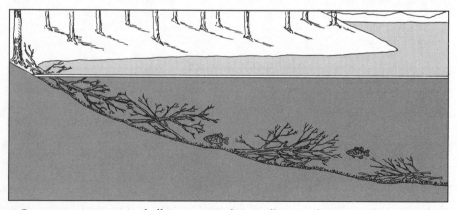

Cove attractors start in shallow water and generally extend in a straight line into deep water. Each site contains about ten brush piles. White, 6-foot poles, or a tree painted white to a height of 6 feet at the heads of coves, mark where attractors are located.

RESERVOIR SECTION TYPES

CANYON	PLATEAU	HIGHLAND	HILL-LAND	FLATLAND	WETLAND
CONDITIONS OF ENVIRONMENT					
COLD	COOL			COOL OR WARM	

TROUT

WALLEYE—(NORTH)

LARGEMOUTH BASS—(SOUTH)

SAUGER

SMALLMOUTH BASS

Key: _____ strongest populations
- - - - - - - - - - weaker populations

Due to the wide geographic distribution of the various reservoir types, it is very difficult to generalize about which species of fish may be present. For example, a shallow, wetland impoundment located in the North may contain walleyes and only a few largemouth bass. A wetland reservoir located in the deep South, in contrast, will not contain a single walleye, but could have lots of big bass!

The geographic area in which a reservoir is situated has a direct bearing on the resulting fishery. In general, reservoirs in the North provide a cooler water environment than those located in the South.

The smallmouth bass is again found in "in between" conditions. Highland reservoirs are mid-way in the reservoir classification type. They are generally in between the cold water canyon and warmer water wetland environments, whether they are located in the North or South. Smallmouths are highlanders! Interestingly, smallmouths are present in highland impoundments located in such diverse areas as Texas, Wisconsin, Kentucky, California and Maine!

A special riverine impoundment type could be created for several of the Tennessee River TVA waters. Pickwick, Wheeler and Guntersville Lakes would fall into this category. These waters are conspicuously river-like in character and don't fit into our "normal" reservoir classifications. Even though these TVA impoundments are situated in a hill-land/highland area, they cannot be assigned to either classification, due to their narrow width and rapid flow-through rate. Similarly, sections of the upper Mississippi River could also be placed in this special riverine classification.

IMPOUNDMENT CLASSIFICATION

Canyon Impoundment

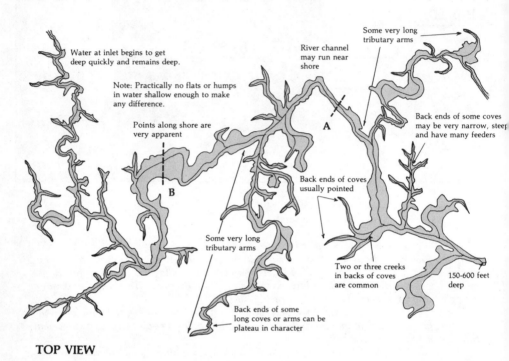

Water at inlet begins to get deep quickly and remains deep.

Note: Practically no flats or humps in water shallow enough to make any difference.

Points along shore are very apparent

B

River channel may run near shore

Some very long tributary arms

A

Back ends of some coves may be very narrow, steep and have many feeders

Back ends of coves usually pointed

Some very long tributary arms

Two or three creeks in backs of coves are common

Back ends of some long coves or arms can be plateau in character

150-600 feet deep

TOP VIEW

CROSS-SECTIONS

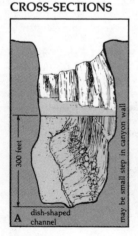

300 feet

A dish-shaped channel

may be small step in canyon wall

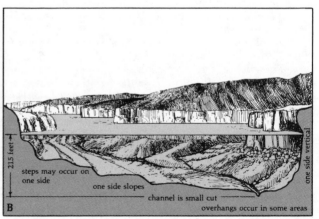

215 feet

steps may occur on one side

one side slopes

B channel is small cut

one side vertical

overhangs occur in some areas

Plateau Impoundment

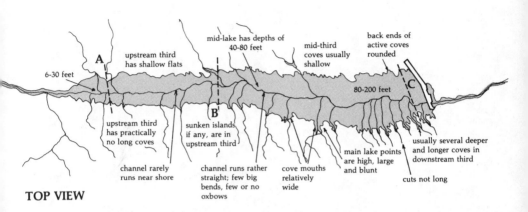

TOP VIEW

- 6-30 feet
- A
- upstream third has shallow flats
- mid-lake has depths of 40-80 feet
- mid-third coves usually shallow
- back ends of active coves rounded
- 80-200 feet
- C
- upstream third has practically no long coves
- B
- sunken islands, if any, are in upstream third
- main lake points are high, large and blunt
- usually several deeper and longer coves in downstream third
- channel rarely runs near shore
- channel runs rather straight; few big bends, few or no oxbows
- cove mouths relatively wide
- cuts not long

CROSS-SECTIONS

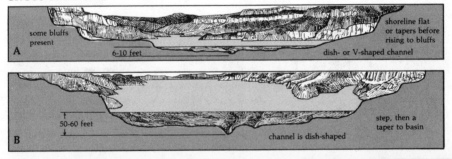

A — some bluffs present — 6-10 feet — shoreline flat or tapers before rising to bluffs — dish- or V-shaped channel

B — 50-60 feet — channel is dish-shaped — step, then a taper to basin

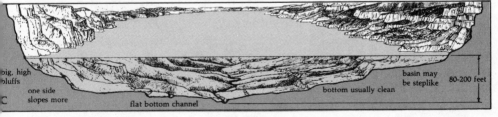

C — big, high bluffs — one side slopes more — flat bottom channel — bottom usually clean — basin may be steplike — 80-200 feet

Highland Impoundment

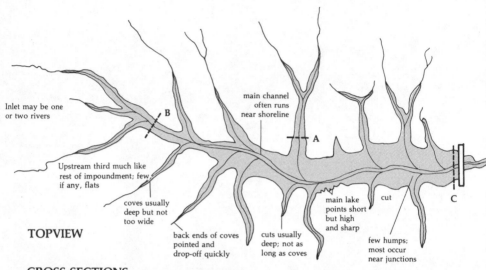

TOPVIEW

Inlet may be one
or two rivers

B

main channel
often runs
near shoreline

A

Upstream third much like
rest of impoundment; few
if any, flats

coves usually
deep but not
too wide

back ends of coves
pointed and
drop-off quickly

cuts usually
deep; not as
long as coves

main lake
points short
but high
and sharp

cut

C

few humps;
most occur
near junctions

CROSS-SECTIONS

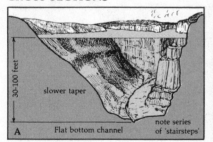

30-100 feet

slower taper

Flat bottom channel

note series
of 'stairsteps'

A

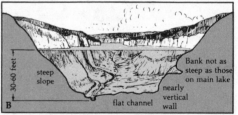

30-60 feet

steep
slope

flat channel

nearly
vertical
wall

Bank not as
steep as those
on main lake

B

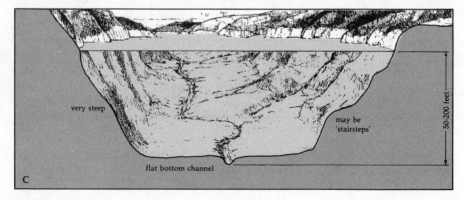

very steep

flat bottom channel

may be
'stairsteps'

50-200 feet

C

Hill-land Impoundment

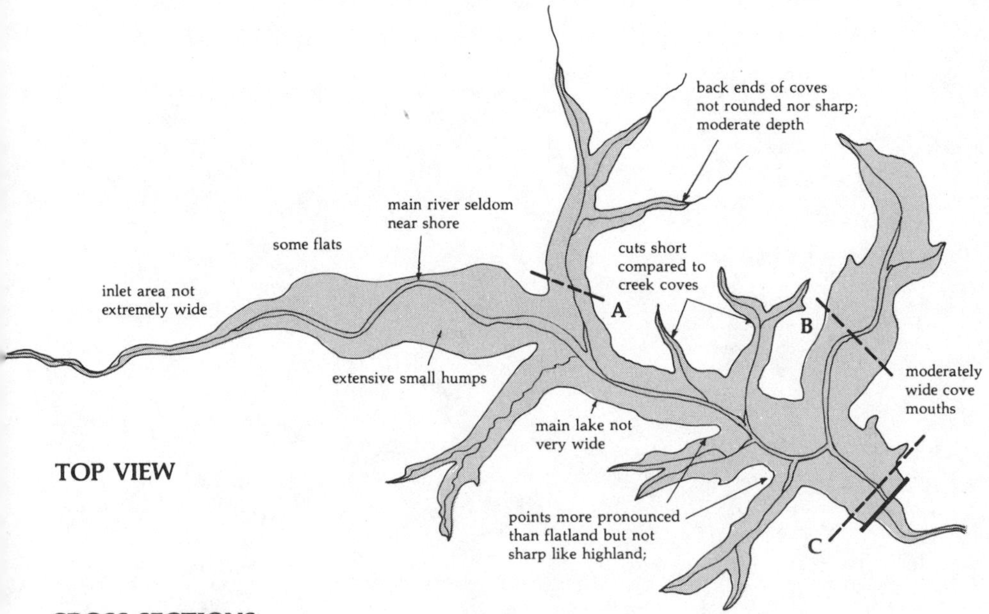

back ends of coves
not rounded nor sharp;
moderate depth

main river seldom
near shore

some flats

cuts short
compared to
creek coves

inlet area not
extremely wide

A

B

moderately
wide cove
mouths

extensive small humps

main lake not
very wide

TOP VIEW

points more pronounced
than flatland but not
sharp like highland;

C

CROSS-SECTIONS

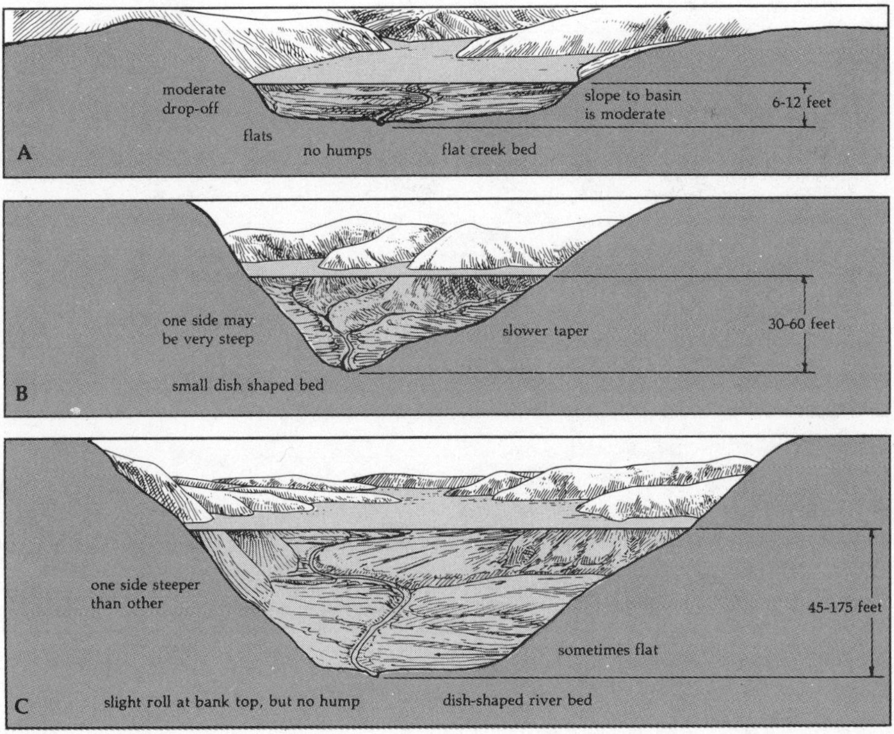

moderate
drop-off

slope to basin
is moderate

6-12 feet

A

flats

no humps

flat creek bed

one side may
be very steep

slower taper

30-60 feet

B

small dish shaped bed

one side steeper
than other

45-175 feet

sometimes flat

C

slight roll at bank top, but no hump

dish-shaped river bed

Flatland Impoundment

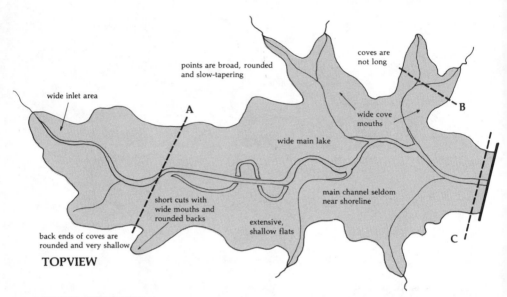

wide inlet area

points are broad, rounded
and slow-tapering

coves are
not long

B

wide cove
mouths

A

wide main lake

main channel seldom
near shoreline

short cuts with
wide mouths and
rounded backs

extensive,
shallow flats

C

back ends of coves are
rounded and very shallow

TOPVIEW

CROSS-SECTIONS

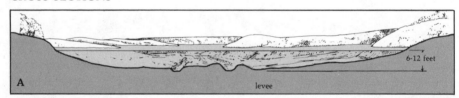

A

levee

6-12 feet

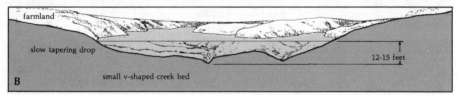

farmland

slow tapering drop

12-15 feet

small v-shaped creek bed

B

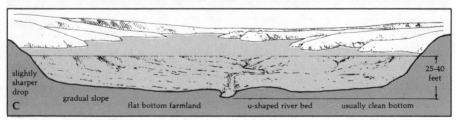

slightly
sharper
drop

gradual slope

flat bottom farmland

u-shaped river bed

usually clean bottom

C

25-40
feet

Lowland/Wetland Impoundment

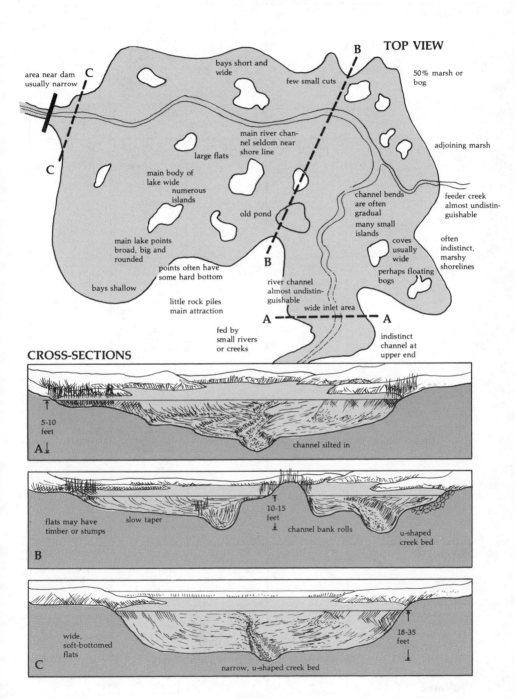

TOP VIEW

area near dam usually narrow C

bays short and wide

few small cuts

50% marsh or bog

main river channel seldom near shore line

adjoining marsh

large flats

main body of lake wide numerous islands

old pond

channel bends are often gradual

many small islands

feeder creek almost undistinguishable

often indistinct, marshy shorelines

main lake points broad, big and rounded

points often have some hard bottom

coves usually wide

perhaps floating bogs

bays shallow

little rock piles main attraction

river channel almost undistinguishable

wide inlet area

fed by small rivers or creeks

indistinct channel at upper end

CROSS-SECTIONS

5-10 feet

A

channel silted in

flats may have timber or stumps

slow taper

10-15 feet

channel bank rolls

u-shaped creek bed

B

wide, soft-bottomed flats

18-35 feet

C

narrow, u-shaped creek bed

COMPARATIVE IMPOUNDMENT CHARACTERISTICS

Impound-ment Classifi-cation	Forage	Depth	Main River Channel Charac-teristics	Feeders
Flatland	Shad, bluegills, frogs, freshwater eels	20-40' at dam 6-12' upstream	Seldom near shoreline, meanders, grealy altered, straightened with levees, dikes. Trees and brush along banks. Oxbows where channel has been straightened.	Creeks or ditches usually less than 20' wide. 1-6' deep, V-shaped bed.
Hill-Land	Shad, crayfish, bluegills, freshwater shrimp	45-175' or more depending on region	Near center of reservoir. Natural state, usually quite straight. River bed is usually rounded.	Most have a distinct channel with sloping banks, brush and/or tree-lined.
Highland	Shad, crayfish, freshwater eels, salamanders	60-200' or more depending on size.	Often runs near shoreline. Natural state has many junctions of creeks and river channels that are mostly too deep for bass use. Flat channel with steep walls.	Some are "dry-wet" (carry water only after heavy rains), rock bottoms
Plateau	Shad, salamanders	50-200' depending on location	Runs through center of reservoir, quite straight, usually not deep with flat beds. Banks are generally clean, some brush may be found. Downstream ⅓ is generally too deep for bass use.	Little gullies or washouts from flash floods. Main feeders have high walls. Feeders most prevalent on downstream third. Short and wide at mouth.
Canyon	Shad, crayfish. Some have no shad.	500-600' downstream; a few feet to 40 or 50 ft. at the inlet	May run near shore. Less distinct downstream. Very distinct, dish-shaped gorge upstream. Usually is too deep to be used by bass.	Very long creeks and small rivers. Can be 40-60 mi. long, and are shaped like main channel.
Wetland/ Lowland	Wide variety; depends on region.	Depends on region	The diversity of lowland impoundments makes them difficult to categorize.	

Cuts and Coves	Points	Shoreline	Bottom Content	Brush, Timber or Vegetation	Common Man-made Features
Coves are short, are shallow with a small feeder creek running through, and have wide mouths. Short cuts with wide mouths and rounded backs. May contain weeds, brush & timber.	Broad, rounded, slow tapering. Some with brush; usually lack timber.	Mainly long, slow tapers. Steeper bluff banks on rare occasions.	Black soil, mud flats, some hard clay.	Standing timber in main lake is common—mainly cypress and willow. Brush in backs of coves. "Moss" is main vegetation.	Dam, roadbeds, causeways, ponds, levees, building foundations, rip-rap, cemeteries.
Coves are deep downstream, and may have large timber stands. Upstream much like flatland coves. Short cuts.	Rounded, usually with standing or cut timber. Some rare cases have boulders.	Slopes quickly to 7-12 ft. of water, then gradually to main river channel.	Sand, clay, loam, some mud flats, extensive small humps.	Brush and timber in coves, "moss" on shallow flats in main lakes. Has most weed growth of any reservoir type in the South.	Dam, rip-rap, high lines and pipe lines, fence rows, rock piles, road beds, cemeteries, drainage ditches, railroad beds, building foundations, marinas.
Coves are deep, but not wide, and can be very long. Brush and timber common, sharp rocky points, some steep walls, some flatter, shallower. Deep cuts, not as long as coves.	Short, but very sharp and steep. Some slick; some with trees or brush. Mostly rocky.	Varies from heavily-timbered, moderate slope to cliffs. "Stair-step" ledges in some cases.	Sand, clay, rock, shale, limestone.	Timber is mainly hardwoods or pines and cedar. Brush varies regionally. Moss or weeds not common.	Same as hill-land except causeways, bridges, and rip-rap are not as common.
Coves have flat basins, short, usually wide in relation to length. Some brush may be present. Shorelines are steep in deep coves, flat in shallow coves. Short cuts with high sloping walls in downstream ⅓. Not as prevalent upstream.	Vary depending on region from very sharp to ,rounded.	Steep bluffs downstream; gradual slope upstream.	Varies from rocky to sandy, to silt depending on region. Usually clean. Upstream ⅓ has shallow flats.	Quite limited. Some in backs of coves. Some vegetation in upstream third.	Dam, roadbeds, marinas, spillways, others as mentioned above not common because of low populations.
Almost all coves are creek or river-fed. Some "dry-wet" with wide mouths can be very long. Some with 2 or 3 creeks.	Very distinct along sheer walls of reservoir and downstream portions of cove. Most composed of jagged rock. Can rise 1200 feet above water and drop 300 feet below water.	Sheer cliffs with mainly, some broken rock, slightly-sloping solid rock faces or "mesas."	Mainly rock, some sand and gravel in backs of coves.	Some sage brush or other scrub vegetation found occasionally. Cottonwood trees and some highland cedar at extreme backs of coves.	Very few, some marinas, dams.

Chapter 9

WATER COLOR— CLEARING UP CLARITY

Take your basic lake—a hole filled with water. Now add fish, weeds, plankton, siltation, and run-off from the surrounding land. You no longer have clean, clear water, but some stained, off-colored variations. Even the clearest of lakes, rivers and reservoirs aren't completely clear. Add even a few goodies, and the water is bound to pick up some color.

Many anglers just head out and flail away using the same lures and the same color patterns, regardless of whether the water looks like distilled water or chocolate milk. Many of these return to the dock, frustrated and skunked. If you're beginning to suspect that water color makes a difference, you're right.

Water color, or more correctly water *clarity*, has several major effects on fish location, behavior and feeding tactics. Once you understand the role water clarity plays in the fish's environment, then you can figure out how smallmouth bass are going to respond in most bodies of water.

How clear is clear? Well, you have very clear, clear, medium-clear, sort-of-clear—it's pretty tough to come up with an exact way to break it down. But you really don't have to. For all intent and purposes, fish response will be basically the same in any of these conditions providing the water is clear enough for the fish to see fairly well. How clear is that? Well, if you want a yardstick to work by, lower a white lure, like a jig, into the water on a sunny day, and if you can still see it at a depth of 6 feet or more, figure the lake to be clear.

When a white lure disappears between about 2 and 6 feet, consider that to be stained; by stained water, we mean discolored. The fish can still see fairly well, and weeds can still grow, but not like in clear water. Even though fish do not have clear vision, they make up for it through their senses of vibration and sound.

See the difference? Clear water fish can do one heck of a job on sight alone, but when you get into stained water, vision begins to lose its primary importance. Stained water fish rely more on a mixture of sight and sound to locate their prey.

Let's carry it a step further. Put a white lure in the water and zap, it's gone at one foot deep. Now that's dark water! How'd you like to be down there trying to find your way around? It's pretty tough to see anything.

In dark water, sound becomes the main program. Fish can't see what's out there, but they can sense vibration and sound through their lateral line and inner ear. You can't count on them to see much unless they are really close. But if you put some kind of noisemaker down there, chances are they can find it.

The Three Basic Degrees of Water Color

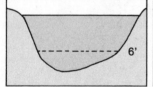 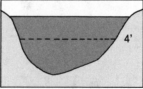 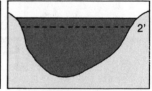

Clear Water	Stained Water	Dark Water
lure disappears at 6 ft. plus	lure disappears at 2-6 ft.	lure disappears at 0-2 ft.

Lower a white lure into the water. Note the depth at which it disappears. This gives you a general idea as to fish behavior and the relative importance of sight vs. sound.

GENERAL TENDENCIES OF WATER COLOR VS. GENERAL FISH LOCATION, PEAK FEEDING TIMES AND PRESENTATION

Most clear water fish tend to feed at low-light hours. They can often be at a variety of depths, and can see your offering. Dark water fish, conversely, feed during the brightest hours. These fish are often restricted to shallow locations, and would welcome a little shake, rattle and roll in your lure to help them find it.

The general rule of thumb is: Use bright, visible, sound-making lures in dark water to help attract fish. Bounce the bottom, dig up the rocks or make some noise on the surface. In clear water, tone down your offering. They can see it just fine, and a lot of extra vibration and flash might even serve to scare them away. Normally, you don't have to tear up the bottom in order to trigger a strike in clear water.

Now, if clear water fish are generally sight-oriented and dark water fish are sound-conscious, what about stained water fish? Well, since that's an in between condition, you get in between reactions. The feeding times tend to be more spread out, fish can be on several patterns, in several locations, and both sight and sound play an important part in lure selection. Slightly stained water makes "sight" lures the higher percentage baits, whereas a darker stain reduces visibility and means you should use a thumper/bumper of some kind. It's an environmental balancing act, and water color is a key ingredient.

Fish Are Tied to Their Environment And React Accordingly

The Balancing Act

CLEAR WATER	DARK WATER
Fish can see well	Fish can't see much at all
Fish rely heavily on sight	Fish rely heavily on sound
Good light penetration	Poor light penetration
Oxygen is deeper	Low oxygen in depths
Weeds grow deeper	Weeds restricted to shallows
Fish can be found deeper	Fish often restricted to shallows
Fish feed more toward morning and evening, or at night	Fish feed more toward mid-day
Fish are more active on cloudy days	Fish are more active on sunny days
Heavy schooling	Fish tend to be scattered
Fish roam	Fish are object-oriented
Fish chase lures	Fish don't chase lures
Fish are spooky	Fish are less spooky
Water warms or cools slowly	Water warms or cools quickly

STAINED WATER FISH FALL SOMEWHERE IN BETWEEN

Clear water fish rely heavily on sight and are generally less restricted in behavior due to their more varied environment. Dark water fish rely heavily on sound and often live in a far more restricted environment, with fewer options. Stained water fish are nearest the balancing point. Depending on the degree of water color, their behavior can swing either way.

PERMANENT VS. TEMPORARY WATER CLARITY

Permanent Conditions	Temporary Conditions
Clear	Normal
Stained	Dirty
Dark	Muddy

So far, we've discussed clear, stained and dark water conditions. They're all permanent conditions caused by the local environment. But what happens when it rains, or when a heavy wind tears up a shoreline and washes all sorts of foreign material into a lake. Shouldn't that have a categorization all its own?

Normally, clear water becomes dirty when rain or wind introduces foreign substances to the lake. It's a temporary condition, which changes the environment for a period of time. In this instance, normally clear water temporarily behaves like stained water, and so do the fish. Similarly, normally stained water temporarily takes on the characteristics of dark water. Sight is reduced, and fish rely more heavily on sound than they normally would.

Ten Timely Tips
Water Clarity Recap

Clear	Stained	Dark
1. Light line preferred (4, 6, 8 lb. test)	In-between condition.	1. Heavier line acceptable (12, 17 lb. test)
2. Small profile lures	Fish have mixed reactions based on amount of stain in water.	2. Large, bulky profile lures
3. Natural lure finishes (crayfish, perch, shad)	Trial and error is the key to proper presentation.	3. Gaudy lure finishes (multi-colored and patterned)
4. Subtle colors (white, yellow, brown, black)	In general, lean toward dark water approach.	4. Bright fluorescent colors (chartreuse, orange)
5. Swimming retrieves		5. Bottom-bumping retrieves
6. Long casts		6. Shorter casts
7. Minimize sound/vibration in lure selection		7. Maximize sound/vibration in lure selection
8. Low light conditions favorable		8. Bright light conditions favorable
9. Smaller jigs best, ($\frac{1}{8}$, $\frac{3}{16}$, $\frac{1}{4}$ oz.)		9. Larger-sized jigs productive ($\frac{1}{4}$, $\frac{5}{16}$, $\frac{3}{8}$ oz.)
10. Live bait effective (natural presentation)		10. Live bait effective (enhanced presentation, such as 'crawler and spinner combos)

Chapter 10

THE PRE-SPAWN PERIOD

"A Time of Anticipation"

The smallmouth bass Pre-spawn Period can be subdivided into three separate phases. These phases are not etched in stone, but are approximate temperature levels for spawning-related activities. The Pre-spawn Period is composed of:

1) Early Pre-spawn - 46°F-47°F
2) Mid Pre-spawn - 48°F-52°F
3) Late Pre-spawn - 53°F-55°F

Each phase is temperature dependent, and smallmouth location and behavior is different in each. Let's examine these phases on two different types of waters—a meso natural lake and a Canadian Shield lake—during the Pre-spawn Period.

MESOTROPHIC NATURAL LAKE

Take a close look at the accompanying illustration (*Figure 1*). It shows a typical, good, smallmouth lake and the areas that may be present. Neverthe-

96

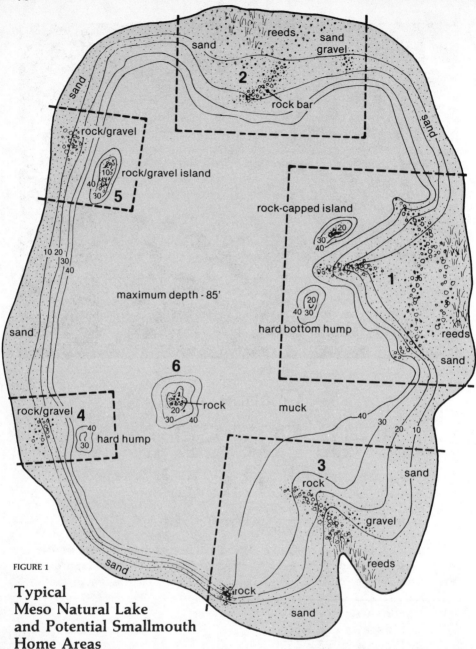

FIGURE 1

Typical
Meso Natural Lake
and Potential Smallmouth
Home Areas

less, even in this classic, meso, smallmouth lake, the topnotch areas are relatively limited. Only *AREAS 1, 2* and *3* provide the necessary combination of suitable year 'round habitat. The other areas are marginal, at best. *AREAS 4, 5* and *6* might produce plenty of walleyes from time to time, but they're not great for smallmouths. *AREA 1* has the best combination of elements for a healthy smallmouth population. Let's take a close look at this area for smallmouth use throughout the changing seasons.

EARLY COLD-WATER LOCATION (ICE-OUT)
(32°F-43°F)

For the first few days after the ice goes out, smallies will generally be located in *AREAS 1-4*. Pay careful attention to deeper areas where a transition from hard to soft bottom (rock/clay to muck) occurs. The fish are probably lying right on the edge, inactive, but still catchable.

LATE COLD-WATER LOCATION
(43°F-45°F)

As the water temperature rises to the mid-forties, a locational change begins to take place. Smallmouths still remain deep; however, they move *toward* the shallows—not shallower, but *toward* the shallows. This is an important concept, so let's refer to *Figure 2*.

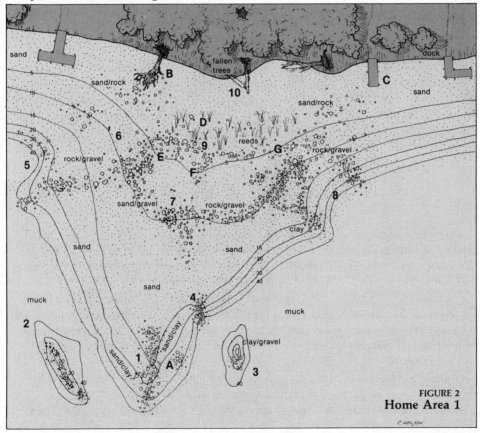

FIGURE 2
Home Area 1

At this stage, smallies begin to desert *AREAS 1-4* and move toward *AREAS* like 5 and 8. They're still deep, but they're *closer* to the shoreline spawning areas. You might still find them in 20-40 feet of water, but they'll be a bit more aggressive than they were earlier.

As they begin to filter toward spawning areas, smallmouths display a marked tendency to move up the *edges* of bar formations, rather than right over the top of them. This, perhaps, displays their reluctance to move shallow at this time, or might be due to the natural tendency for hard bottom to be found at inside corners (*AREAS 5* and *8*) of a shoreline projection (a prime spawning area). Whatever the case, be aware of this tendency.

EARLY PRE-SPAWN LOCATION
(46°F-47°F)

Once the water temperature reaches 46°F-47°F, the fish enter a transition stage. They begin filtering into the shallows. A period of stable, balmy weather with bright skies will lure some fish up from the depths to begin cruising shallow water. Whether they are seeking spawning sites, searching for food (crayfish also spawn in the shallows at this time), or are simply stimulated by the warmth of the sun, some fish enter the shallows. *AREAS 6, 7, 9* and *10* begin to draw fish.

MID PRE-SPAWN LOCATION
(48°F-52°F)

As the water nears 50°F, the smallmouths are in a full-fledged pre-spawn migration. The bulk of the fish should now be in the shallows. Rocks, reeds, docks, fallen trees—any shallow cover may draw fish. Males and females are shallow, feeding, moving, and very aggressive—and catchable! This is the time when big fish are easier to catch. *AREAS 9* and *10 (Figure 2)* would be loaded with "biters."

LATE PRE-SPAWN LOCATION
(53°F-55°F)

Aggressive behavior begins to take a downswing at this stage. Males begin sweeping out nests in shallow gravel, rocks, sand or other suitable bottom. They spread out in the prime areas along the shore, sometimes near prominent features, like a large rock, dock piling or fallen tree.

The exact bottom compositions that males choose for nesting varies from lake to lake. It depends, naturally, on what's available. In very sandy lakes, a short stretch of mixed sand and rock might be a prime spot. In a very rocky lake, the main attractor might be a stretch of sandy shoreline with only a few rocks. If reeds are present, they might be the ticket. It all depends on what is available to the fish. Once you determine the preferred type of bottom composition, you can locate similar areas on the lake.

Water clarity is another factor that's vital in locating males at this time. Smallmouths, particularly in dark or off-colored lakes, tend to build nests at a precise depth level. The depth depends largely on water clarity and the resulting sunlight penetration. Nests might be 2 feet deep in one lake, 3 feet in another, or even 5 feet in a third. But whatever depth is used, the vast majority of nests in any given home area are often built at the same level.

We're still talking about pre-spawn fish—not spawning fish. Spawning smallmouths, especially in smaller, fragile, northern, natural lakes, should be left completely alone. It's difficult enough for fish to spawn successfully in the face of natural occurrences without bothering them on the nest.

What about late pre-spawn females? Well, strangely enough, they're conspicuous by their absence. Few anglers catch them at this time. Where did they go?

The chief mistake anglers make at this time is to fish only the *extreme* shallows. Perhaps the previous week they loaded up on mid pre-spawn fish—big and lots of 'em—in 2 feet of water. Now they're catching males, but not the females, though the fish haven't spawned. What happened?

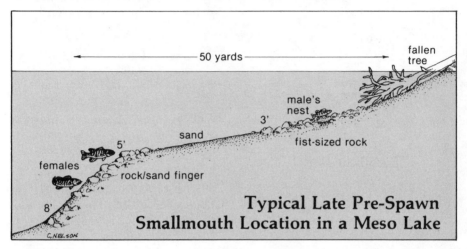

Typical Late Pre-Spawn Smallmouth Location in a Meso Lake

Apparently, the female fish move out into slightly deeper water. After the initial, mid pre-spawn frenzy, females leave the extreme shallows and wait for the males to build nests. Later, when they're ready to spawn, the females move back in. But during the late pre-spawn stage, if you only fish the shoreline, you'll miss the females.

Did the females run all the way back out to the drop-off? Probably not. Instead, they drop back part way and relate to minor drop-offs or rocky spots on top of the flat.

A good place to find late pre-spawn females would be *AREAS 6* and *7 (Figure 2)*. Perhaps they'll hold on the deep edge of the rocks at about 10 feet. If the weather is stable and mild, they may be as shallow as the edge of the rocks in *AREAS E, F* and *G*. These little rocky fingers are natural attractors. So, even though the females are deeper than the males, they're still close by—and catchable.

PRESENTATION

Spring smallmouth success depends upon correctly matching your presentation to the depth and aggressive tendencies of the fish. Let's examine several options that work well during the various phases of spring smallmouth activity.

COLD WATER PRESENTATIONS

As we've seen, most smallmouths remain deep and sluggish until water temperatures rise above 45°F. Therefore, choose a presentation that not only enables you to effectively fish deep water, but is also slow and precise enough to entice a strike from inactive fish.

Live bait rigs, and the "old reliable" jig, are top choices for this condition. Both give you precise depth control and can be worked ultra-slow. Let's look at each presentation.

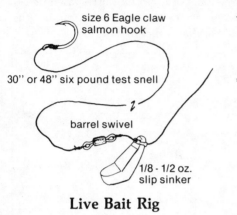

Live Bait Rig

SINKER WEIGHT BY DEPTH

depth	recom-mended sinker weight	distance from boat
15' or less	1/8 or 1/4 oz.	45'-60'
15' to 25'	1/4 or 3/8 oz.	30'-60'
25' to 45'	3/8-1/2 oz.	fish almost directly beneath boat
beyond 45'	3/4 oz.	"

Note: Almost all of your fish will be caught between 15'-45'. The most productive depths are usually from 20'-35'.

Live bait rigs are especially good for locating deep, inactive fish. Lip-hook a lively, 3 or 4 inch chub or shiner, and slowly backtroll the base of the drop-off in *AREAS* like *1-5* or *8*. Carefully lift and drop the sinker, feeling for the transition from hard to soft bottom, where the drop-off levels out and meets the lake basin. This is where inactive, cold-water fish will lie.

The best part of fishing these fairly large minnows is that you don't have to get a hit to determine if smallmouths are there. When you even come close to the bass, the minnow panics, jerks around and starts sending vibrations up the line. If you pay close attention to the feel of your rig, you'll sense the activity. When this happens, go back and make a few more passes. Enough dedicated effort will get a response from even inactive fish. Pause a few seconds after each strike, take up the slack, and then slam the hook home. Bring the fish up quickly to avoid spooking the school.

If fish take the rig with any regularity, perhaps they're active enough to strike a jig. In this case, lower a ¼ ounce jig to the bottom and slowly lift it up and down, a few inches at a time. Active fish will strike a plain jig. If they're fussy, try adding a small minnow (perhaps a 2-inch fathead) to the back end of the jig. That should do the trick. Continue to backtroll, drift, or hover over the area to determine the extent of activity.

If the fish are really active, toss out a floating marker and carefully anchor within casting distance of the spot. Cold-water fish concentrations are often massive, and you might be able to pop quite a few nice fish while casting. Let your jig sink to bottom and lie still; then twitch it a few times. As long as you're fishing a relatively small area, you can even fish deep water effectively by casting. If nothing happens, resume backtrolling to locate the next concentration of fish.

PRE-SPAWN PRESENTATIONS

As the smallmouths begin to move shallow, presentation techniques should be adjusted to suit those conditions. Live bait rigs or jigs aren't necessarily the best approaches. Let's see what you can do to put the odds in your favor.

Sure, you can cast the entire shallows, but some smallmouth lakes are so expansive that you'll cast your arm off before you find the fish. What's needed is a quick, efficient way of locating some of the more subtle holding spots. Common sense dictates a trolling approach.

Rig a casting rod with premium 12 or 14 pound test line. Attach a small crankbait like a Bagley Balsa B, Rebel Wee R, Lindy Shad, etc.; any good small crankbait will do. Just make sure it's small, because smallmouths show a decided preference for smaller lures.

Make a short cast behind the boat and begin trolling the shallows. In *Figure 2*, for instance, start outside *AREA C* and begin trolling across the bar. Keep your speed *very* slow. Idle speed is all you need to start a small crankbait wobbling. With a little experimentation, you'll soon determine how deep your crankbait will run. Most small, short-lipped models will troll from 3-7 feet deep.

Try to maintain a consistent depth level as you proceed along. Once you determine how deep a particular crankbait runs, you can run at a pretty consistent level just by feeling the bait strike the bottom. If it digs too hard, you're too shallow. Head your boat out a little deeper. If you lose your "bottom feel" and the bait starts running free, head back into shallow water until you contact the bottom again.

Between this "feel" approach and keeping an eagle eye on the depth finder, you'll start to notice things. Perhaps the rocks end at a consistent depth, say 6 feet. You'll feel the change from rock to sand. Moving along you might encounter little, rocky fingers such as *AREAS E, F* and *G* on *Figure 2.* Those are prime holding spots that other anglers may miss, especially while trying to find those late pre-spawn females.

Let's assume that your bait runs at 4 feet. You've trolled the shallows back and forth a few times, and you've struck out or only caught small fish. Simply tie on a deeper running lure. Again, select a small crankbait, but this time try one with a deep-running lip. Repeat the trolling procedure again, but this time, run at 6 or 7 feet. The procedure is the same; only the depth is different. By eliminating water, you'll eventually be on fish. Be versatile!

Let's look at another situation. It's mid pre-spawn, and you suspect there are fish very shallow—about 2 feet deep. Kick your outboard up into a shallow tilt position (to save your propeller) and start running the extreme shallows. Switch to a small Rapala-type lure so you'll only run a foot or so deep.

Since you're very shallow, you'll have to run a long line, say 40 yards, to minimize the spooking factor. Smallmouths will move aside as you pass overhead, and then return after the boat passes. By the time your lure travels the additional 40 yards and reaches the fish, they'll be willing to strike.

Sound strange? It works. In order to allow the balsa minnow lure to wobble properly, you may need to switch to lighter line (6 or 8 pound test) and a spinning rod. Sometimes you'll catch fish by trolling in water so shallow that your propeller will occasionally bounce off the rocks. But don't despair! Once you locate a concentration, you can stop trolling and start casting.

Don't try to sneak up on a concentration of shallow-water smallmouths and cast while the outboard is running. You'll have to switch to a silent, electric motor, or you can try drifting. The fish are usually too spooky to stay within casting distance of a running outboard.

Lure selection depends on the type of cover the fish are using. Fallen trees in *AREA B* or docks in *AREA C (Figure 2)* are quickly and easily fished with a crankbait. You may wish to pitch a small Panther Martin or Mepps type spinner.

If the lake contains reeds like *AREA D*, a more snagless, ⅛ or ¼ ounce spinnerbait might work best.

Finally, let's say you locate fish holding out on rocky fingers like *AREAS E, F or G.* In this case, it would be hard to beat a little ¹⁄₁₆ or ⅛ ounce jig. Hover just outside the rocks, within casting range, and slowly drop those little jigs down to the fish. This will be particularly effective where there are few snags and when the fish aren't very aggressive.

CANADIAN SHIELD LAKE SMALLMOUTHS

Shield-lake smallmouths also tend to be *homebodies.* If conditions are right, they'll spend their entire lives in a small area. However, forage is often sparse in shield lakes, and one area may not offer all the smallmouths' seasonal needs. For shield-lake smallmouths, it is, "Have needs; will travel!"

Certain rather isolated rock humps may attract summer smallmouths. However, don't expect this during early season. Smallmouth spawning water

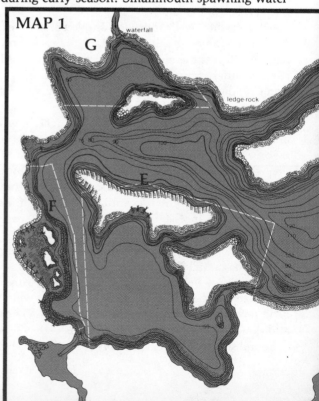

Smallmouth Location in Shield Lakes

Locating smallmouths is fairly easy on shield lakes. Just "think mesotrophic!" In other words, stay away from very deep, slab-rocked lake sections and concentrate on sections with plenty of relatively shallow (less than 15 feet deep) water with boulders, rock/rubble and gravel. Rock/rubble and gravel is especially important during the early season because smallmouths spawn on such bottom composition. Bays with the proper bottom composition offer more protection than shallow, main-lake areas, and are also more likely to hold early-season fish.

Let's look at seven general lake areas on Map 1.

AREA A—Boulders, rock/rubble, gravel, the proper depth range, both shallow and relatively deep (15-20 feet) holding areas, cover in the form of fallen trees, plus running water. This is more than a great early season spot; it's a year-'round smallmouth home area. AREA A is the epitome of what you're looking for.

AREA B—This will likely be the best summer smallmouth area in the lake, but it will also have a year-'round smallmouth population. Thus, AREA B is worth fishing anytime, although good bays offer higher percentage fishing during the early season.

AREA C—Another superb year-'round smallmouth holding area. One prominent note here: Narrow areas with water moving through them from one lake or lake section to another are particularly good during tough, cold front conditions.

AREA D—Muck bay areas are unlikely to hold shield smallmouths during any period.

AREA E—Small sections of AREA E (the mesotrophic areas) will hold smallmouths all year long. However, this is not a prime smallmouth holding area. Concentrate on areas such as A, B or C if they are available.

AREA F—Another good early season smallmouth area. Pay particular attention to the shallow, sheltered, gravel-based shoreline. Purely boulder areas such as those found in the southern section of AREA F are summer holding areas.

AREA G—During Pre-spawn, any inlets are possible fish attractors, so check the waterfall. But this particular waterfall isn't likely to attract many smallmouths because it isn't located in a year-'round holding area. Generally, forget deep, slab-rock lake sections.

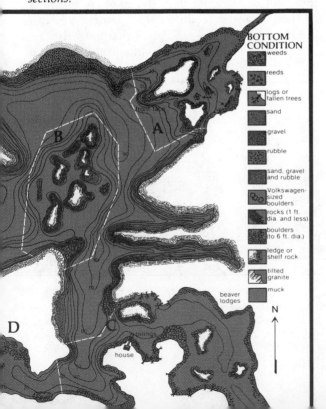

will often be located near the very best rock humps, or in shallow bays.

In shield lakes, catchable smallmouths are rarely found deeper than 20 feet. They prefer warmer water—as warm as it can possibly get in these lakes. They also need rock/rubble/sand for spawning. Smallmouths are limited to the upper, shallow water levels, and they need broken rocks, boulders, rock/rubble, or perhaps weedgrowth and fallen trees, at all times. These productive, shallow areas house crayfish and attract minnow-type forage.

There are two types of lake areas which consistently hold smallmouths: (1) bays and (2) lake sections with closely-grouped, shallow, sunken or protruding islands. Bays are particularly attractive during the early season, because they offer protection from wind. But, the perfect all-'round condition is a combination of closely-grouped bays and islands. This is year-'round smallmouth habitat, and smallmouths rarely move from such areas.

Running water is a fairly unusual condition that draws smallmouths during the early Pre-spawn Period. The best creek inlets are near prime, year-'round smallmouth habitat. Running water attracts forage, so check any creek.

PRESENTATION

We use artificial lures from four basic families: spinnerbaits, crankbaits, surface baits and jigs. Fly rod buffs will also do well with streamers, surface bass bugs and poppers. Minnows, nightcrawlers and leeches are good live bait options.

When and where you use a particular bait is as much a matter of personal preference as it is dictated by conditions. Because very aggressive fish will often be quite shallow, it may be hard to distinguish between the fish-producing potential of a spinnerbait or a surface bait. If you enjoy fishing a surface lure (and who doesn't), you may wish to choose that method. You can cover 6 foot deep water using a crankbait or a jig, and you can usually fish the crankbait faster than the jig. Still, your choice of baits in many situations is a matter of personal preference.

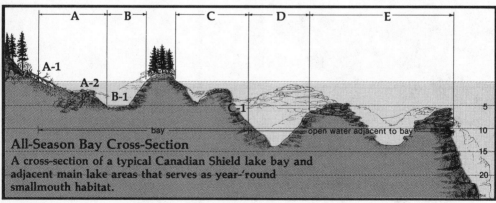

All-Season Bay Cross-Section

A cross-section of a typical Canadian Shield lake bay and adjacent main-lake areas that serves as year-'round smallmouth habitat.

To illustrate general, seasonal, smallmouth bass location in shield lakes, we've taken a cross-section of a typical bay and its adjacent main-lake areas. Because this features mesotrophic characteristics—shallow boulders, rock/rubble, and sand, as opposed to extensive, deep-dropping slab rock—it will hold smallmouths unless they've been fished down. This area is year-'round smallmouth bass habitat.

Generally speaking, AREA A will attract most early-season (pre-spawn, and especial-ly spawn and post-spawn) smallmouth. AREAS C and E will hold the most summer and fall fish.

During the early season, AREA A is usually the most attractive to smallmouths. You might expect the larger females to hold near overhead cover (A-1) during the day or to drop into the slightly deeper water provided by the rock drop-off (A-2). During the ear-ly morning, and especially the late afternoon and evening, expect the fish to roam the shallows. These fish will eventually spawn on the shallow, rock/rubble flat.

Cold fronts may drive fish out of the shallow water near shore. As they drop back from the bay, they'll seek deeper water. Although the 6 foot water (B-1) in AREA B might hold some fish, AREA C is a more likely holding area. Expect the turned off fish to hold along the main-lake drop-off (C-1). Prime drop-offs offer rock/rubble or boulders, but if they aren't available the fish may hold on slab rock. It's one of the few times they do so. The shallow areas of AREA C are worthwhile spots to check during the early season, too.

AREA E is basically a summer and fall holding area. Because they offer nothing but slab rock, AREAS B and D can generally be considered poor, smallmouth holding areas during any season.

One basic guideline for fishing early-season, shield-lake smallies is to start fishing fairly fast and shallow. This usually requires a crankbait. If this doesn't produce action, continue fishing shallow, but slow down. Slow your crankbait retrieve, or switch to a small jig, spinnerbait, surface lure, or live bait on a plain hook, weighted with split shot. Concentrate your efforts close to cover like fallen trees, large boulders, weeds, or quick-breaking shores that don't drop into very deep water. If that isn't producing, try fishing deeper and slower. Jigs tipped with live bait, or plain hook/live bait/split shot rigs, are good choices.

Early-season baits are usually small. Spinnerbaits and jigs should weigh ⅛ or ¼ ounce; crankbaits, ¼-½ ounce; and surface baits should be 3, 4 or 5 inches long. Use crankbaits resembling minnows or crayfish. Wobbling minnow baits (Rapala, Bagley Bang-O-Lure or Rebel minnow) are very versatile because they can be fished subsurface, as well as twitched on the surface. These lures are a must for early-season, shield-lake smallmouth fishing.

Use these small baits on appropriately matched casting or spinning tackle. Generally, that means ultralight, light, or medium tackle and 4-10 pound test line. Use heavier 8 or 10 pound test line only when fishing either larger crank-baits or spinnerbaits, or when fishing near downed trees.

LIVE BAIT

Live bait is deadly on early season smallmouths. However, when fish are really "on," artificials allow you to cover more water and will usually produce more fish. This may also hold true for fishing neutral fish. With few excep-tions, live bait is the best option for taking fish under tough, changing weather conditions.

Which live baits are the best? Big fathead minnows or 3-inch shiners are deadly. Unfortunately, they're often impossible to get or to transport, and may even be illegal in Canadian park areas. A good option for tipping jigs is freeze-dried bait.

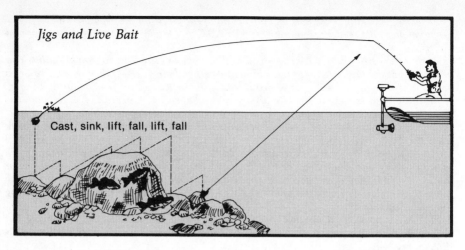

Jigs and Live Bait

Cast, sink, lift, fall, lift, fall

Fish jigs or live bait on a plain No. 6 or 8 hook and weighted with a split shot 6-12 inches above the bait. Use a lift, drop, lift, drop retrieve around and over likely areas.

If you can take leeches with you, by all means do. Smallmouths love 'em. Leeches, however, become more productive as the season progresses. Crawdads are another option you may wish to try. We've caught shield fish by suspending small craws below a slip-bobber.

CASTING

Because most early-season fish are relatively shallow, most of your fish will be taken while casting. Move along slowly with either your electric or gas motor. If you're in a canoe, simply paddle/halt/cast, paddle/halt/cast. Even when fish drop back out of bays into relatively deep, quick-breaking areas, casting is still more likely to trigger fish, although backtrolling and live bait rigging is also an option.

Trolling is useful when covering a very large area, searching for fish. In this instance, toss out a shallow-running crankbait and troll it 50-100 feet behind a slow-moving boat. You can troll with a canoe, too, but that's more difficult. Hold the rod between your legs with the tip over your shoulder. If a fish hits, thrust the rod forward with one hand. Keep the line tight and the fish will usually stay on.

FISHING A BAY

We've covered good, early-season, shield-lake smallmouth habitat; which basic baits to use; and how to present these baits by casting. Let's take a short trip through a good looking smallmouth bay in order to show you one good, basic fishing approach.

The bay we've chosen is perfect, year-'round, smallmouth habitat. It is the only shallow, rock/rubble bay in a deep-lake section that is composed of

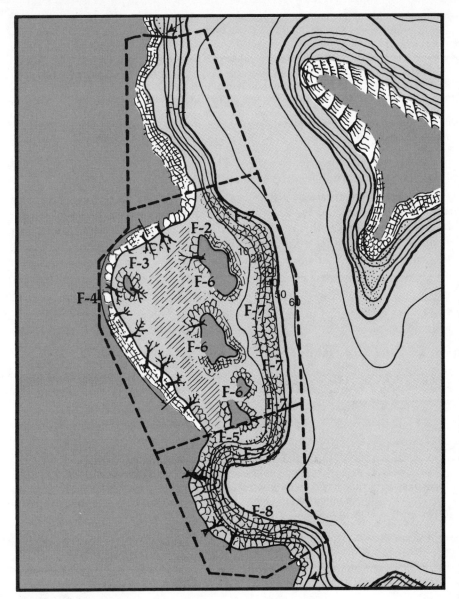

Fishing Area F

Although AREA F *(from Map 1) wouldn't be a first choice on this particular lake, we'll use it as an example of how you might consider fishing an area. First, forget sections F-1 and F-8 during the early season. F-8 would be a summer holding area. Start your fishing on either point F-2 or F-5. Let's start on point F-2. We're going to fish fast, so tie on a crankbait. Toss it up to the boulders on the point and crank it in quickly. Proceed down shoreline F-4, fishing the shallows and the fallen trees as you go. Pay particular attention to boulder pile F-3 when you discover it. Continue down shoreline F-4 even though it's ledge rock; the fallen trees may still attract fish because it's shallow and there's plenty of gravel bottom nearby. Upon reaching point F-5, turn your attention to the boulder areas F-6 of the islands.*

If we catch fish doing this, we may have established a pattern that will hold up in similar lake areas. If we haven't found active fish while fishing the shallows with a fast-moving crankbait, proceed back to point F-2 and refish it as before. This time, however, fish slowly with spinnerbaits, surface lures or live bait and split shot rigs. Again, if we find fish, we may have established a pattern.

If we still haven't found many fish, perhaps they've dropped back out of the bay. The fish won't go far, but if they've moved out, they're definitely "off." This time, concentrate on fishing deeper (to about 15 feet) and slow. In AREA F, we'd concentrate on point F-2, or the areas marked F-7 near the main lake. If we still haven't found fish, things are likely to be slow all over. Concentrate your fishing in a lake section with current, such as AREA C on Map 1.

steep-dropping, slab-rock formations. This *mesotrophic habitat* is located in an otherwise oligotrophic surrounding. That's smallmouth water!

We prefer to start fishing just outside the bay point that's most protected from wind. On one rod we'll use a crawdad-imitating crankbait which runs about 4-6 feet deep. On the other we'll use a surface lure or a spinnerbait. On a third rod we'll use either a jig (preferably a dark color), or a plain hook/live bait/split shot set-up. For live bait, we'll use either a live minnow or a leech.

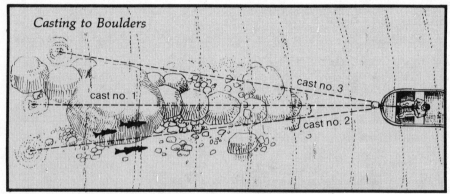

When casting to cover, such as submerged boulders, your first cast should be made directly over the boulder. This way you cover any fish laying in back, over, or in front of the boulder during your retrieve (see "zinging" rocks with crankbaits and flutter fishing). Your second cast should be directed to the shady side of the boulder, while the third one should cover the opposite side. Some rather large boulders could hold two, three or even five fish.

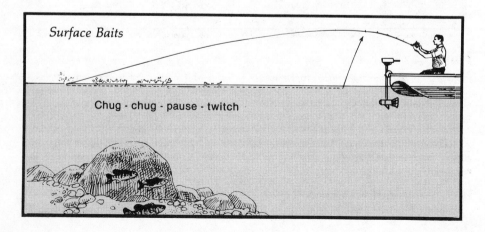

Twitch surface lures over boulders, occasionally pausing to let the lure lie motionless. The same basic presentation, with appropriate modifications, works for fishing downed timber or any other cover.

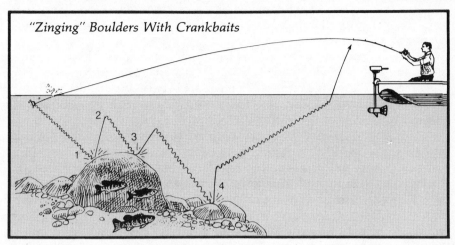

"Zinging" Boulders With Crankbaits

For this delivery, use a floater-diver crankbait. After the lure hits the water, it is cranked until it "zings," or strikes the rock (Point 1). Now you can continue cranking or pause to let the lure rise. If you crank, the lure will often veer to one side and begin diving again. If you pause, begin cranking after the lure reaches Point 2. Zing the rocks again, if possible, and repeat the procedure.

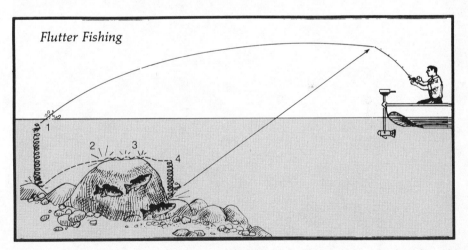

Flutter Fishing

When using a spinnerbait, be sure to strike any boulders. After the lure hits the water, allow it to flutter down behind the boulder. Begin your retrieve and strike the boulder with the lure. Then slowly crawl the lure over the top (Point 3). At Point 4, you can allow the lure to flutter toward the bottom again before retrieving. The flutters at Points 1 and 4 are the most probable strike-provoking stages of this presentation.

Unless the bay is huge, make your entire first pass using primarily a crankbait. Move quickly, looking for groups of "active" fish. Toss the bait up to steep shorelines and past rock crevices; bounce it over and along each side of, and over, huge boulders; run it down the branches of fallen trees; bounce it along a rock/rubble bottom; cast it past rock points, searching for suspended fish; but in any case, keep it moving! Stop using the crankbait only if you find fish. Switching to other baits may put a fish or two in the boat once you've identified a prime holding area.

If the fish aren't aggressive, go back and start over again. This time, continue fishing shallow, but slow down. Run the crankbait very slowly, often stopping the bait during the retrieve; or alternate between fishing the surface bait or spinnerbait and the jig or live bait set-up. Concentrate on fishing tight to cover.

If this doesn't produce fish, try only productive-looking, 8-15 foot deep areas using a jig or live bait rig.

There's a reason for going through the same bay perhaps three times. If you've identified a good mesotrophic area, there *will be* fish there, unless they've been fished down by the catch and kill brigade. The key is often to pattern what the fish are doing at a particular time during the day. In other words, if the only way you take fish in a "perfect bay" is on falling spinnerbaits, surface baits, or live bait fished close to cover, you can expect the same results to hold true in other bays as well.

Chapter 11

THE SPAWN PERIOD

"A Time of Tension"

Other areas of this book mention "Catch and Release" and what it means to the future of smallmouth bass fishing. Now we come to the most critical Calendar Period of year for protecting fish, the Spawn Period.

Our *IN-FISHERMAN* policy is to avoid fishing for any spawning species of fish. We'll fish pre-spawn or some post-spawn fish (fish that don't build and protect nests), but when fish are actually spawning, it's best to let nature take its course and fish somewhere else. This helps ensure a successful spawn and good fishing for future generations.

In the southern portion of its range, the smallmouth spawns as early as the latter part of April; in southern New York and Michigan, the usual period is May and early June; and in Ontario and northern New York, spawning may continue throughout June.

Temperature is the most important factor in initiating the spawning period. Nest-building activities and spawning generally occur at water temperatures from 59°F to 65°F, assuming that the fish's eggs are ripe. In addition, evidence suggests that most spawning activity commences when these water temperatures coincide with the full or dark moon.

THE NEST

In basses and other members of the sunfish family, the duties of selecting and constructing the nest and guarding the eggs and young are left to the male alone. One prime concern is the selection of a suitable site for nesting. While largemouths frequently make their nests on soft bottoms where they will expose such hard objects as roots, twigs and snail shells, smallmouths select such locations as a last resort; their nests are almost always found on a bottom composed of gravel, rubble, coarse sand, bedrock or a combination of these materials.

When the temperature becomes suitable, the male leaves his resting place in deeper water and inspects the shallower parts of spawning shoals. Under natural conditions, the smallmouth places his nest in a location sheltered from direct wind and wave action. Nests are ordinarily located on nearly level bottoms at depths of from 3 to 5 feet, but they have been found in water as shallow as 10 inches and deeper than 12 feet.

After selecting a satisfactory nesting site, the male begins to construct the nest. He assumes a nearly vertical position in the water—head up—and fans the bottom vigorously with his caudal fin. The silt, sand, and small stones are displaced and settle to the sides, forming a circular ridge around the edge of the nest. Using his mouth, the bass will remove large objects from the nest. In the same manner, he will remove foreign objects from the nest after it is completed.

Nest construction requires from 4 to 48 hours or more, depending on the temperature and type of bottom. The completed nest is a concave, saucer-shaped depression, usually 2 or 3 feet in diameter, but large males may build nests as large as 4 feet across. The normal width of the nest is about twice the length of the male.

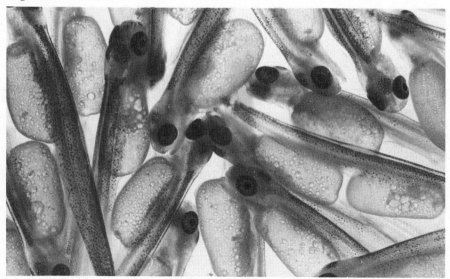

SPAWNING

If the temperature is suitable, actual spawning may take place immediately after the nest is completed, or may be delayed for several days until the water warms. In any event, the male usually remains on or near his nest, protecting it from other males. During the period of nest building, or during any delay, his future mate remains in deeper water.

When the female is at last induced to enter the nest to spawn, a sudden transformation occurs in her color pattern. Her color becomes paler and her dark blotchings more intense, repeating the color pattern of the young. Within a period of a few minutes, her entire body becomes mottled, and the white spot on the opercular membrane stands out in strong relief against the dark opercular blotch. The male develops only a slightly mottled appearance—the same black and white contrast on the opercle. The upper, rear part of his iris becomes scarlet; that of his mate usually remains brown.

During the period of color change, both fish move slowly over the nest, and the male frequently nips the female gently on the head. She swims slowly in a

Development

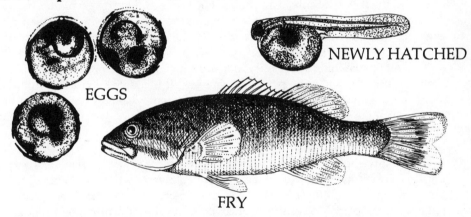

EGGS

NEWLY HATCHED

FRY

The eggs, when deposited, are greyish-white and about 2.5 millimeters in diameter. The embryonic bass develops on the upper side of the egg, protecting it from possible injury or suffocation at the bottom. These embryos, however, are super-sensitive to changes in temperature. They are killed with a rise from 61°F to 73.5°F, whereas newly-hatched young are not so affected. Three or four days after the eggs are laid, the developing fish reaches a length of about 5 millimeters—one fifth inch, and then hatches out of the egg membrane. For some time, the growing fish is nourished entirely by the yolk.

The newly-hatched young, lying in crevices between the stones, are entirely colorless, and therefore very inconspicuous. Within a day after hatching, the eye becomes darker as pigment forms in the retina. Soon after, black pigment spots (chromatophores) form on the body, first in two longitudinal streaks, and later over the entire body. As they swim slowly about in schools, the young appear entirely black, quite unlike the young of the largemouth bass which are pale with a median lengthwise streak of black.

When they rise in a swarm from the nest—7 to 16 days after the eggs are deposited, depending on the temperature—the fry are about 9 millimeters long. Most of the yolk has been absorbed, the eyes are iridescent, the dorsal and anal fins are beginning to separate from the caudal fin, the pelvic fins are still unformed, and the whole body except the fins and lower surface of the yolk sac is covered with deep black pigment.

circle, partially turned over on one side, or remains quiet with the male beside her. Occasionally, she resumes a normal position in the water and rubs her belly against the stones in the bottom of the nest; at the same time she bends her body, first to one side, and then to the other.

If an intruding male or female appears during any stage of the courtship, the male rushes out and drives the intruder away, while the female remains on the nest. If she does move away, the male immediately drives her back.

During the egg-laying, the fish lie side by side, usually facing in the same direction, with the head of the male slightly behind that of the female. He retains a normal upright position in the water, while she drops to the bottom. The female seems to become rigid just before the eggs are emitted, then rapidly vibrates her body and fins, especially the partly-depressed dorsal fin, during the actual extrusion of the eggs.

About 20 to 50 eggs are deposited during each emission, which lasts 4 to 10 seconds. The eggs have the appearance of a string of beads, but soon this string breaks and the eggs settle to the bottom of the nest where they adhere to the cleaned stones. The milt, emitted at the same time or immediately afterward, also appears as a whitish thread, which also breaks apart. Several such periods of egg laying follow at intervals of about 30 seconds. During each interim, the female rests or swims slowly near the edge of the nest, while the male seems to examine the eggs. He then swims around the female, biting her about the mouth, cheeks, opercles and anus.

The end of spawning apparently indicates that either one or both parents are spawned-out for that given period of ripeness. If the male still retains milt, he seeks out and finds another female, and immediately spawns with her in the same nest. Likewise, the female will accept the attention of another male in another nest if she still retains eggs. This often happens if the spawning has been interrupted.

One to three hours usually elapses from the time the female first enters a nest until she leaves it, either voluntarily or driven away by the male after spawning is completed. Both fish then lose their mottled appearance and rapidly regain their normal, greenish-bronze coloration. All subsequent duties— caring-for and guarding the eggs and young—are perfomed by the male.

GUARDING THE NEST

The devotion of the male in guarding the nest is pronounced throughout the period of parental care. He frequently remains on the nest until an intruder actually drives him from his post. He immediately attacks any other fish or trespasser who approaches the nest site. At times, however, schools of white perch and eels have been reported successful in destroying the contents of the nest.

When the young rise from the bottom of the nest, the male circles about, keeping them in a compact school. They remain over the nest for a short period, but usually the parent soon drives them into the protection of shallow water near shore, where he patrols up and down past them. During this time, the fry begin to feed independently.

As they grow, the young tend to disperse. After they attain a length of nearly an inch, the school usually breaks up. The young are usually protected from 2 to 9 days, but at times the male guards them for as long as 28 days.

Chapter 12

THE POST- SPAWN PERIOD

"A Time of Recuperation"

Indeed, the Post-spawn Period can be a tough nut to crack. The rigors of spawning have taken their toll on female smallmouths; in most waters, they appear to be as scarce as flamingos in Minnesota. In addition, the fish seem to feed only sporadically and are very difficult to catch consistently. Post-spawn, female smallmouths filter out of the nesting area and appear to relate to available cover in deeper water. For example, an emerging cabbage bed adjacent to a gravel/rocky finger, extending toward deeper water, is a good bet.

Male smallmouth bass, on the other hand, remain in the shallows, guarding the nest and fry from predators. Male smallmouths are very aggressive at this time, and will strike at almost anything that invades their territory. Do not fish for the males, however, because protection of the fry is essential to a successful hatch.

One of the best ways to tackle the post-spawn condition is to fish very slowly and carefully—often with live bait. You might even try fishing at night. Yes, it's tough fishing, but that's what you're faced with when you're after post-spawn, female bass.

This approach works in many environments, but is usually *the* bread-and-butter system for fishing strip pits. These small bodies of water often contain huge fish, yet seldom receive much fishing pressure, due to their tough-to-fish reputations. Therefore, by discussing strip pit techniques, we can accomplish two valuable lessons at one time: (1) We'll explore several deadly techniques for hard-to-catch, post-spawn smallmouths, and (2) learn a dynamic system for catching fish all year long from hard-to-fish bodies of water. As you'll see, "tempting" smallmouths from strip pits is remarkably similar to "extracting" non-aggressive, post-spawn bass in many other waters.

Pits offer a unique alternative to the post-spawn blues. Fishing is never easy during this time. However, due to the smaller size of most pits, they can be fished thoroughly and efficiently—and that's what it takes to catch post-spawn bass. We'll begin by examining a typical pit environment, and then detailing exactly what it takes to catch fish in them.

PIT FISHING BASICS

Although strip pits come in many complex forms, the key pits to concentrate on are those with a large amount of "productive shelf." A productive

Inflatable boats provide easy access to waters where boat launches don't exist. They come in all sizes, from one-man rafts to multiple-angler, outboard motor-powered models.

shelf is an area located above the thermocline with the capacity to support gamefish. Pits that are nearly all productive shelf—shallow pits—usually have a better capacity to produce a larger and more extensive food chain than deep, steep-walled pits. The end result is that shallow pits generally host more and bigger fish than extremely deep ones.

In this environment, bass tend to relate to available cover. This may occur in simple or complex forms depending upon the fertility of the pit. Simple pits have only a few cover options. Complex pits, meanwhile, may have extensive weedbeds, rock piles, sand and gravel bars, points and flooded timber. You may have to fish several areas and use various techniques to be consistently successful. The key is to be versatile and to logically consider the environmental options available to the fish.

Peak-period fishing can be fantastic on small pits; the best peaks occur during *low-light* periods. In shallower pits, the entire lake basin is often subjected to extreme light penetration. Consequently, you should adapt your methods and concentrate on low-light peaks when the bass are more active. What are the low-light periods? Basically, the period from dusk to dawn.

LOCATION

The following chart gives a basis to work from, though not all conditions occur in every pit. The more complex the pit, the more versatile your approach must be. Typical, key fishing areas in pits include:

AREA #1
CHUNK ROCK AREAS

AREA #2
TAIL-OFFS AND ROCK SLIDES

AREA #3
CUTS OR DIPS IN
SPOILBANK BARS

AREA #4
ISOLATED ROCK PILES

AREA #5
WEEDBEDS

AREA #6
FLOODED TIMBER (usually
seasonal)

For those of you who wonder what a "spoilbank" is, spoil is a generic term for "what's left" after a mining operation. The mining company simply deposits the leftover spoil into large, mid-pit humps or piles along the shoreline. This creates points, humps, islands, bars, etc., once the pit fills with water.

The other areas are all fairly obvious. Flooded timber exists all year in some pits, although in many it's only a seasonal, high-water pattern caused by rain and melting snow. In any case, note the parallel between pit bass and post-spawn bass in other waters. Post-spawn females usually relate to the *available cover* just outside a spawning area, much the same as pit bass relate to available cover in a pit.

Now that we have established the primary pit areas, study the accompanying lake map, take a closer look at each of these areas, and compare daytime and nighttime bass locations.

PIT PRESENTATION

Strip pit presentation is very simple if approached properly. For the most part, the fishing situation calls for a tremendous amount of versatility. Both

Pit Savvy

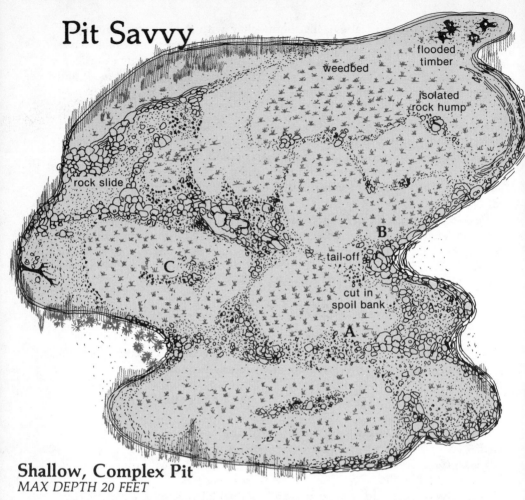

Shallow, Complex Pit
MAX DEPTH 20 FEET

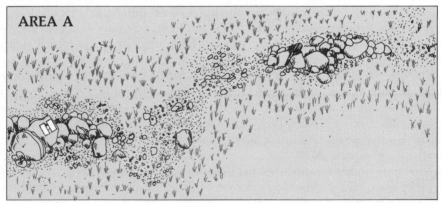

One of the keys to understanding bass location in a complex pit environment is recognizing that there are relatively few combinations of structural elements to consider. If you look at AREA A a little closer, you'll notice that essentially the same structural features are present over the entire area, whether it covers 25 yards or 125 yards. It is made up of boulder piles and sand/chunk rock areas, and is largely bordered on both sides by heavy weedgrowth. Without the option of depth, the fish tend to relate to the heaviest areas of cover in conjunction with available food.

It's easy to see why predator/prey relationships are relatively simple in this environment, with only crayfish and panfish as the two dominant forage options. By understanding how these lakes function, it's actually rather simple to put together a consistent approach.

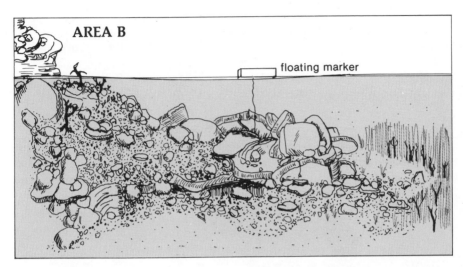

Let's examine a side view of AREA B in detail. This type of area occurs in many different portions of a shallow pit, such as a tail-off or point, a rock slide caused by eroded cliff walls or even a small finger along the length of a long bar (such as in AREA A).

AREA B is a light chunk rock, sand and gravel bank dropping off into a slab rock pile. There is also a clean, hard bottom lip extending from the rocks, tapering into an adjacent weedbed.

We all know that active fish relate to edges. In this situation, active fish tend to relate to the obvious edges of the rock pile. Here we have an excellent chunk rock break on the inside and outside edges of the pile, with adjacent weedbeds nearby. These areas can be loaded with crayfish and bluegills.

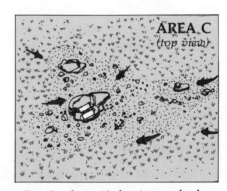

AREA C is an isolated sand flat (with a small rock pile on it) that is completely surrounded by a weedbed. Bass generally bury among the thick weeds and boulders during the day, but because the area is a bit more "open" than most of the other areas in this pit, you have a shot at catching a few fish here during the day. Fish the weed edges and scrape a jig and worm down between the rocks. Once night falls, however, the fish will probably roam the entire area.

artificials and live bait have their place at certain times and in the right situations. What are the right situations? Let's go back to the low-light periods and the general mood of the fish, and match our presentation accordingly. The accompanying chart lists the results.

Presentation vs. Low-Light Period

Low-Light Period	Mood	Presentation
Pre-twilight	Inactive/Neutral	Live Bait
Twilight-Dusk	Active	Live Bait/Artificials
1st Stage Night	Active/Aggressive	Artificials
Mid-Night	Neutral	Live Bait
Twilight-Dawn	Active	Artificials/Live Bait

EQUIPMENT

We again impress upon pit fishermen that versatility is a must. Many pits are impossible to fish from the bank. Walking carelessly along the rocks will spook most of the fish in the area, and possibly the whole pit. On the other

A "belly boat" is simply an inner tube with a harness to support you. Toss one in the back of your car, and you're always prepared for smallmouth action.

hand, most situations don't allow you to launch a large boat, either.

"Belly boats," or inflatable rafts with a small trolling motor, are probably your best choices. Both are extremely quiet and very easy to handle on the water. A good pair of chest waders is a must with the belly boat. It's also a good idea to wear warmer clothing, since it can get quite cool after dark.

The basic rule of clear water fishing is to use the lightest line and tackle possible, or, put another way, the heaviest line you can get away with. One excellent way to fish pits with live bait is to use a 7 foot, two-piece, graphite spinning rod designed to present a live bait (crayfish or waterdog) in a delicate manner. The rod should have a fast taper, sensitive tip for casting even the lightest baits, and yet enough power in the butt to turn a 6 pound smallmouth away from any cover! It should also handle lures from ⅛ to ⅝ ounces and 4 to 10 pound test line! You'll be very surprised at the amount of pressure you can apply to 6 pound test line with this type rig! Once you maneuver the fish into open water, take your time and enjoy the fight! After dark, you can go to heavier line and still fish all types of live bait.

One important and very effective technique for use after dark is waxed line. On a night with any moon at all, your line is much easier to see on the surface, and you can quickly see any slight evidence of a strike. A floating, waxed line glides over the surface as the fish moves off with your bait. This keeps your line free from tangling on submerged obstructions, such as boulders, timber, etc.

Simply rub your line lightly across a piece of wax or a candle to give it a light film of wax. Be sure to leave the first ten feet or so of the line free of wax, however. This allows proper sinking action so your live bait will appear more natural. Add a ¹⁄₆₄ or ¹⁄₃₂ ounce slip sinker and you're ready to go fishing.

It is necessary to use reliable and comfortable tackle when fishing with artificials after dark. We use spinning tackle at night, because we have fewer problems with it. A graphite rod and a quality reel, loaded with 8 pound test (carry a spare spool of heavier line for after dark, if you desire) will handle any lure or bait you wish to cast. Sometimes it's a good idea to have an extra rod rigged for artificials, since this saves time changing lures and eliminates having to use a flashlight as often.

LURES

A small variety of surface baits, spinnerbaits, crankbaits, jigs and worms are all the artificials you'll need to fish shallow pits. Match your lure selection to the conditions until you establish a pattern that works.

It's easiest to work flooded timber with weedless lures like single-spin spinnerbaits and Texas-rigged plastic worms. Active fish will smash a steadily-retrieved spinnerbait, although it pays to pause occasionally and let the bait flutter downward to trigger a hesitant bass. Bounce and smack the lure into and off the trees whenever possible. This drives 'em nuts. When they're just not chasing, though, drop a plastic worm deep down inside the thickest brush and timber tangles, and let it sit. Wiggle it a bit, and pause again. Inactive pit bass are *tough*, and you have to extract them, as opposed to just catching them.

Fish in more open water—around rock piles, weed edges, tail-offs, etc.—are

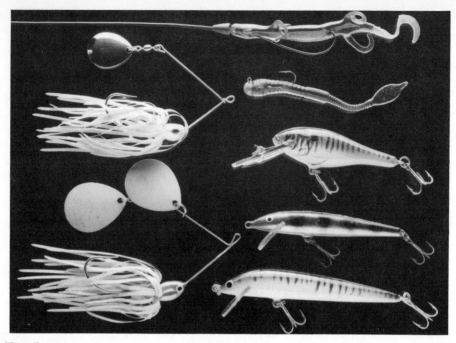

Pit Lures

Here's all you will need to get 'em in the pits.

Spinnerbaits: The single spin is best for fluttering into heavy cover, and the tandem spin is used with a steady retrieve over shallow water cover.

Plastics: A Texas rigged worm or salamander can be slithered through cover while the jig/worm can be ripped through weeds or crawled over rocky areas.

Crankbaits: Floater-diver lures are super, because they can be fished on the surface or subsurface. For deeper areas, use a deep diver with a sturdy lip.

easier to get at. Try pitching a tiny jig/worm combination, crawling it down the rock face or ripping it through the weeds. Rattle their cages by zinging a deep-diving crankbait across the rocks, or by rustling it over the tops of the weeds. The point is, experiment! Pit fishing calls for a versatile approach.

Died-in-the-wool fans of artificials won't like it, but they'd better accept the fact that they should at least try live bait. In fact, for pits, it's the way to go, under most conditions, most of the time.

LIVE BAIT CHOICES

There are two main bait selections to consider—the crayfish and the water-dog. Both are excellent, high-percentage baits.

Crayfish can be seined in any stream. Many people believe that you need softcraws to be successful, but we feel as confident with hardshells as with softshells. Hardshell crayfish are easier to use, and their durability allows you to use the same bait, even after repeated casts. Seining your own crayfish provides the most economical live bait you can fish with.

We advise you not to import non-native crayfish into your area. Recent introductions of the "rusty crayfish"—a ferocious and detrimental species—has

Top Live Bait Choices

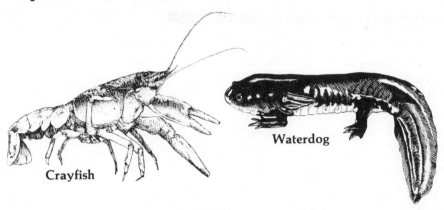

Waterdog

Crayfish

led some states to consider banning the sale of crayfish for bait.

The "waterdog boom" is on, and if you fish a couple of days a week, you know that it doesn't take long to run out of waterdogs. They are a super bait. The only drawback to using waterdogs is that you don't know how big a fish you'll get. Waterdogs are trophy smallmouth food!

We prefer the "Super Hook" for casting craws and waterdogs. However, you can simply hook a crayfish through the back of the tail (a waterdog through the snout) with a standard #6 or #4 hook.

Whether you're using crayfish or waterdogs, simply cast them out, let them sit awhile, and slowly inch them back while pausing frequently. This method is deadly!

Leeches fished on Lindy Rigs are a third choice, and also have their place in pit fishing. We've had our greatest success later in the year using leeches, when bass stop taking crayfish.

During bright, daytime conditions, bass exhibit their classic behavioral tendencies by relating to cover in shallow, pit environments. During these periods, most bass move into the thickest available cover where they bury themselves. They are not normally found near the outside edges or openings. Daytime is a good time to get out on the water to map, interpret and mark the areas you plan to fish at night.

Chapter 13

THE PRE-SUMMER PERIOD

"A Time of Transition"

Basically, Pre-summer is a time of transition, when a body of water transforms from the cooler-water environment of spring to the warmer environment of summer. Fish begin to regroup, and classic patterns begin to emerge.

Pre-summer is characterized by a variety of fishing patterns. You might catch several smallmouths by rigging (backtrolling) live bait in deep water, a couple more while crankbaiting the mid-depth flats, and you may even find a few fish in extremely shallow water. While no absolute temperature level indicates just when fish enter the Pre-summer stage, the surface water will have warmed to a point at which the smallmouth's metabolism demands more food to sustain its energy levels. When the surface water temperature reaches 70°F, you can assume that smallmouths are "back on the bite."

During this transition period, many lakes can be tough to fish. Some of the most consistent smallmouth action at this time occurs on rivers. Here's a simple, effective method for catching lots of smallmouths and a few bonus walleyes. All you have to do is apply a few basic rules of the road to rivers and cast a crankbait. Have fun!

CRANKING RIVERS FOR SMALLMOUTH BASS

Why fish rivers? World-class river-rat, Dan Gapen, says it all in his book *River Fishing.* ". . . This was river fishing . . . on a day when the thermometer was hovering around the 100°F mark. Certainly not a time to expect the kind of action which sees a pair of men boat over 100 fish, of four varieties, and then carefully release most of them." Yes, river fishing can provide some of the fastest action you've ever experienced. Also, it's not unusual to fish some rivers and not see another angler all day long! OK, here's how you can get in on these fast-action hotspots.

What types of rivers? Generally, the methods and techniques described here work best in adult, mature, and also parts of middle-aged river stretches. *It is important that you recognize the basic differences between river stretches so that you understand just what type of bodies of water this method is most effective on.* Some prime examples of ideal rivers for cranking are: the upper Mississippi, the St. Croix, the Kankakee, the upper Ohio River, the Tennessee River, portions of the Cumberland River in Tennesee, the Susquehanna in Pennsylvania, and the St. Lawrence in New York. Generally, this method will be effective anywhere you can find a shallow stretch of river less than 12 feet deep that contains smallmouths and/or walleyes, and has a moderate-to-fast current flow.

Cranking involves retrieving lipped-diving plugs (crankbaits) at a rapid pace. Very few anglers realize how effective cranking is on river smallmouths. Do not hesitate to combine this overall approach with jig and live bait combos, either.

EQUIPMENT

The equipment, along with presentation, is also relatively simple. In fact, you can take fish with no more than a rod, reel and a crankbait, as you walk along the bank from spot to spot. Nevertheless, there is no question that fishing from a boat allows you to take maximum advantage of this deadly system.

The boat and motor you use are very important. The ideal boat for shallow rivers is a Jon boat powered by a small outboard. A Jon boat is lightweight and maneuvers well in current. It is easy to launch when you're faced with tough river landings. On larger rivers, bigger boats are a better choice.

A good anchor is a useful tool. In very heavy current, 2 anchors may be necessary to ensure a solid grip on the bottom, to maintain the best possible boat position. A minimum of 30 feet of rope is necessary under most conditions, but a 100-foot rope allows you to adjust your position without lifting the anchor.

We suggest baitcasting tackle for practically every type of crankbait fishing. This type of tackle will give you the best possible lure control, because you can "thumb" your reel and control the distance of each cast. This is important when you're pinpoint casting to objects in the river. Spinning tackle would be our second choice; it works best with smaller crankbaits in very shallow water. In either case, we prefer a lightweight rod with a sensitive tip and plenty of backbone.

A baitcasting reel with a 5 to 1 gear ratio will pick up line quickly in current without wearing out your arm and shoulder. Cranking a reel with a 3 to 1 gear ratio for an entire day can be exhausting. Finally, the extra speed of a 5 to 1 will keep your lures ahead of the current, even if you are quartering upstream.

We suggest a high visibility line with little stretch. For most river situations, 12 or 14 pound test will be sufficient. Lighter line increases the chance of losing expensive crankbaits on river snags. A heavier line, meanwhile, prevents your lures from achieving their maximum depth.

The first 3 feet of line above the crankbait takes a terrible beating while cranking, as repeated contact with rocks and logs can fray the line in a very short time. Remember to check your knot and line every 15 minutes or so.

The best lures for river cranking are thin, sinking, tight-action crankbaits. Some good examples that we use are the Cordell Spot and Gay Blade in the ⅓ or ½ oz. sizes. The Bill Lewis Rat-L-Trap, Heddon Sonic & Sonar, and Rebel Racket Shad are other good baits. They feature a lip that is part of the body rather than an extension of it. The eye is on top, and the top of the lure forms a vibrating, diving lip. Tight action and rapid, side-to-side motion makes them unique among crankbaits.

A superior action in current also makes these baits ideal for rivers. Their thin shape works easier in moving water than a more bulky plug. More importantly, these baits ride head-down with both treble hooks facing back, which gives you a better chance to hook a *striking* fish. Chunkier plugs will work, but longer casts and/or rapid retrieves are required in order to achieve proper action and depth.

LOCATION AND PRESENTATION

Fishing rivers for smallmouths and walleyes is unique because it is so visual. As you look for spots, you can actually imagine the bottom by reading the telltale clues on the water's surface. Once you understand how the current reacts to bottom contours and creates visual signs, you will be able to spot the areas that hold fish well *before* you come into casting range.

Remember, river fish tend to shelter themselves from current whenever possible. They don't want to fight the current anymore than we would like to walk uphill into a 40 m.p.h. wind. Most rivers are strewn with objects such as rocks, logs, boulders, gravel and sandbars, which retard the current flow. When these objects occur in shallow water, the river will react by forming eddies, riffles or boils.

To better understand some types of areas which hold fish in an adult river stretch, we've prepared a map to help you visualize the river bottom.

As we head downriver, the first area that attracts fish is a wing dam, *AREA A*. A wing dam is a man-made structure of alternating piles of submerged rock and sometimes brush. These structures are designed to direct the current flow away from the shoreline and into the main channel. Because they break or disrupt the current, they form ideal fish-holding areas.

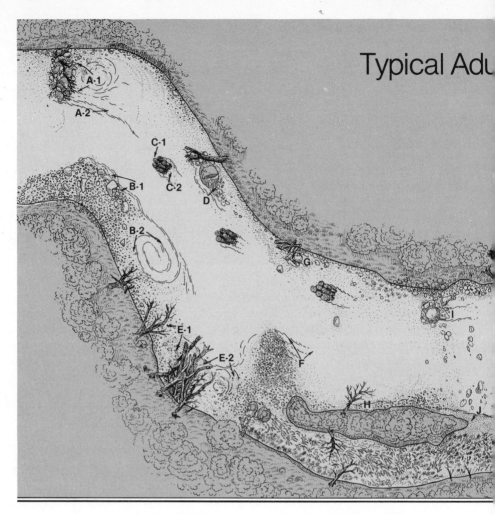

Typical Adu

In most cases, a small hole will form at the tip of a wing dam. The wing dam will also create an eddy and current break downstream behind the dam.

This current break is an excellent spot for both walleyes and smallmouths. Smallmouths tend to hold shallower and closer to the wing dam (*AREA A-1*). They can often be taken all along the downstream side, but they're usually at the tip, near the edge of the fast water.

Walleyes usually hold slightly downstream from the wing dam during the summer (*AREA A-2*).

Let's take a closer look at *AREA A-1*, immediately behind the wing dam. To cover this spot thoroughly, drop the anchor towards the very tip of the dam, and let out about 8 to 10 feet of rope so that the boat settles behind the wing dam.

Smallmouths will inevitably hold tight against the structure, so make your casts as close to it as possible. Casts should also be made parallel to the dam (as much as possible) and retrieved along its entire edge. Also cover the small hole at the tip of the dam where fish often school heavily.

After casting, engage the reel immediately, making sure the line is tight. If

ver Stretch

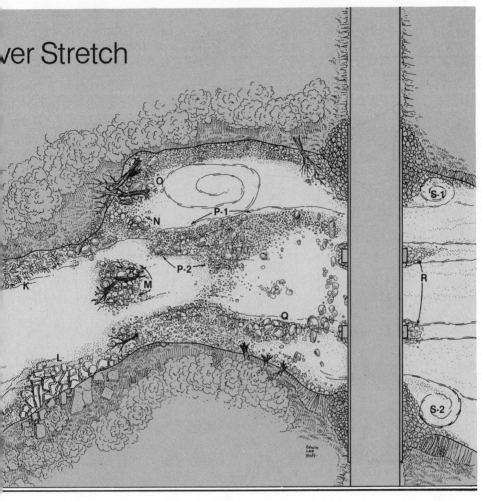

you are casting to a shallow spot, begin cranking quickly by lifting up the rod tip. As your lure leaves the shallows, slow your retrieve a bit and drop the rod down so that the bait covers deeper water. (Remember, we're using a crankbait that sinks.) If you cast to a deeper area, engage the spool immediately and keep a tight line. This time, however, let the bait work itself down into the current before you begin cranking.

AREA A-2 is the current break that forms below a wing dam. It is usually a little deeper here, and there will most likely be a visible boil or stream of roiled water. Walleyes will lie along the current break or edge where the fast and slow water meet.

In AREA B, there is a shallow, gravel tongue with larger rocks on the inside bend of the river—a very common fish magnet in rivers of this type. In AREA B-1, a riffle forms where the current flows over the shallow rocks. Depths may range from 2-4 feet on top of the tongue, usually dropping quite abruptly to 6 feet or more in the channel. In this area, larger submerged rocks will hold smallmouths, both on top and down the drop-off. The eddy in AREA-B 2 will generally be a bit deeper than the shoal, and will likely attract walleyes rather than smallmouths.

AREA C includes several log pilings in the center of the river. These man-made structures were created many years ago to aid lumberjacks in floating logs downstream. Groups of these logs are commonly found in a row, along one side of the main river channel, and are usually spaced anywhere from 30 to 50 yards apart. When present, they are excellent current breaks that attract smallmouths.

AREA C-1, a small, slack-water area in the front of the piling, could possibly hold feeding smallmouths. It is best to cover this smaller spot quickly from a mobile position, casting as close to the pilings as possible, because smallmouths will be located next to and in between the individual logs. It is a good idea to bump the logs as you retrieve your crankbait.

AREA C-2 includes the slack water directly below the pilings, and the current breaks on both sides. There are usually more fish behind the pilings than in front, both in the slack water and strung out along the two current breaks.

Maneuver your boat so that you adequately cover both sides of the pilings. Accurate casting is the key in this situation; you should be able to tell if there are any catchable fish behind the pilings with 5 or 6 good casts. If you catch a fish or two, take the time to work the area thoroughly.

In AREA D, a submerged log has jammed against a large boulder. Large boulders (both above and below the water) are very common in these kinds of rivers. There will be small riffles downstream from this obstruction. This would be a good spot for a few smallmouth bass and possibly some walleyes. It would not hold a lot of fish, but such spots often have big fish.

It's best to work smaller objects like this from a mobile position. Place your casts ahead of the rock, at the tip of the sunken tree. Don't hesitate to cast near or on top of obstructions. Smallmouths often strike as soon as the plug hits the water. Follow with consecutive casts downstream, below the boulder. Make your casts across and beyond the rock, retrieving the lure so that it hits the rock. You'll be surprised how often this will trigger a fish. Remember, the current break downstream from the rocks usually holds fish, so don't forget to fire a few casts in this area.

AREA E combines an abandoned beaver lodge with dead trees that have fallen into the river. Wherever you find this situation you'll find fish, because both smallmouths and walleyes are attracted to large amounts of submerged timber.

The top arrow in AREA E-1 points to the fallen trees. Begin here. Cast well up into the timber; make your casts as close to the base of the tree as possible, and work the plug all the way out to the tip. Cover both sides of the tree, as each side could hold fish.

The entire stretch between the fallen trees and the beaver lodge should be fished as you work your way down. The beaver lodge could have fish on all sides, so work it thoroughly. You may even want to anchor when you reach the lodge, especially if you picked up a fish or two while you were moving.

AREA E-2 features a current break that runs downstream from the beaver lodge. This area will hold both smallmouths and walleyes, and is one of the better spots on the map. Why? Because it is found in combination with a number of desirable conditions in a relatively small area.

AREA F, like *AREA B*, is a shallow gravel bar that could be anywhere from 2 to 4 feet deep on top and drop down to 6 or 8 feet in the channel. Providing it's shallow enough and there's enough current, riffles would form on top of the bar and a current break would trail behind the shoal. This current break would correspond with the edge of the drop-off. The base of the drop-off along the current break is ideal smallmouth and walleye habitat.

AREA G is an unusual situation that you'll find on some rivers—logs from the logging era that have been driven into the riverbank by the current. Many times, we've found that these old logs shelter a few smallmouths. There's no need to anchor here, as it takes only a few casts to check for fish. Cast as close as possible to the logs, because the bass inevitably hold tight against them.

In AREA H, a large tree has fallen into the water alongside an island, forming a small current break behind the deadfall. Most of the time this area will hold more smallmouths than walleyes. Spots like this rarely hold large numbers of fish and should be treated much like *AREA E-1*.

AREA I is a giant boulder—above or below the surface depending on water level—on top of a stretch of gravel. A few smallmouths or walleyes could be found in a spot like this. Cast beyond the boulder, hitting the rock as you retrieve your lure. For some reason, this technique seems to trigger reluctant fish. Remember to fish the trailing current break downstream.

Above *AREA J* is an island that is common on rivers of this type. These islands generally have a lot of bushes and trees on them which become partially submerged during periods of high water. Behind the island is a shallow side-channel. These side-channels are usually only 2-4 feet deep, and have a very soft silt and sand bottom with little current. Stringy river weeds often bloom heavily in spots like this, making presentation next to impossible.

AREA J is a long sandbar extending from the downstream tip of the island that holds smallmouths and walleyes. This is very common on an adult river and almost always draws fish. The sandbar will most likely only be about 1 to 3 feet deep, but will quickly drop off into the channel, and will have a harder bottom than the side channel because of the flushing action of the current. A noticeable current break will form alongside of and downstream from the bar. Work the entire edge by casting on top and parallel to the sandbar. Sometimes smallmouth bass will be right on top of it, next to the edge of the weeds that sometimes extend out from the side channel.

You might also try front-trolling upstream, parallel to the bar. Let out about 30 to 40 yards of line and troll slowly, occasionally pumping your plugs up and down. You can't troll into the current very fast or you'll have problems controlling your lures. Vary your trolling speed until you find a successful pattern. Watch carefully for any little dip or irregularity in these kinds of sandbars, as they can be important, fish-holding spots. You should anchor, of course, if you make contact with a substantial number of fish.

AREA K is another small gravel shoal adjacent to a group of weeds growing in sand near shore. These weeds can be long, thin grass, or a miniature version of cabbage. If adjacent to the main channel, these weeds will often hold walleyes—especially if gravel is present.

AREA L is a makeshift landing with a pile of broken cement slabs (these often appear below dam and bridge pilings) which have fallen into the river from one bank. Areas of fractured concrete or transplanted rock (rip-rap) along river banks are very common, since many of these rivers were the transportation routes of yesteryear. These broken slabs act much the same as boulders, and create a current break. Fish lie along the current break which forms downstream, reacting in the same manner as in areas with large boulders.

A pile of rocks and sticks lies in the middle of the main channel in *AREA M*. This large structure drops into 6 to 8 feet of water rather quickly on all sides, and is one of the better spots on the map for big schools of both walleyes and smallmouths. Since this area should be covered thoroughly, it's best to anchor twice and fish each side, casting as close to the pile as possible. The upstream edge will often hold aggressive smallmouths, and should be worked carefully. Distinct current breaks form downstream on either side of this structure.

AREA N is simply a series of three medium-sized boulders near the river bank. Only a sharp eye on the water's surface can spot these if they are a couple feet underwater. The only clue would be a few boils 20 feet downstream, with a trail of foam. These hidden spots are deceiving, and often harbor a real trophy.

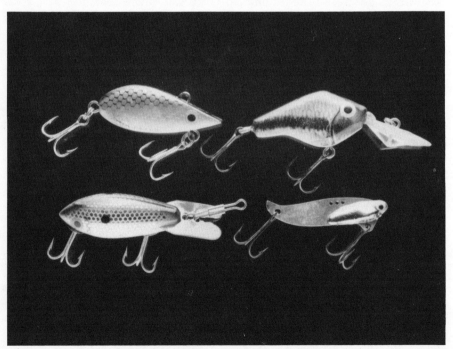

As a rule, smaller, tight action crankbaits are preferred for river smallmouths. The best lures for river cranking are thin sinking baits (note the eye on the top of lure).

AREA O is a small, sheltered, slackwater area with rocks, boulders and fallen logs. Quiet spots like this with heavy cover often hold big smallmouths, but are ignored by many fishermen because they are hard to fish. Your best bet here is to cast the plug into the shallow-water obstructions and carefully work it back. You may get a few more snags, but you'll also catch more fish. Be sure to work the entire inside edge along the rim of the hole formed by the eddy.

The combination of *AREA O, AREA P,* and the large eddy formed by the outcrop of land at this point in the river combine to make this one of the best spots on the map. In *AREA P,* a shallow gravel bar expands in width and is surrounded by the channel on both sides. Alongside *AREA P-1,* just below *AREA O,* is a large eddy that has molded a small depression in the bottom. The gravel bar would likely be 3 or 4 feet deep, dropping to 8 to 10 feet in the middle of the eddy. These larger eddies are usually not as visible as the smaller ones. Larger areas like these combine several desirable conditions that attract large schools of both smallmouths and walleyes.

AREA P-1 is the current break formed along the edge of the gravel bar. This is a key spot for both species. Smallmouths will favor the part of the eddy closest to *AREA O.* During periods of low water, both species will concentrate in the deeper part of the eddy.

Begin by trolling, as described in *AREA J,* along the current break and through the heart of the eddy. This spot should be big enough for several trolling runs, beginning at the bridge and extending upstream through *AREA P.* When you contact fish, note the exact spot. Then, slip downstream and cast toward that spot. If you catch another fish immediately from the same area, you're probably into a good school. In this case, drop the anchor and work the spot thoroughly.

AREA P-2 is the other side of this small gravel ridge where a current break has also formed. While this spot would probably not have as many fish as the eddy side, it would be well worth a few casts.

At the base of *AREA P-2* (where the right arrow is pointing), the entire midstream area turns into a shallow gravel flat with intermittent rocks. The shallower portions would most likely hold smallmouths. Take the time to cover this spot, both by trolling and casting.

AREA Q features a gravel bank that drops off into deeper water. Again, a current edge is created that will draw fish. Both trolling and casting will work here.

AREA R, a very important part of the river, contains pilings supporting a highway or railroad bridge. The type of pilings depends largely on the age of the bridge or where it is located. Some have a very gradual drop-off into deeper water, while others are sharper. Most pilings have an underwater pile of rip-rap at their base. These pilings are excellent current breaks, and will hold both smallmouths and walleyes. Both the front and back of the pilings will hold fish, but the downstream side will be better—especially the current break trailing downstream. Again, quickly cast this area, and if you run into a concentration of fish, drop the anchor.

AREAS S-1 and *S-2* are eddies created by the rip-rap from the bridge foundation. Always be alert for eddies in these locations. Place your casts as parallel as possible along the rip-rap bank, and gradually work deeper. The larger the eddy and the more extensive the rip-rap, the better chance for a big school of fish.

SUMMARY

This map contains representative samples of the better spots on an adult river. Many of these conditions can be found on a mature river as well. Though they are grouped closely together for the sake of convenience, they would probably not occur quite so close together on an actual river. It is, of course, impossible in a single chapter to cover all the conditions that hold fish on this type of river. Furthermore, since rivers differ and have their own unique characteristics, on every trip you'll find new types of spots that produce fish. This system will enable you to take fish on practically any adult or mature smallmouth river, *even if you are a novice river angler.*

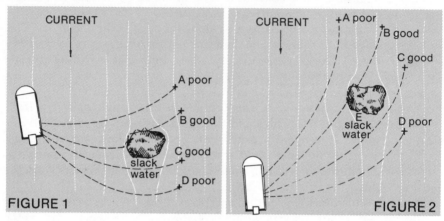

Figures 1 and 2 *show the difference between a good and poor cast with a crankbait in current. Figure 1 shows how your approach should be from the upstream side of an object; Figure 2 from the downstream side.*

Figure 1: Casts A and D are poor casts, because the lure is too far from the stump. Remember, a fish won't move very far into the current to strike. The correct way, shown by B, is to cast past the stump and hit the upstream side on the retrieve. This is exactly where an active, feeding smallmouth would be.

Below the stump, D represents the wrong way to cast. Cast C is a better choice, since it covers the slack water directly behind the stump. A resting fish would be here. The lure should be cast past the slack water and pulled directly into it as close to the stump as possible. Be sure to engage your reel immediately—any delay will allow the current to push your crankbait downstream.

Once the lure is in the slack water, you can slow your retrieve a bit. The crankbait is now in that narrow band of productive water behind the stump. Unless speed seems to be necessary to make the fish strike, it's a good idea to slow down your retrieve to keep the bait in the fish zone as long as possible.

Figure 2 shows the right casting position once you've drifted past the stump. Again, A and D demonstrate poor casts—too far from the fish zone. Cast B strikes the upstream side of the stump, which is perfect. Cast C is fine, since the lure passes through the slack water.

Take a look at point E. This would be an excellent spot to place a jig. But with a crankbait, it would be best to cast beyond point E. Then, once the plug reaches E, it will have achieved the proper action. It is always to your advantage when fishing a crankbait to cast past your target. This way by the time your retrieve brings the lure alongside the target, it will be running at the right depth and be vibrating properly.

When drifting past a stump like this, you and your partner will only be able to get about three casts apiece before the river carries you out of range. That's why it's so important to make sure your casts are covering productive water.

Chapter 14

SUMMER PEAK

"A Time of Fulfillment"

Here are some basic rules of thumb for recognizing the onset of the Summer Peak. First, the surface temperature of meso (middle-aged) lakes is usually in the low 70°F's. It may eventually climb into the upper 70°F's, or even low 80°F's, but this typically happens very slowly. Thus, the Summer Peak Period seems to begin with the end of the rapid, early-summer rise in water temperature. In cooler Canadian lakes, the water temperature might only reach the mid-60°F's, yet the principle is the same.

While the Summer Peak can be one of the best times of the year for walleye fishing, it's not necessarily so with smallmouth bass. Apparently, the combination of environmental factors that stimulate a walleye feeding binge does not have the same effect on smallmouths. Smallmouth bass don't display the intense feeding activity demonstrated by other species. At this time, the larger smallmouths may still be affected by the rigors of spawning, or they may be selectively feeding on insects. Further, the period may be extremely short and difficult to pinpoint.

As the season progresses, smallmouths relate more heavily to the points, turns and humps in drop-off areas. If plenty of good habitat exists (a good, better, best situation), some scouting will be necessary to locate the "best" area. One tip for locating these spots is to look for schools of baitfish in the area; smallmouths will usually be nearby. However, smallmouth bass have a tendency to move up and down a lot, so you'll catch them 18 feet deep on one trip and in 6 feet of water the next time!

The Great Lakes offer a situation where there seems to be an abundance of habitat, yet smallmouths are still only found in certain areas. Thus, they provide an excellent example for locating and catching smallmouths on any large body of water, be it lake, reservoir, or one of the Great Lakes. The following approach works well under these conditions, and you can use it just about anywhere you fish.

THE GREAT LAKES

It's a *huge* region. From the St. Louis River harbor at Duluth, Minnesota, to the St. Lawrence River where Lake Ontario exits to the sea, stretches a course some 1000 miles long. The wealth and variety of local habitat across such a vast region is monumental, indeed! And so are fish behavior and fishing techniques.

Kind of intimidating, isn't it? Thousands of miles of shoreline, islands, rivers, harbors, plus countless points, bays, nooks and crannies in the shoreline. And everywhere you go, the locals have their own fishing tricks!

BASIC LOCATION

Perhaps the most important things to keep in mind are that smallmouths are *not* (1) cold water or (2) open water, suspended fish. You won't find them in vast areas of deep, cold, open water. That's trout and salmon country.

Since the vast majority of the Great Lakes *is* deep, cold, open water, *most* smallmouth bass are limited to bays, canals, harbors, rivers, connected lakes, etc. These function as small, cool-water environments connected to gigantic, cold-water ones. This fact narrows your search considerably; it's *the* key.

The big bonus is that these areas receive seasonal influxes of Great Lakes baitfish like smelt, alewives and emerald shiners. When this occurs, "bay" fish like smallmouths, walleyes and northerns gorge themselves on the feast. The abundant prey produces a growth rate seldom matched on inland waters.

FISHING THE CONNECTED WATERS

Smallmouth fishing in the bays and connected waters of the Great Lakes is really very simple. The fish generally see little fishing pressure, and are very willing to cooperate. Simply find their "home" areas, and you're on the fish.

When shallow, connecting waters provide suitable spawning and rearing habitat, cool (not icy cold) water, and abundant food, the result is *big* smallmouths. Fish *over* 4 pounds are common, and 5's and 6's are a real possibility. A good example of this kind of smallmouth home area is shown in *FIGURE 1*.

FIGURE 1

Smallmouth Location in "Connected" Waters

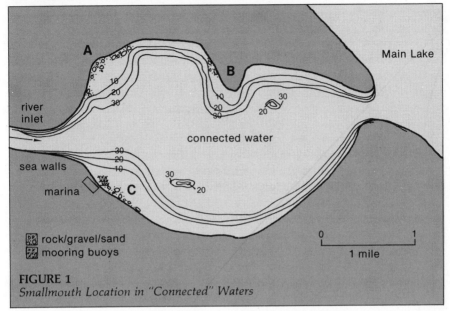

FIGURE 1
Smallmouth Location in "Connected" Waters

There are many bays, rivers, canals, harbors and small lakes connected to the Great Lakes with abundant smallmouth bass. How strong the population is depends on the local habitat. If suitable spawning and rearing areas, structural elements and food are all present in a favorable combination—presto—smallmouth bass. These areas function as small, cool-water environments connected to large, cold-water ones.

The accompanying illustration depicts a typical "connected water" with three distinct smallmouth home areas (A, B and C). The local "families" would probably have very little interaction with each other. Some fish from B and C might make seasonal use of the sunken islands near each area, but A's fish wouldn't stray that far. Chances are that a few fish from C would occasionally use the seawalls, or patrol amongst the sailboat mooring buoys. Basically, it's that simple.

Prime "home areas" are generally larger, multi-depth-level bars and shoals. These areas provide smallmouths with suitable habitat and prey, all year long. However, the fish don't simply spread out in random fashion. There are definite key spots that attract smallmouths.

By the Summer Peak, the smallmouths will have completed spawning, and they'll be in deeper, summer habitat areas. Smallmouths appear to make "classic" deep to shallow water movements, so they might be located deep, shallow, or in between.

Look for concentrations of smallmouths on gravel/rock points, projections and humps. On some waters, the presence of cabbage weed adjacent to these areas could enhance the potential of the spot (more cover for prey). The transition area from weeds to gravel/rock can be excellent. Another choice spot is a clam bed, which can be tough to locate but worth the effort.

PRESENTATION

Trolling crankbaits, casting jigs and rigging live bait are all effective techniques for catching smallmouths. Here are several game plans to help you locate and stay on smallmouths.

Because of the large size of some smallmouth areas, we often troll to locate the areas of major fish use. Tie on a Countdown Rapala or crawfish-colored crankbait and start trolling. For terminal gear, we recommend a 5½ foot, medium-action, fast-tip casting rod, equipped with a casting reel. Use about 8-12 pound test line, and let out 150 feet of line behind the boat to minimize the spooking factor.

Follow approximate depth contours. Make a pass at 8-10 feet deep, moving just fast enough to wobble the lure and occasionally smack the bottom. If fish are present, they'll hit. If they're out a bit deeper, you may need to put on a slightly larger, deeper-diving lure and make another pass. Trolling eliminates a lot of water while looking for active, biting fish.

Feel for rocks or a change in the bottom. Somewhere, *something* will change, and all of a sudden, smallmouths will be there. Once you locate a key area, shut off the outboard motor and drift back through the area, casting a crankbait. If the fish are aggressive, they'll smack it.

When the fish are a bit less aggressive, you can still catch a bunch by switching to a jig. For jigging, use a quality 6 foot spinning rod and an open-face reel. Try a ⅛ to ¼ ounce jig, like a Lindy Fuzz-E-Grub, or a jighead with a 3-inch Mister Twister Meeny tail. Pitch it out on 6 pound test line, and let it sit. Then move it a few feet and let it sit again. Be sure to use a sensitive spinning rod to help detect the often-subtle hit as the bass just barely sucks the lure in. Another good retrieve is a "swimming" technique that seems to trigger fish which are slightly suspended off the bottom.

Backtrolling a live bait rig is a very effective technique for catching neutral-feeding-attitude smallmouths. The backtrolling method allows a nearly vertical presentation with live bait. By using the outboard motor in reverse gear, or an electric motor, you can creep along, keeping the bait in the prime fish zone. Top live bait choices are: leeches, crawlers, crayfish, waterdogs and shiner minnows. The secret is to fish slowly while maintaining contact with the bottom.

A sensitive rod is essential, because many times a waterdog or shiner will "go nuts" and indicate the presence of fish. An astute angler can *feel* the minnow struggling while trying to escape from the bass. Use the lightest sinker you can to maintain bottom contact, and match the hook size to the size of the live bait, so as not to spook the fish. This method works, and accounts for many trophy smallmouths!

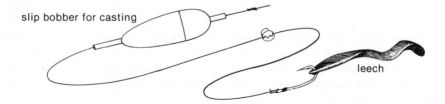

slip bobber for casting

leech

A secret walleye anglers have been using for years can be dynamite on smallmouths. Slip-bobbers are easy to use and are beneficial in many situations. For example, a slip-bobber rig can be used to float a leech or crayfish onto a rocky reef with minimum hang-ups. It's a great method for taking non-aggressive fish; the bait literally wiggles under their noses. Try it; you'll like it.

FISHING ON THE "BIG WATER"

The Western Basin of Lake Erie is a *logical* exception to the cold waters of the rest of the Great Lakes. True, it has many miles of open water, but it is definitely *not* trout and salmon water. The average depth of the Western Basin is only about 30 feet, and the water temperature climbs up to 70°F in summer, much like an inland lake.

Smallmouths generally do not wander, suspended, chasing schools of baitfish, either! Rather, they relate to rocky islands and reefs in typical smallmouth fashion. So, even though the water is gigantic, you're still faced with *localized* populations of smallmouth bass in well-defined island, reef and bay areas.

During the month of June, the smallmouths are largely scattered across, and along the edges, of rocky flats and large points around the islands. Some fish are working their way toward nearby, offshore, shallow reefs. At any rate, they'll be in general areas, but will not be heavily grouped.

A crankbait trolling technique, similar to the one we discussed earlier, is a very efficient technique for locating fish. You'll need deeper-diving crankbaits, and you can probably pick up speed a little, but the nuts and bolts of the system is the same. Put the lines in the water, and start trolling the general drop-off area next to the islands.

When you catch a fish, swing back around for another pass. If you pick up 1 or 2 more, toss out a floating marker. Then drift through the area, casting crankbaits or switching to a ¼ ounce jig and minnow combination. Fancast the entire area. If there are numbers of fish present, you might even anchor.

In July, August and September, the smallmouths regroup into *awesome* schools. We're talking *hundreds* of fish! It's something you have to see to believe. This can provide an unbelievable fishing experience.

KEY SMALLMOUTH AREAS IN THE BASS ISLANDS

Top-notch smallmouth charter captain, Jim Fofrich, has made it easy for all bass chasers who want to try smallies around the Bass Islands. He's marked some of the better spring and summer smallmouth areas. Try the techniques described in this chapter and you'll catch fish.

We don't often see such an unselfish gesture. However, Jim feels that the smallmouth population is so good, and that the average *IN-FISHERMAN* reader is so catch-and-release minded, that a little extra pressure won't hurt.

If you'd like to take a trip with an experienced smallmouth bass guide, we highly recommend the guides headquartering out of Floro's Marina, Lacarne, OH 43439 (just west of Port Clinton). These knowledgeable guides use 25-35 foot boats that'll tackle the big water. In addition, they know *where, when, and how* to catch fish.

Top Smallmouth Areas in the Bass Islands

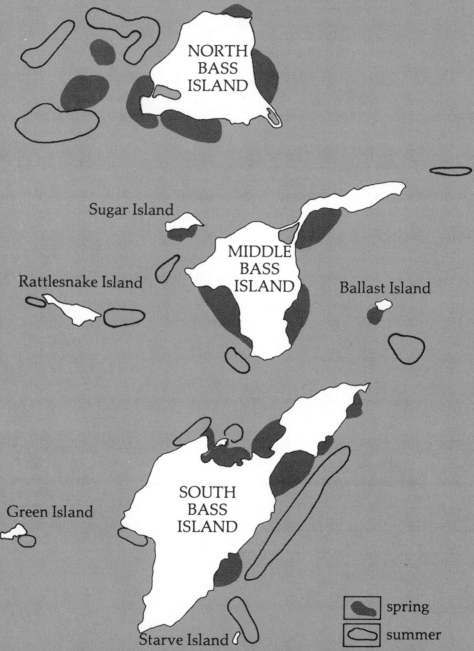

The Bass Islands, and nearby Pelee and Kelleys Islands, host perhaps the finest smallmouth bass fishery on earth. Yet, even in this huge area, smallmouths still display their typical stay-at-home tendencies. Ohio Department of Natural Resources' tagging studies confirm that smallies live most of their lives within a relatively small home range. Nearly 90% of the recaught, tagged fish were captured within one-half mile of their spawning sites.

Some charter captains drift the edges of the reefs and shoreline drop-offs with live bait. Others prefer to anchor along fast-breaking, rocky drop-offs. It may take a number of anchoring positions to get on the fish, but it's worth it. Once you start catching smallies, the activity will progressively attract more and more fish, and you'll have all the action you can handle. When Jim Fofrich calls this a "hernia-provoking experience," it's hard to tell if he means the anchor or the smallmouths.

The standard, Lake Erie, live bait rig is an egg-sinker slip-rig with about a #1 hook. Lindy Rig, walking-sinker rigs have also caught on recently, and work equally well. Regardless of the exact rig, the most commonly used live baits are shiners and small crawfish. Both baits are available at local tackle shops, and we must admit that those baby crawfish look mighty good!

For still-fishing, hook craws once through the tail, and shiners *lightly* through either the back or the upper portion of the back, near the tail. Then lower 'em down, let 'em squirm, and be ready for action. Keep the rig a foot or two off the bottom to thwart the ever-present sheepshead. Raise and lower the rod occasionally to entice the bass. That's all there is to it; go get 'em!

Things get hectic when the smallies attack! They don't come in ones or twos—but in waves. Catch a few, get the rest in a frenzy, and you'll have all the action you can handle.

Small crawfish and shiners are the two top smallmouth live baits on Lake Erie. We've done very well on "connected" waters with chubs, waterdogs and leeches, too! Apparently, smallmouths never lose their affinity for live bait, no matter where they live!

Chapter 15

THE SUMMER PERIOD

"A Time of Plenty"

Smallmouth fishing during the summer can be a real challenge, because the fish are scattered over a large habitat area. Some fish may forage in the shallows; others may choose to feed on the flats; and still others may opt to feed in deeper water. As groups of fish become less concentrated, you need to cover more water to contact them. In addition, feeding activity can be of short, intense duration.

On many clear bodies of water, low-light conditions seem to trigger smallmouth feeding activity. In fact, nocturnal feeding movements are common on clear-water natural lakes and reservoirs. At night, smallmouths may be up on the flats, foraging for insects, small fish, crustaceans and other targets of opportunity.

In many northern, natural lakes, summer smallmouths forage on rock-capped, sunken islands and rock/gravel bars. Slow-tapering flats with sand-grass on their deeper edges can be overlooked, smallmouth, home areas.

Canadian Shield lakes of the North and southern TVA reservoirs both offer excellent, summer smallmouth fishing. The name of the game is habitat, and each body of water offers smallmouths a different set of options. How fish react to these options determines exactly where, when and how to catch them. Here's how it's done on typical southern reservoirs and Canadian Shield lakes.

THIRD-SHIFT SMALLMOUTHS— A SUPER SUMMER SMALLMOUTH SYSTEM

An old adage states, "Night fishing is only for people who can't catch fish during the day." No doubt this phrase has been coined by the banker's hours brigade of anglers. Granted, nighttime fishing can be frustrating; however, with a little planning and practice, it becomes enjoyable. Who wouldn't enjoy catching a 5, 6 or even a 7 pound smallmouth bass?

Why should you fish after dark? During the summer, daytime temperatures can easily hit the 90°F's (or more). If you combine this with a hot sun, speed-boaters and water skiers, you have a rush-hour traffic jam on the water! This situation is not very enjoyable or productive. However, it exists throughout the U.S. of A. Yes, there is a logical alternative to this aquatic rat race—night fishing.

This nocturnal (after-dark) approach is especially effective on clear water natural lakes, strip pits and impoundments. For example, in many southern TVA impoundments, smallmouth bass in the 4-6 pound class are regularly taken at night. Occasionally, these southern good ol' boys catch a 7-9 pound smallmouth! This is, obviously, world-class fishing.

THREADFIN SHAD

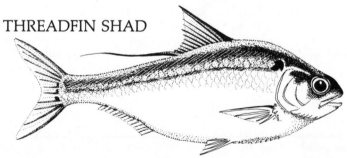

Shad are members of the herring family, which includes threadfin and gizzard shad, plus the skipjack herring. All are prime forage for smallmouths in many southern waters. The threadfin shad closely resembles the gizzard shad, but because of its smaller size, the threadfin remains available longer as forage for smallmouth bass. Adult threadfin only reach 6-8 inches, compared to adult gizzard shad which can grow to 12-18 inch lengths. However, the young-of-the-year gizzard shad are prime smallmouth food. Apparently, the abundance of these high-fat forage fish is one of the major factors in growing huge, southern impoundment smallmouths.

WHERE'S THE BASS?

Nighttime smallmouth fishing is an effective approach to the summer reservoir dilemma. The following method is effective on both crystal-clear water impoundments like Dale Hollow, and the stained water impoundments of the Tennessee River.

All TVA impoundments offer a real smorgasbord of structure. Typically, points, bluffs, bars, weeds, stumps, islands, tributary creeks, channel and main lake areas are all present to some degree. All these spots could house smallmouths; in essence, these are ideal smallmouth bass habitat. Additionally, shad, crayfish, panfish, small fish and insects provide a superb food base for adult smallmouths.

At night, smallmouths, which may have been located in adjacent deeper-water areas during the day, move into shallower water to forage. These smallmouths are catchable during the day; however, they're usually far more active at night.

Prime shallow areas are normally located near a drop-off. For example, stump flats, gravel/rock points, submerged islands or humps, underwater ridges, channel banks, brush piles and weedbeds are potential spots. All these spots may hold a few fish. However, if any of these areas are located adjacent to a river channel or deep water area, the spot can be sensational.

Many times, local anglers enhance these spots by sinking old Christmas trees, brush or tree branches on them. This added structure is a real bonus. Apparently, smallmouths use these areas to prey upon threadfin and young-of-the-year gizzard shad. This type of environment appears to be ideal habitat for smallmouth bass. There's cover, plenty of forage, and deeper water nearby.

All these spots have the awesome potential to hold large concentrations of fish—big fish. Catches of five smallmouth bass, each weighing more than 5 pounds, are not uncommon, even during the heat of summer! Interested? Good; read on!

Most of these areas can be located with a little intelligent scouting, using a topographical map and a graph or fish locator. By studying the map, asking a few questions and applying some common sense, you can locate the better areas. Even though some homework may be involved, it's worth the effort.

Research your potential hotspots during the day, so you can locate them at night without too much trouble. (You must exercise extreme caution at night, and it's always safety first.)

Let's assume you've located a shallower water stump flat near a river channel. OK, just exactly how do you approach and fish it? Here's a logical plan that works!

Slowly approach the stump flat from the river channel or deeper-water side and locate the outside edge (drop-off) using the locator. If you motor into the middle of the stump flat, chances are good that you will spook the fish into the next county. Once you locate the edge of the flat, begin searching for the best areas on top of the stump flat.

Sometimes a stump flat contains isolated "islands" of stumps near an extensive stump field; these isolated groups can be super. In addition, irregularities in the stump field may be productive. For instance, a creek channel may cut through the stumps, creating a natural break; or the flat may contain a finger with stumps that extend into deeper water. Additionally, underwater stump

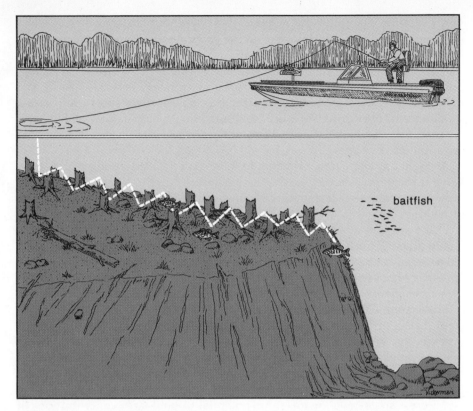

The accompanying illustration shows how to retrieve a spinnerbait through a stump flat using the lift-and-drop technique. Note the position of the boat on the drop-off area; the angler is casting a stump row. Proficient smallmouth anglers take the time to learn good areas. You must be able to visualize what's on the bottom in order to fish properly.

rows are good; look for the upcurrent end of a row of stumps nearest deep water.

The smaller turns and pockets in the stump field are overlooked, big fish spots. Also check out the ends of the stump field, especially if the end of the field is created by a turn in a river channel. These spots can be located and marked prior to fishing them to help you find the exact spots.

OK, now we know when and where to fish. How are we going to catch 'em?

Basically, the presentation options are simple. Terminal tackle could be a 5½ to 6 foot, medium-heavy action, fast taper, casting rod with a good quality casting reel spooled with 14-20 pound test line. Heavy gear is necessary to horse these hard-fightin' fish out of cover. A second choice is a 6½ to 7 foot, medium-heavy action, fast taper, spinning rod with a good quality spinning reel. The decision is yours. Both will do the job, so pick whichever outfit you can fish most efficiently. A third option is our personal favorite—a 7½ foot flippin' stick, rather than a shorter casting rod. The added length allows a better hook set and more leverage to pull a fish out of cover. Try it!

The spinnerbait is the number one lure for nighttime smallmouth fishing. Most anglers use a ¼ or ⅜ oz., black, single spin model, with a No. 4 or No. 5

blade attached by a ball bearing swivel. Both short arm and long arm styles are excellent. The lure should have a rubber skirt, and as an added feature, you should put on a pork chunk or twister tail.

The purpose of the ball bearing swivel is to ensure that the blade turns freely as the lure is falling, since the most productive retrieve is generally an up-and-down, yo-yo motion. To make this retrieve effective, the blade must continue to rotate when the lure is allowed to fall.

The pork chunk provides extra weight for easier casting, but its main purpose is to add a slight buoyancy to the lure so that it actually falls a little slower. It also adds bulk, and may keep a smallmouth holding on just a split second longer so you can set the hook easier.

Cast the spinnerbait out and allow it to fall to the bottom. Remember, you're generally fishing less than 10 feet deep, so the fall won't take long. Once the lure has settled, reel in slack line. Then pull the lure up off the bottom by raising the rod tip to about the 10 o'clock position. Don't bring the spinnerbait completely to the surface, but rather keep it closer to the bottom.

Once you raise the rod tip, slowly lower it again, and reel in slack line as the lure falls. When it reaches the end of its fall, raise the rod tip again, and repeat the sequence without hesitation.

What happens is that the spinnerbait blade changes speed from the climb to the fall, and again from the fall to the climb; these speed changes apparently

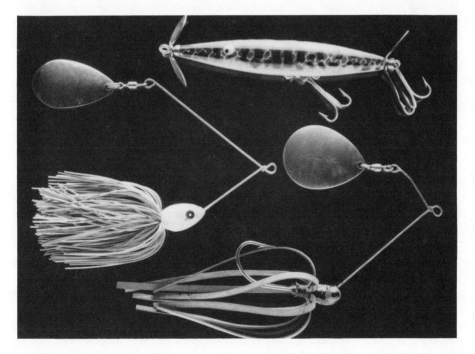

Basic ammo for third-shift smallmouths! Topwater baits can trigger explosive strikes (upper). Spinnerbaits are numero uno for nighttime smallmouth fishing (lower) and both long and short arm styles are good—note ball bearing swivel on blade of short arm spinnerbait.

attract smallmouths. Strikes most often occur just after the lure begins to climb or right after it begins its fall—right when the blade changes speed.

You should not have any problem feeling the blade rotating with a ball bearing spinnerbait. In fact, if you ever do feel it stop, it's time to set the hook. Although most smallmouth strikes are sudden jolts and the fish frequently hook themselves, some are very soft and barely distinguishable.

With this lure and retrieve, it's imperative that you keep a tight line at all times—not only to aid in hook-setting, but also to help you feel the spinnerbait. It's also important to establish a constant rhythm in your retrieves. Instead of changing speeds, as in daylight fishing, keep every retrieve as much alike as possible. You already have the necessary change in the up-and-down motion of the spinnerbait.

Work your target area at night the same as you would during daylight hours. Simply fan cast the area. Be thorough and methodical. Begin at one end or along an outside edge, and gradually cover the entire zone. Remember, too, that errant boat noise or excessive light will spook shallow water fish.

Topwater plugs can be used successfully on after-dark smallmouths. It's just as exciting, perhaps even more so, as using spinnerbaits, and the fish seem to prefer surface lures to blade baits at times.

Several topwater lures draw strikes, but the most popular seem to be those with one or more propellers. Surprisingly, it doesn't seem to be actual prop action that attracts strikes, because one of the most successful of all tactics is to cast and simply let the lure lie motionless for half a minute or longer. Smallmouths may suddenly blast it, more out of anger or frustration, it appears, than hunger.

If no strikes occur as the lure is motionless, try an ever-so-slight twitch that spins a propeller—just enough to cause a tiny ripple to ride the water; then leave the lure alone again. If there is a smallmouth nearby, this trick might take him. It works well in Dixie, and it's been used summer after summer in clear northern lakes, too.

Oddswise, live bait is the answer to fishing ultra-clear water impoundments. In many parts of the country, live bait is used in daytime bass fishing, and the same baits and techniques can also be used successfully on big reservoirs at night. The primary baits used are small minnows and crayfish, although nightcrawlers, frogs, leeches, water dogs and grasshoppers all work. These baits are often used with artificial lures.

Crayfish are probably the most popular smallmouth bait, simply because these crustaceans form a major part of the fish's diet in many lakes. Rigging crayfish for smallmouth fishing is simple. Slip a No. 2 or No. 4 hook through the tail of the crayfish, pinch on a small split shot 8 to 10 inches above the hook to sink the bait to the bottom, and you're set.

Try freelining crayfish over gravel bars, around rock piles, and along sloping points. Once the bait falls to the bottom, you can reel it back very slowly. When a smallmouth hits, you'll know it, and you can normally set the hook immediately.

If the bottom is extremely rocky, you may prefer to use a slip bobber to keep the crayfish suspended just above the rocks. Hook the bait through the top of the shell, and adjust the bobber stop to keep the crayfish floating just inches

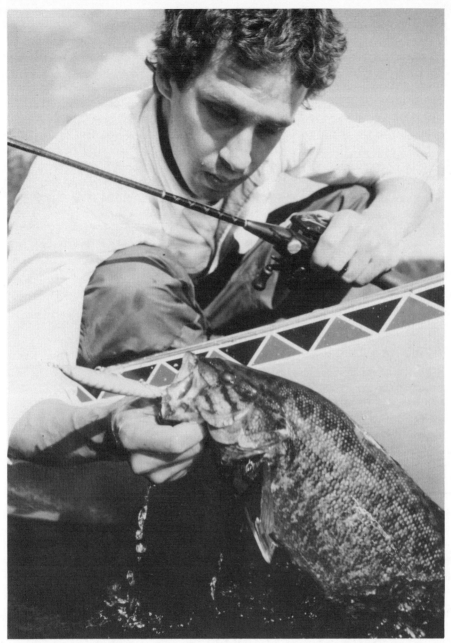

Canadian shield lakes also offer some super, summer smallmouth fishing. Here's Jim Lindner with a trophy sized smallmouth bass!

above the bottom.

Insects like crickets, hellgrammites and grasshoppers are fished much the same way crayfish are. Pinch split shot on your line to take the bait to the bottom, and either let it drift naturally in the current or reel it back with a slow, steady retrieve.

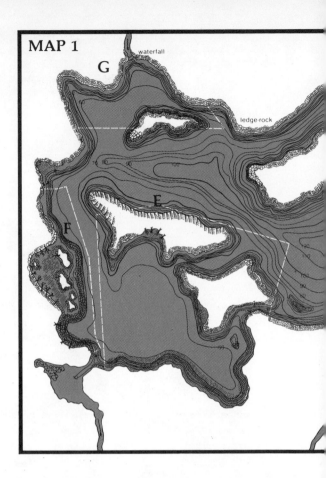

In many reservoirs, small minnows also form a large part of the smallmouth's diet, and some anglers hook them on spinners or jigs. Hook the baitfish through both lips from the bottom up; then cast and retrieve the rig as if the lure had a pork or plastic trailer, instead of live bait.

On lakes with relatively clear, gravel bottoms, some night anglers fish light-weight hair jigs, tipping them with minnows. Bucktail jigs, weighing ⅛ ounce, require relatively small minnows, but they can be quite effective. Cast and retrieve them very slowly, just inches above the bottom. A variation of this retrieve includes periodic jumps or falls, controlled by rod tip movement.

SUMMER SMALLMOUTHS ON THE SHIELD

Early season smallmouth fishing can be fantastic. The fish are generally shallow, and when the weather's fine, the fishing's great. Toss poppers, hair bugs, plastic worms, Daredevles or Rebel Minnows in shallow water, and the bass will try to nail 'em!

Many of the bass'll be big—4's and 5's, or perhaps even an honest 6 pound fish. Experience that kind of fishing once, and you'll be back year after year.

Such utterly unbelievable fishing may only occur on one out of three early

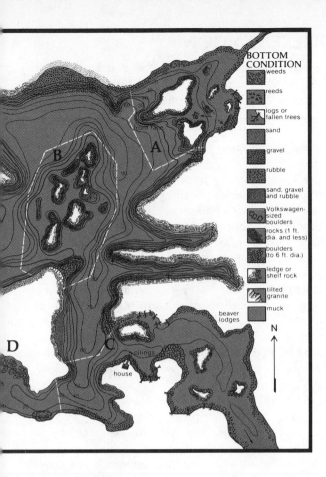

BOTTOM CONDITION

weeds
reeds
logs or fallen trees
sand
gravel
rubble
sand, gravel and rubble
Volkswagen-sized boulders
rocks (1 ft. dia. and less)
boulders (to 6 ft. dia.)
ledge or shelf rock
tilted granite
muck

beaver lodges

N

season trips, however. Tremendous, early season fishing depends on stable weather, and there's only so much of that to go around. Much of the time, the fishing's just "good."

Transitional fishing occurs between early season and summer fishing, and is unpredictable. This transition begins after the fish spawn, when they move from shallow bays or shorelines to areas in, or closer to, the main lake. While fish are moving, it's tough to catch them. On the border waters between Ontario and Minnesota, this transition period usually occurs during late June.

Fishing doesn't have to be terrible during the transition, but don't expect to find concentrations of fish in any one type of habitat. Search shallow and search deep. Search bays and search in the main lake. Try many different areas and many different methods, and you'll find enough smallies to keep you busy.

The situation is different during summer, however. Once smallmouths establish summer patterns, they're predictable, and the fishing is reliable. It's a different sort of fishing, however. Subsurface and live baits are productive, instead of topwater baits that worked so well during spring. By comparison, summer smallie fishing is a sure thing, or at least as "sure a thing" as exists in fishing. During summer, fishing is "good" *most* of the time.

PRESENTATION

Shield lake smallmouth presentation is difficult only because there are so many methods and baits that work; crankbaits, surface poppers, streamer flies, nightcrawlers, leeches, crayfish or minnows on live bait rigs, leadhead jigs—if the bait looks reasonable, it'll catch fish.

Obviously, however, certain presentations catch more fish at certain times. It's always a good idea to have a presentation plan, and to fish as efficiently as possible. Let's put together a plan.

Before proceeding with "the plan," consider John Herrick's observations on presentation, based on over 10 years of serious, daily guiding on shield lakes. John says that you can almost always catch fish on artificials, but live bait— particularly leeches and 'crawlers—produces more and larger fish. At least part of the reason relates to another of John's prescriptions for shield small-mouths. Simply put, no matter what time of year, a slow presentation usually produces more and bigger bass.

Does that apply to crankbait fishing, too? You bet. John has spent a ton of time in the back of a canoe, guiding hundreds of folks to big bass. He's emphatic. An angler who retrieves a crankbait slowly, even during mid-summer, usually catches more bass in a day's fishing than a fast-cast-and-retrieve angler. That's so, even though Mr. Fast Cast usually covers more water. When it comes to crankbaits, John says it's even better to work 'em slow, in a stop-and-go manner.

Live baits are, as a matter of course, presented slowly; plus there's the added attraction of natural scent. Live baits are also presented more effectively in deeper water than crankbait-type artificials, and can also be added to artificials that go deep, such as leadhead jigs.

But live bait isn't always the most effective summer approach. At times, even during summer, a minnow-imitating bait like a Cordell Red Fin, twitched on the surface, may be just the thing for shallow bass. But again, fish the bait slowly. Twitch it and let it sit. Twitch it again. Then retreive it a bit to make it dive; stop it, and let it pop back to the surface. Again, John says that "slow" takes more and bigger bass.

Other artificials are also effective. Shield lake smallies feed extensively on insect larvae and minnows. We have one approach that most effectively imitates this larvae. Slip a Garland Mini Jig Skirt over a number 2 or 4, long shank, thin-wire hook. Add a split shot about 18 to 24 inches above the hook/skirt combo. The hook and skirt is so light that any rod-tip movement makes it hop and dance.

We've fished this rig down 12-15 feet with success. Simply use a lift-drop, lift-drop retrieve. Cast out and let the split shot carry the rig to the bottom. Lift your rod tip to about 10 o'clock. Then lift your rod to 11 o'clock, and immediately reel back down to 10 o'clock. Now watch your line as the skirt falls back to the bottom.

It may surprise you, but plastic worms, preferably 4 to 5 inch worms rigged Texas-style for fishing shoreline brush, or with an exposed hook in other situations, also account for a lot of smallmouths. The exposed-hook rig is akin to our Garland skirt rig; that is, a plain hook is inserted in the plastic 'crawler and

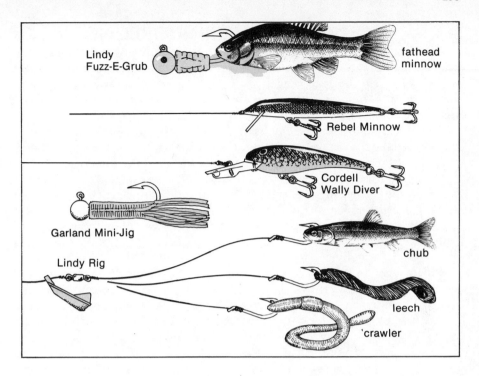

Lindy
Fuzz-E-Grub

fathead
minnow

Rebel Minnow

Cordell
Wally Diver

Garland Mini-Jig

chub

Lindy Rig

leech

'crawler

a split shot is used for weight. Place the shot about 12 inches ahead of the worm. This rig can be fished shallow (without weight) or down to about 15 feet (weighted).

THE PLAN

Now here's one plan that works. John uses a high/low approach for fishing different structural elements such as points, sunken islands or shorelines in bays. "High/low" equates to searching both shallow and deep with different baits. How shallow? Fishing the surface is as shallow as you can get. And how deep? Most of John's summer fish are taken from 10- to 15-foot deep lips, associated with sunken humps, points or shorelines in large bays. But he'll poke around in water down to 50 feet deep, especially at the end of the summer when fish aren't biting shallower. Obviously, John uses a portable depth finder when he's fishing from a canoe.

During most of the summer, John expects to find the *most* smallmouths in about 8 to 15 feet of water. That's where he usually begins fishing, only moving to other depth levels if he doesn't find fish.

The Lindy Live Bait Rig is used most often. Slip a ¼ ounce sinker onto your 6, 8 or 10 pound test line, and tie onto the swivel on a commercially-made snell. Of course, you can also make your own snell from the following components: a size 10 barrel swivel, a 1½ to 2 or 3 foot section of 6 or 8 pound test monofilament, and a size 6 or 8 hook. Size 6 or 8 hooks work well with either nightcrawlers or leeches.

DON'T FORGET THE SHORELINE

The most consistent, summer smallmouth fishing usually occurs on sunken islands, points and bars. However, even though most bass are taken from water in the 8 to 15 foot range, casting to shorelines is always an option. Sometimes it's the best option available, although it usually just provides a welcome change of pace. It can be exciting fishing.

The best shorelines are usually located inside large bays or towards the outside (main-lake section) of smaller bays. Look for cover like boulders or fallen trees. Concentrate on shaded banks if you're fishing during midday.

Perhaps the best lure choice is a floating/diving plug that can either be fished on the surface or subsurface. Long, thin, minnow-imitating baits, such as the Cordell Red Fin or the Rebel Minnow, hook more fish than short, fat plugs, such as the Rebel Deep Wee R, that do a great job of imitating crayfish. Baits that aren't quite so fat, or long, are a good compromise. An example is the Heddon Tadpolly.

Whether you're fishing without power from a canoe, or from a motorized boat, another method is to troll live bait slowly along the bottom. Keep the reel bail open and your trigger finger perched on the line. When a fish hits, release line. Don't wait long—ten seconds should be sufficient—before closing the bail and striking, or the bass may swallow the bait.

Because most of your shield lake, smallmouth fishing should be catch and release fishing, we believe a live bait rig modification is appropriate. Use the same live bait set-up as before, but instead of only one hook, tie two hooks in tandem about 3 inches apart. When a fish takes a 'crawler or leech on this rig, you can strike almost immediately. Few fish are deeply hooked, so they can be released quickly without serious injury.

Thus the first part of a plan might be to start fishing with a live bait rig along a lip, or often the first major drop-off breakline on a structural item. If you catch a fish on the live bait rig, drop a marker and back off the spot. It's common to find summer smallies grouped in an area. Either cast to the spot with a live bait rig, a leadhead jig tipped with live bait, or the Garland skirt option.

If you don't find fish, try casting or trolling crankbaits along the same lips or breakline. But begin a bit shallower—say at about 5 feet—and work out to 12-15 feet. Keep your bait close to the bottom when you fish shallower water, but as you get deeper, it's OK to fish several feet above the bottom. Small-mouths often suspend along structural items, so even mid-depth running baits may catch fish when fished over, say, a 10 to 15 foot deep lip.

If crankbaits don't take fish along lips, move up shallow. If you're fishing the lip along a shoreline, move up along the shoreline. If you're fishing the lip along a bar, point or sunken island, move up onto the flat on top of these structural elements. Expect the fish to be a bit spooky up shallow, so make long casts with shallow-running crankbaits, or drift a slip bobber/live bait rig across the flat.

If you've identified a smallmouth holding area, and have effectively fished different portions of it, both shallow and deep, chances are you'll catch smallmouths. Of course, there are many other approaches for fishing for shield smallmouths during summer. Once you get a feel for the fishing, you can modify these approaches to suit either the situation or your personal preference.

We're often asked if we prefer to fish shield lakes where we can use boats and motors, or if we prefer canoeing options. We don't actually prefer one type of trip over another. The trips are just different. It's true that more heavily-fished, motorized waters usually have fewer smallmouths because of fishing pressure. However, canoe-in trips take more time. There are advantages and disadvantages to both. If you can, try both and decide for yourself.

Summer smallies from shield waters remain one of the most appealing fishing opportunities available anywhere. The best advice is simply, go! Good fishing when you get there!

SUMMARY

Main-lake orientation doesn't mean there are no shallow fish, so be sure to check both deep and shallow habitat. Typical good summer spots usually have both shallow and deep-water options, with gravel, rock/rubble or boulder bottoms. Look for rubble or boulder points, either at the mouths of spawning bays, farther out into the main lake, or on sunken islands. Be prepared to systematically check both shallow and deep until you find fish.

Although most smallmouths will be shallow, John catches *big* fish as deep as 40 feet. The type of habitat varies, but hard-to-soft bottom transition points are good, usually near obvious, shallow smallmouth habitat like a rock reef or shoreline bar. He also fishes with a portable depth finder, since it's tough to find the best summer smallie spots without one. While many presentation methods and lures work during the summer, John is emphatic about the productivity of nightcrawlers for truly big fish.

Chapter 16
POST-SUMMER

"A Time of Impending Change"

Basically, Post-summer is a time of impending change, when a body of water goes through the transition from a warmer to a cooler environment. In effect, Post-summer is the reverse of the Pre-summer process. Typically, hot, calm days are followed by cool nights.

Most of the food in any lake, river or reservoir has already been produced for the year, and the time of plenty is slowly giving way to reduced food stocks.

In some rivers, the water may be near the lowest level of the year. Smallmouths which spent the summer scattered in shallow stretches might begin regrouping with other fish and relate to deeper pools. Let's take a look at a sure-fire method for catching some of these overlooked fish.

Most river smallmouths spend much of their time in a limited range, not migrating long distances in their daily movements. In fact, in some streams, smallmouths occupy the same pool all their lives. Studies indicate that some fish move less than 100 yards or so in several years! In streams that have alternating riffles and pools, smallmouths actually treat the riffles as boundaries. These streams have a series of independent resident populations, rather than a huge mass of interacting fish.

However, in some smaller rivers where only shallow pools are available, smallmouths must migrate long distances to find wintering habitat. This wintering area could be a large, deeper pool, or possibly the deeper water adjacent to the face of a dam. In any case, the fish are very tightly grouped in huge numbers.

Besides pools, smallmouths use numerous other river structures such as wing dams, eddies, current breaks, etc. The key to catching these fish is to present your bait effectively. Dan Gapen, an expert on river fishing, has developed a system of boat control that makes fishing various river structures easy.

THE RIVER SLIPPING METHOD

"River slipping" is similar to backtrolling—a system of exact boat control. It

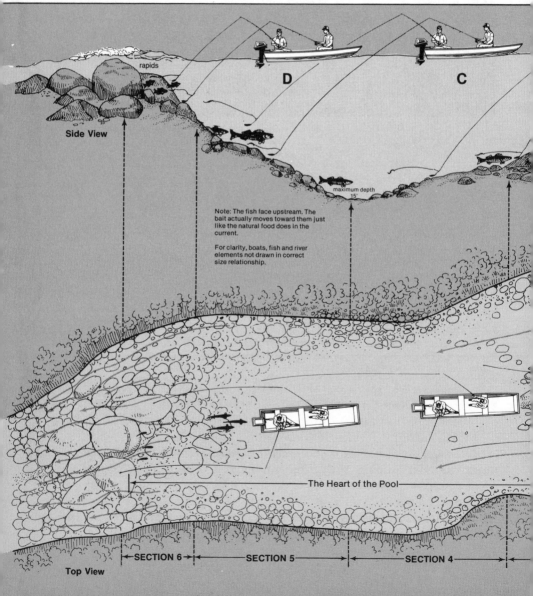

rapids

Side View

D

C

Note: The fish face upstream. The bait actually moves toward them just like the natural food does in the current.

For clarity, boats, fish and river elements not drawn in correct size relationship.

maximum depth 15'

The Heart of the Pool

|←SECTION 6→|←——SECTION 5——→|←———SECTION 4———→|

Top View

Study the drawing and notations on the illustration carefully; the anglers are not front trolling upstream. They are slipping backwards! It appears on the drawing that the boat and the lures are moving upstream. The opposite is true. Instead, lure, line, and boat are all slowly slipping downstream!

In the SIDE VIEW we see the fast current as it flows out of the rapids (SECTION #1), into a deeper pool area below. This area will hold crappies, smallmouth bass, and small walleyes. Cast this spot with jigs before you begin to work the pool with live bait rigs. From this point on (SECTION #2) the stream bed gets gradually deeper and the speed of the water slows—this is where the "pool" begins. The side view shows some good walleyes "hanging" on the downstream side of a few boulders. The top view shows that the river makes a slight bend here and forms an eddy on each side (in SECTION #3). The outside "current breaks," adjacent to the eddies, probably hold fish.

By the time the boat "slips" to SECTION #5, which is just downstream of the deepest part of the pool (SECTION #4), we have covered what is called the "heart of the pool." At SECTION #5 the bottom begins to rise and we encounter rocks as the pool merges with the next rapids at SECTION #6. SECTION #5 is an example of a "slick"—the

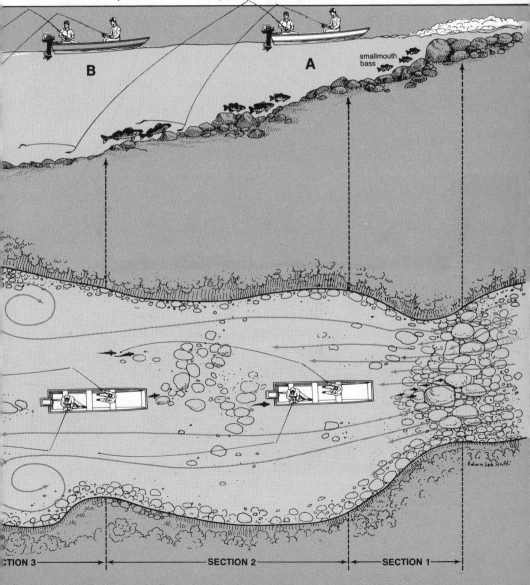

resting place for big walleyes—and is the best spot in the pool. Both walleyes and smallmouths will tend to congregate in this area—the walleyes in the deeper areas, the smallmouths slightly shallower. In this area the water would appear smooth just before it breaks into the rapids.

OK, let's start our "slip trip." In the top view our boat is in position at A just below the first rapids (SECTION #1 in the side view). In this case we would be using a bait walker rig or heavily weighted, three-way set-up. Since it's summer, we'll use either leeches or nightcrawlers. The bow of the boat is facing into the current and the boat is in the center of the stream.

With the motor in forward, against the current, we drop our rigs behind the boat (BOAT POSITION A). Usually about 50 feet of line and a heavy weight are necessary to keep contact with bottom. In moderate current, a ⅝ oz. Bait Walker rig would be enough, but a 1 or 2 oz. rig might be needed if the water was deeper or faster. The current will "lift" too light a rig, and the boat will overtake too heavy a rig. We work the slick by setting the throttle so that the boat "slips" backwards downstream.

With our lines out we start "backing" our baits into the face of the fish. Our bait moves directly into fish, facing upstream. We always keep a tight line as the current takes our rig naturally downstream. Remember, a lure or weighted live bait rig travels faster downstream than a "slipping" boat. The nightcrawlers or leeches appear to be fighting the current in a forward swimming motion. The current does the work for us— our motor acts only to control the speed that we travel downstream.

In this manner we slip our way back through BOAT POSITIONS B, C and D. If we make fish contact we'll "gun" the motor upsteam a short distance and "slip" down again. We continue this maneuver as long as we continue to take fish. We could also completely rerun the pool to include sections that we didn't cover on the previous run. This process would be repeated as long as we caught fish or until we worked the entire pool thoroughly. Simple? You bet! and deadly, too.

is particularly effective in the faster water of young to mature rivers. Slipping allows you to correctly position your boat to make the most efficient use of each cast or troll. There are few wasted casts. In the course of a day, this can add up.

This photo illustrates what the basics of slipping are all about. ARROW #1 symbolizes the force of the downstream current. ARROW #2 is the speed of the motor. Note

that the motor's forward thrust is less than the force of the current. This means that although the boat is facing the current and the motor is running in forward, the boat is actually losing ground. ARROW #3 is the difference between the current and the thrust of the motor. With a little practice you can hold a boat virtually motionless by balancing the forward speed of the motor with the downstream speed of the current.

Slipping results when the forward speed is reduced to a point where the forward thrust of the motor cannot overtake the speed of the current. But be careful! Once you begin to slip, when you start casting, your lure will travel much faster than the amount of slip (ARROW #4), so your lure will come back to you faster than you are slipping. You must always keep a tight line to maintain proper "feel." Steadily retrieve and keep a high rod tip to reduce slack and bows in your line. This is very important, because with too much bow, the current will tend to lift your lure off bottom. In a nutshell, this is the secret to slipping.

Note that the motor is in forward gear. This approach generally works best with small outboards (less than 10 hp) which lack the power to back up in reverse gear against the current. With larger outboards, however, you may find it easier to work in reverse gear. The choice is yours.

Just like backtrolling, the secret of slipping is to keep your bait in the fish zone as long as possible on each cast or trolling run. And, like backtrolling, you can hold your boat virtually motionless without anchoring, or move with precision as the occasion calls for. Mobility is the key; it is easy to use the force of the current as an aid to lateral movement.

There are many other benefits, too. You can follow the current path of an eddy with the same ease as a leaf on the water's surface, but just as easily change direction and pull out. One of this method's primary strengths, along with its speed and mobility, is that all-precious commodity, versatility. You can jig, cast plugs, or troll live bait—all effectively.

The Jigs

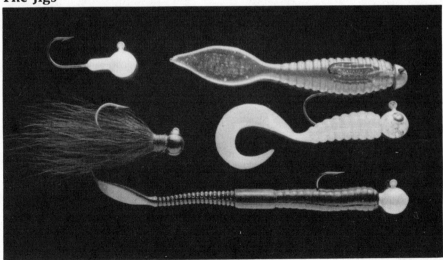

Here is a lineup of small (⅛ oz. and ¼ oz.) jigs that are riverworthy. Each has its own little peculiarity which can be an asset or a liability depending on the particular set of circumstances. The ballhead jigs work best in slower water. The bullet shaped or wedge heads are best in a more moderate flow.

The 3-Way Rig

Slip sinker rigs are not the way to go in current. Instead, a stationary sinker set-up is best. Here is a recommended rig to use in current. A 3-way, drop line rig is an old, river standby. Note that you can use a multitude of live baits or even a streamer fly on these 3-way rigs.

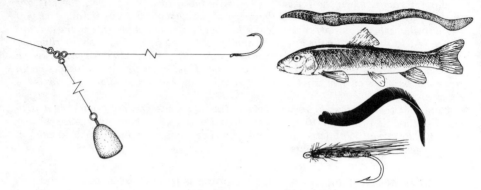

HOW TO RIG FOR RIVERS

In order to fish rivers effectively, you must rig properly. River fishing is a different ballgame and should be approached as such.

The ideal rig for river slipping is a Jon boat. A 14 foot, flat-bottomed boat is perfect for control in current. In addition, it's fairly light and durable. Due to the super-shallow water, a light, 5 or 6 horsepower motor is best. In order to "slip properly," the motor should have a reverse gear.

For working rivers with small jigs and live bait rigs, there is no question that an open-face, spinning reel is the top choice. A 6 to 6½ foot, medium-action, spinning rod with a fast tip, equipped with a good quality spinning reel (5:1 gear ratio) fits-the-bill. The reel should be spooled with either 8 or 10 pound test, high visibility line. With this outfit, you can handle light, ⅛ oz. baits, and yet be able to pull free of most snags.

Chapter 17

THE TURNOVER PERIOD

"A Time of Turmoil"

The mere thought of fishing during this period fills even die-hard anglers with despair. Turnover! What is the dreaded Turnover, and how does it affect smallmouth bass?

During the summer months, the Calendar Periods were determined primarily by the ecological conditions of a body of water. However, after autumn's cooling process starts, the Calendar Periods are primarily determined by water temperature. Actually, the Turnover Period is a period of transition, and is an extremely important event in the annual rhythm of some waters. Let's take a look at the turnover process.

Not all bodies of water experience the Turnover Period. The most classic turnover situation occurs in bodies of water which stratify into distinct temperature (and density) layers during summer. Basically, water generally stratifies into a warmer upper layer and a colder bottom layer. In between these two layers lies a narrow band of water which displays a rapid temperature change.

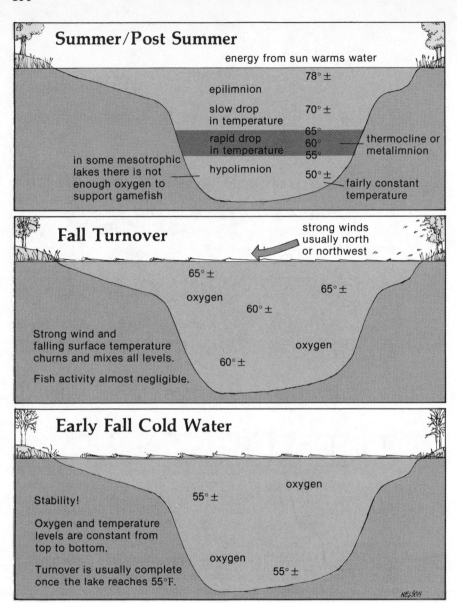

This band is called the thermocline.

In these waters, this thermocline condition usually remains in effect throughout most of the Summer Peak, Summer and Post-summer Periods. However, during the tail end of the Post-summer Period, as the sun grows less direct, seasonal, driving, cold winds and rain begin chilling the surface temperature of the water very quickly. As the heavier (colder) water begins sinking, it comes in contact with the warmer water below. This action forces the lighter, yet warmer, deeper water, back to the surface. Eventually, the narrow thermocline layer ruptures and a mixing or "turning over" process takes place. As the wind whips the water, the mixing action continues until it thoroughly homogenizes the water to a point where the whole body of water is the same temperature. This process also re-oxygenates the deep water.

The actual turnover process takes place once the thermocline layer has ruptured. But the turmoil that occurs usually adversely affects the fish for a period of time before and after this event. Fishing doesn't improve until these conditions stabilize. In general, once the water temperature drops to about 55°F and the water clears perceptibly, cold water fishing patterns emerge.

Typically, a turnover condition is the bane of anglers who are confronted with it. Here are a few tips to help you survive this trying time.

Fishing during the Turnover Period on bodies of water that thermocline is tough! However, since all bodies of water do not turn over at the same time, it is usually best to switch to waters which have already turned over. Alternate strategies would be to fish bodies of water which have not yet begun to turn over, or try waters which don't thermocline at all.

Remember that small, shallow, dark-water lakes cool rapidly and will turn over before large, deep, clear-water lakes. Plan your fishing trips to minimize battling the turnover by picking waters that are not in the midst of a turnover condition.

Another good choice would be to fish a river which isn't affected by the Turnover Period. Obviously, small rivers won't thermocline, and even larger rivers may not thermocline if there is sufficient current. Rivers can provide fast action, while a nearby lake is a "dead sea." This approach also applies to current areas where a river or feeder creek enters a reservoir. In short, current usually minimizes the turnover effect.

If you're forced to fish a turnover condition, concentrate your efforts on the shallow water cover. For example, a shallow gravel/rubble area with boulders or wood present may produce a couple smallmouths. Usually, shallow-water smallmouths are affected least by this time of turmoil.

Chapter 18

THE COLD
WATER PERIOD

"A Time of Stability"

There are several keys to understanding smallmouth bass during the Cold Water Period. One is realizing that the combination of falling water temperature and diminishing light levels (plus other factors) appears to stimulate smallmouths to shift location into deeper-water habitat areas. Remember, the turnover has literally opened the door to deeper, formerly unusable areas which thermoclined during summer.

During the fall restaging process, smallmouths in natural lakes are usually tightly grouped in drop-off areas at the end of a bar, as far from shore as possible, and close to the lake basin. Additionally, they seek out transition areas from harder to softer bottom, such as the edges of rock-capped, sunken islands and hard-bottom humps. A forage base near these areas is an essential ingredient for smallmouths.

At this time, highland reservoir smallmouths tend to congregate near steeper-dropping points and bluffs. Typically, prime areas have cover in the form of boulders, rock, rubble and/or stumps, as well as a steep drop-off. For trophy fish, try the 25-40 foot depths, using a jig 'n pig, jig and grub, or a tail-spinner.

During the Cold Water Period, the smallmouth bass's activity level and feeding attitude may be anywhere in the active/neutral/negative range. As a rule of thumb, falling water temperatures slow down metabolic processes, and fish activity decreases. Consequently, you must be versatile in order to contact and catch fish consistently.

Both natural lakes and reservoirs offer an opportunity to catch lots of fall smallmouths. It's also time for trophy fishing! Here's a super secret smallmouth system for locating and catching "wallhangers" from natural lakes and reservoirs.

FALL SMALLMOUTHS IN NATURAL LAKES

The fall Cold Water Period is a peak time for catching trophy smallmouths. During fall, the best deep water spots will typically be as far from shore and as close to the lake basin as possible. This means that a long, shallow bar, protruding far into the lake before dropping sharply into the lake basin, is a prime spot. The closer the drop-offs are to shore, the more marginal they become.

The best drop-offs usually aren't completely rock-covered, but instead have groups of rocks scattered here and there on the drop-off. This, of course, concentrates the fish, and makes contacting them much easier.

Prime areas that smallmouth anglers usually neglect to fish are the transition points from harder to softer bottom. This means that any transition point from: 1) rock to gravel or clay, or 2) rock to muck, or 3) clay to muck, all qualify as possible fish concentration areas. Most meso lakes also display a general hard-to-soft bottom transition point in the 25-50 foot range. This can be an important concentration area during the fall Cold Water Period.

Obviously, most smallmouth lakes also have walleye populations, and the two fish must interact with one another. Each fish fits into a certain niche within a lake's ecosystem.

In fall, both fish spend time near a lake's basin. Yet, as can be expected, they don't relate to a lake basin in the same way. As fall progresses, smallmouths make more consistent use of deeper water, finally spending much of the Cold Water and Frozen Water Periods near a lake basin transition (from harder to softer bottom) zone. During fall, walleyes in most deeper mesotrophic lakes position themselves near quick (usually the quickest) breaking lake areas (usually off a bar or hump) adjacent to the most massive area of deep water in the lake.

Walleyes relate to a variety of basin depths at some time during the year; during fall, it's usually the deepest possible basin area. Smallmouths, by comparison, prefer to relate to basin areas of a relatively shallow or moderate depth! That's the difference.

The best smallmouth home areas usually have adjacent, relatively shallow or moderate depth, basin areas for fish to use during the late fall, winter and early spring. Shallow basins usually begin in about 25-30 feet of water, and mid-depth basins can be as deep as 50-60 feet. Again, there are exceptions, but the most appropriate basin depth for smallmouths in meso lakes seems to range from 25-60 feet.

This concept enables you to evaluate the potential of smallmouth home areas, even before getting on a lake—providing you have an accurate lake map. More than this, however, you can actually evaluate the basic smallmouth potential of many natural lakes.

Smallmouth Bass Location

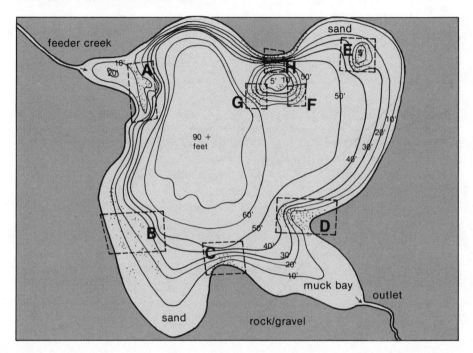

Let's look at a typical smallmouth lake. Remember, the best smallmouth areas will have: 1) a suitable rock/gravel spawning area, 2) plenty of other features (flats, weed areas, rock piles, etc.) to attract and hold forage during different Calendar Periods, and 3) suitable, moderate-to-shallow depth, lake basin areas for use during Cold Water Periods. Keeping these things in mind, let's evaluate the on-paper potential of AREAS A thru H.

AREA A— *A fine looking spot where, unfortunately, too many smallmouth anglers would spend too much time. AREA A will not be home to large groups of smallmouths because it doesn't have enough basin water in the shallow-to-moderate depth range. It's a fine, fall walleye spot because it provides a shallow bar to attract forage and is next to a precipitous drop-off into the largest area of deep water in the lake.*

AREA B— *It provides many of the things that smallmouths need, but the fish in such an area probably won't be concentrated. The area doesn't have distinct enough turns or drop-offs to concentrate fish in small sections. It's a secondary area which would be difficult to take fish from consistently during late fall.*

AREA C— *If only the bar was larger! It will probably hold a few smallmouths, but isn't a major population area.*

AREA D— *AREA D provides all of the characteristics needed to be a great smallmouth area. Note in particular the 40-50 foot basin water available off the tip of the bar.*

AREA E— *This spot provides the characteristics needed to hold smallmouths, although there's limited spawning area. Some shore spawners could be attracted to the island.*

AREAS F, G, and H—*The entire island is an attractive, fish-holding area. Even though walleyes and smallmouths might mingle, one would expect AREA F to attract the most smallmouths, and G to attract the most walleyes. What about H? AREA H isn't a prime fall walleye or smallmouth area. It doesn't drop into the deepest area of the lake for walleyes, or into a shallow-to-moderate depth basin area for smallmouths.*

To review, all the spots mentioned here may attract some walleyes and smallmouths. AREAS A and G, however, are the two high-percentage walleye areas, while D and F would constitute high percentage smalljaw water. AREAS E and C would also be worth fishing for smallmouths. If time allows, attempt to find some concentration spots in AREA B, too.

Fishing A Smallmouth Home Area

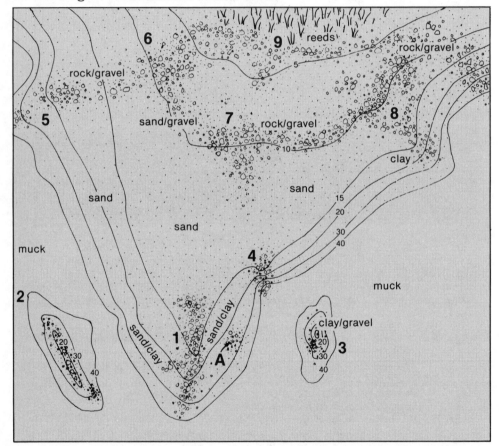

The accompanying drawing depicts a good, smallmouth bass home area. AREAS 5 and 8 are prime, spring, Cold Water spots. These areas provide deep water immediately adjacent to potential spawning grounds. AREAS 1 thru 4 are the best fall, Cold Water spots because they provide good, deep-water habitat as far away from shore and as close to the lake basin as possible. AREAS 6 and 7 are possible pre-spawn locations, and AREA 9 is a spawning site.

AREAS 1 thru 4 also represent four, basic, fall smallmouth fishing patterns. AREA 1 is a hard-bottom, drop-off area that extends into the lake basin. The best of these drop-

offs occur as far from shore and as close to the lake basin as possible. Don't neglect the bottom transition (from harder to softer bottom) in such areas. Also pay close attention to tiny rocky spots like A which might concentrate fish.

To keep from spooking fish, you should generally work the area by keeping your boat over deep water. You might want to make several very long casts with a leadhead jig to check out the shallow top of AREA 1 first. If you find fish, anchor and concentrate on them. If you can't find shallow fish with one or two long casts, start backtrolling the deeper areas with a live bait rig. Once you find fish in deeper water, you can continue to backtroll, but vertical jigging is a faster and more efficient means of taking pinpointed fish. In either case, don't forget to jig the transition area from softer to harder bottom.

AREA 2 is a rock-capped, sunken island adjacent to smallmouth home areas. Of course, very large, rock-capped sunken islands can actually be smallmouth home areas if they have the characteristics necessary for smallmouth spawning. But isolated islands, far from spawning areas, seldom produce any number of fish.

Unless you have pinpointed a particularly productive area of the hump before, it would be best to start fishing the live bait rig. Again, don't forget to check the bottom transition areas. Because of the island's depth, pinpointed fish can either be vertically jigged, or continued to be worked with the live bait rig.

AREA 3 is only different from AREA 2 in the type of island you are fishing. In this case, the island is a hard-bottom hump composed of gravel and clay. Because this island is slightly shallower than AREA 2, casting may be an option. Otherwise, work the area as discussed for AREA 2.

AREA 4 is a rock-strewn, inward break on a smallmouth bar. Because this area is so compact, it is possible to cast, jig and backtroll the area all at once if you have three people in the boat. The rear man casts, the middle man jigs towards the outside of the bar, and the front man rigs with live bait. Otherwise, attack the area as discussed in AREA 1.

These are four basic patterns (locations) you should key on for your fall smallmouth fishing. One final note: Be sure you don't leave with the idea that fall smallmouths will only be found in water deeper than 15 feet. On this particular bar, there seems to be little chance for fall fish to be found very shallow, but if 5 foot water extended out to the drop-off in AREA 1, the fish would occasionally use it under prime weather conditions.

FALL SMALLMOUTH TACTICS

Live Bait Rigs—Live bait rigs are an excellent, all-'round, fall smallmouth fishing option. They are among your best bets when searching for fish, because you can cover large areas relatively quickly. It's best to fish live bait rigs by backtrolling with your electric motor. If it's windy, though, use your big motor or a controlled drift.

size 6 Eagle claw salmon hook

30" or 48" 6 pound test snell

barrel swivel

6-10 pound test

1/8 - 1/2 oz. slip sinker

SINKER WEIGHT BY DEPTH

depth	recommended sinker weight	distance from boat
15' or less	1/8 or 1/4 oz.	45'-60'
15' to 25'	1/4 or 3/8 oz.	30'-60'
25' to 45'	3/8-1/2 oz.	fish almost directly beneath boat
beyond 45'	3/4 oz.	"

It's easiest to fish live bait rigs on a medium-to-heavy action spinning rod/reel combo. How you fish live bait rigs depends on the type of bottom you're over. Relatively smooth, snag-free areas can be fished by dragging the rig or alternately lifting and skimming the bait along for two-to-three feet, and then setting the rig down and allowing the bait to do its thing for a short time. A definite lift, set, lift, set is also the ticket in snag-filled areas or areas that drop off precipitously.

During fall, you normally let the fish run after it hits. If they grab the bait and swim off aggressively, however, stick 'em right now. If they swim off slowly, give 'em about 20 seconds.

Casting Leadhead Jigs—Leadhead jigs can be used to cover shallower areas by casting. If you can't get good live bait (like chubs), backtroll jigs tipped with a small minnow. Again, a medium-to-heavy action spinning rod/reel combo works best, with line ranging from 6-10 pound test. During very cold weather, a limp line is a definite advantage.

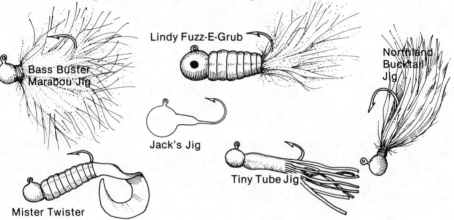

Use jigs ranging from ⅛ ounce (for shallow water to about 15 feet) to ¼ ounce (a good all 'round option) to ⅜ ounce (for deeper water of 25 feet plus). An Uncle Josh 3 inch leech or 4 inch twin tail pork strip (black or brown) are particularly favorite dressings for bucktail jigs.

Leadhead jigs are best fished by allowing them to sink to the bottom and then retrieving them with a gentle lift, drop-on-tight-line, lift, drop-on-tight-line manner. Watch your line for a telltale twitch as the fish inhales the bait.

Vertical Jigging—Vertical jigging is an option for moderate or deep water, mainly after fish have been found by live bait rigging. However, if you've previously pinpointed potential fishing areas, vertical jigging is also a quick and effective method for checking them out. Use the simple lift and drop technique.

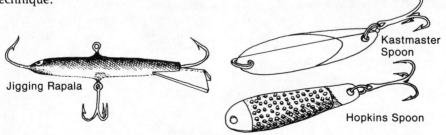

Working a Jigging Rapala

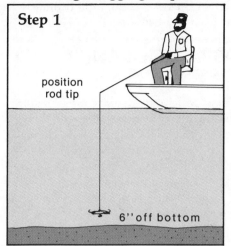

Step 1

position
rod tip

6"off bottom

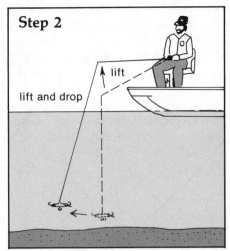

Step 2

lift

lift and drop

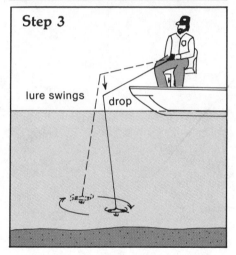

Step 3

lure swings   drop

Working the Jigging Rapala is easy. Step 1: Drop the lure to the bottom; engage the reel and take up enough line to place the lure about 6 inches off the bottom. Your rod tip should be positioned about one foot above the water. Step 2: Now sharply lift the rod tip approximately 1½ feet, and Step 3: quickly return the tip to its original position. The lure will scoot off to the side, turn, and then swim back below you. Wait just a bit and then repeat. As you slide the boat slowly along, the lure will follow and you can keep right on pumping.

Vertical jigging is an effective way to check out a specific area, and the Jigging Rapala is one of the most effective smallmouth jigging lures. Be sure to give it a try.

Bait Types—Chubs are a terrific fall smallmouth bait, as are 3 to 5 inch shiners. Shiners are hard to keep alive in warm weather, but in fall you shouldn't have much trouble. Waterdogs appear to be great until the water temperature drops below about 45°F; then stick to minnows.

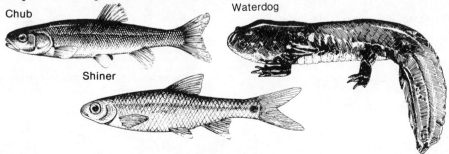

Chub

Waterdog

Shiner

Here's a last minute tip to remember.

Get out on the water early, because some of the best smallmouth fishing occurs during the hours surrounding dawn! It's a big-fish time.

FALL SMALLMOUTHS IN HILL-LAND/ HIGHLAND RESERVOIRS

As a rule, impoundments have a much more varied environment than natural lakes. Rather than one pattern holding up all over the lake, you'll find it applies in one section of a lake. In sections with remarkably different charac-

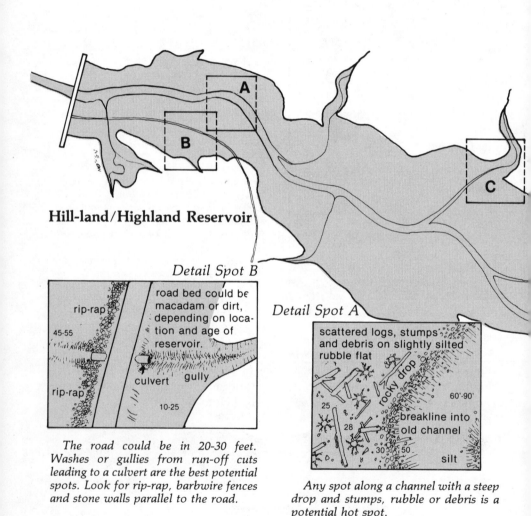

Hill-land/Highland Reservoir

Detail Spot B

road bed could be macadam or dirt, depending on location and age of reservoir.

rip-rap

45-55

rip-rap

culvert gully

10-25

Detail Spot A

scattered logs, stumps and debris on slightly silted rubble flat

rocky drop

25

60'-90'

breakline into old channel

28

30 50

silt

The road could be in 20-30 feet. Washes or gullies from run-off cuts leading to a culvert are the best potential spots. Look for rip-rap, barbwire fences and stone walls parallel to the road.

Any spot along a channel with a steep drop and stumps, rubble or debris is a potential hot spot.

teristics, you'll find strikingly different patterns. Our example impoundment is basically a highland type, with strong hill-land tendencies in its upper reaches.

We're going to look quickly at 4 different patterns on this lake—each relating to a specific type of area within the impoundment.

AREA A is in the lower ⅓ of the reservoir, and is a common pattern on highland impoundments. Here, the flat between the shoreline and the creek channel runs about 25 to 35 feet deep. As is the case with most smallmouth reservoirs, this area is almost slick, with only cut stumps as cover. But highland reservoirs are also typically rocky-bottomed, and rubble is common. Our potential hot spot is basically an area where the drop-off from the flat into the original creek bed is rather steep and well-defined, and occurs in conjunction with an accumulation of debris, rubble or stumps.

Most of the smallmouths in the lower ⅓ of a highland impoundment will use areas like this during the Cold Water Period. The problem with this type of area is that with so much creek channel and so many similar spots, it takes a

Detail Spot C

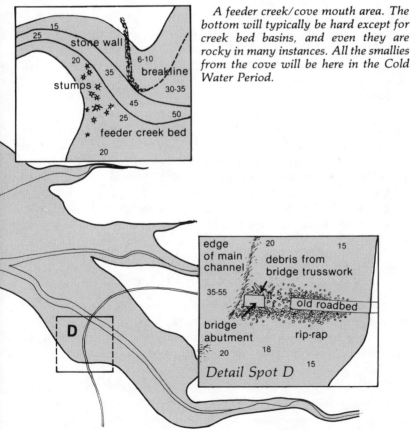

A feeder creek/cove mouth area. The bottom will typically be hard except for creek bed basins, and even they are rocky in many instances. All the smallies from the cove will be here in the Cold Water Period.

lot of checking to find fish concentrations. Invariably, they're in areas with the most debris-strewn bottoms.

AREA B is also in the deep, steep, highland section of the lake. It's a 30 foot deep roadbed running parallel to the bank. Early in the Cold Water Period, the top of the roadbed will serve as deep water for the smallies; and as the season progresses, you'll more likely find them off to the side of the road rather than up on the shore drop-off.

Most of these roadbeds either have stone walls built along them at intervals, or have a rip-rap base along the deep water edge. Either case enhances your prospects. A jigging spoon is the most effective tool for checking these deep areas, but on calm days you can usually catch more fish with a light jig if you have the patience to get it down to the fish.

AREA C, the area of the reservoir which starts to display some *hill-land characteristics*, is a prime spot at the *mouth of a cove*. Here, the channel of the feeder creek forms a home base of varying depth, with areas of sharp drop-offs falling into it. The main lake point on the upstream side of the creek mouth also holds promise as a forage area. In this illustration, there are stone walls and stumps to further add to the high forage potential.

This area is home to the fish all through the Cold Water Periods, and they don't ever leave it completely. But they can range far and wide over the area. It takes a lot of checking with a variety of lures to pinpoint them at any particular time. If you get action on the spoon, which you can fish much faster at these depths, that's fine. But if not, start tossing ¼ or even ⅛ oz. jigs, and you'll eventually contact them.

Our last sample area is *AREA D*, and it's a honey. In a rather bland area, this old inundated roadbed and bridge abutment stands out like a sore thumb. It provides cover, rip-rap, foraging areas and depth variation in an area without many other promising spots. Since it covers a lot of area, and is surrounded by "nothing" water, it's going to attract just about all the smallies in the general vicinity during the Cold Water Period.

In contrast to natural lakes, reservoirs typically are more complicated environments, due to their variety of structural features. As our example shows, localized patterns exist in different areas of the lake, according to what's available.

PRESENTATION OPTIONS

There are several options for putting fish in the boat. Simply match your presentation to the activity level of the fish you've located. Generally, once fish contact has been made, you should take the time to strain the area. Cold water fish can be fairly concentrated, yet they aren't very aggressive. Fish 'em slow.

For spoon jigging, use the heaviest bass tackle you own. A 6 foot, medium-heavy, graphite or boron casting rod with 14 pound test line is perfect.

Jigging spoons like the Mann-O-Lure and Salty Dog are productive. The best finishes are chrome or gold, with a black back. The ¾ oz. size is most useful, but any compact spoon or hammered spoon like a Hopkins or C.C. Spoon, in any size from ½ to 1½ oz., will do the job.

Use the spoon as a fish-finding tool with a cast and rip technique. Use a fairly fast motion and 3 to 4 foot sweeps of the rod. Allow the spoon to sink to the bottom between sweeps. In deep water, vertical jigging with slow rod movements will take lots of fish.

Jigs come in a "zillion" varieties. However, a few will generally do the trick. As a rule, light to medium spinning tackle will work best for casting jigs. And, depending on the conditions, lightweight could range from 4-10 pound test; simply match the line weight to the jig size and the fishing conditions. Jighead weights can range from ⅛-⅜ oz.

Working Shallow and Deep Simultaneously

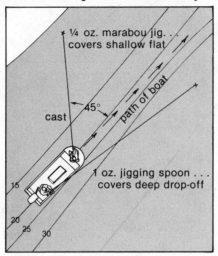

This illustration shows the correct procedure to pinpoint smallmouths in an area you've determined has potential. The angler in the front of the boat (the rear if you're backtrolling) checks the shallower water (12 to 15 feet) by casting a ¼ oz. marabou jig at a 45° angle, as shown. The angler in the rear strains the deeper water with a ¾ oz. or 1 oz. jigging spoon. This way, you'll get a relatively quick idea, at any particular time, of exact smallmouth location.

Normally, if you're going to use a feathered jig, marabou is preferred since it breathes even at slow speeds. The jigs can be tipped with a variety of plastic grubs, pork rind, or live bait. Under tough conditions, though, a plain jighead with a minnow can be the answer. It's very effective in northern waters, yet is rarely used in other areas of the country; it's a *deadly* combo.

Live bait rigs are one of the most popular northern smallmouth and walleye techniques, and are also effective on impoundment smallmouths. There are numerous live bait rigs that present bait naturally to the fish. A slip sinker and snell set-up, a simple split shot and hook, or a slip bobber all allow you to present live bait in a natural manner. Just follow these few simple rules: 1) Match the hook size to the bait used; don't kill a smaller bait by gaffing it on a shark-sized hook. 2) Light line in the 4-10 pound test range is usually best. 3) Light to medium spinning tackle is preferred. 4) Fish very, very slowly, and let the live bait do the work.

With these set-ups, you can fish slowly and effectively. You can also follow exact depth levels simply by using an electric motor and a depth finder. In addition, the rigs can be cast to likely spots and fished stationary, or slowly retrieved.

Live bait options include various minnows, shad, waterdogs, crayfish, plus any other local, common baits. Give live bait rigs a try the next time you strike out with your favorite method. Remember, when the goin' gets tough, the intelligent angler switches to live bait!

Here's the result of one of Rich Zaleski's fall smallmouth outings. His sidekick is his son Tommy. Even though they were fishing a strange lake, their knowledge of bronzeback habits allowed them to take these fish in a few hours.

Chapter 19

THE FROZEN WATER PERIOD

"A Time of Rest"

Ice-cover is common in most northern areas of the smallmouth's range. Yet, there was a time, not so very long ago, when bass lay almost exclusively in the domain of summer anglers.

So far, few fishermen have taken advantage of the opportunity to try winter bass fishing, possibly because of the persistent belief that bass could only rarely be caught through the ice. However, any ice fisherman worth his salt *can* learn to catch smallmouths by applying his angling skill and by the following basic hints.

1) Bass are strongly object-oriented. In winter they tend to congregate

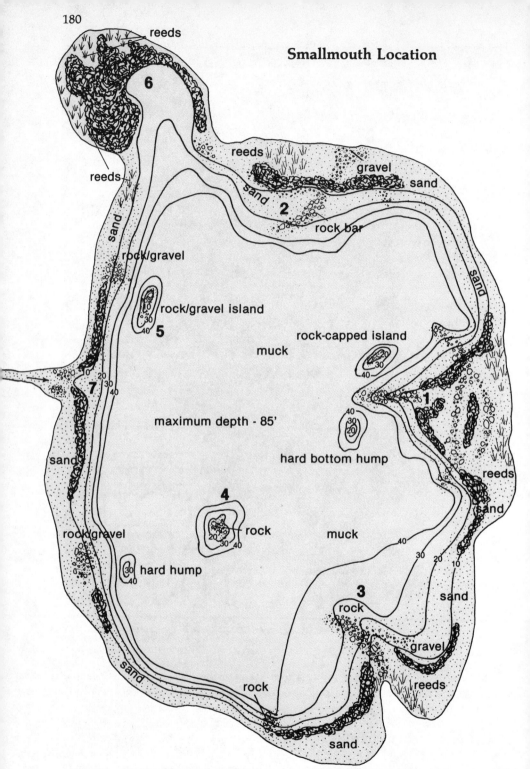

Smallmouths! Each lake area will hold some, except perhaps BAY 6. But the most distinctly grouped smallies will be off the point of, and on the sunken humps near, BAR 1. BAR 3 doesn't drop off so distinctly, but would be our second choice. SUNKEN

HUMP 5 *is close to good shoreline habitat and will also hold fish, but* SUNKEN HUMP 4 *is too far away from other prime yearly habitat to be good.*

around rocky reefs, bars, points, and shoals. The more rocks and boulders in any given area, from 5 to 40 feet deep, the more bass that area is likely to have. 2) Bass are quite sluggish in cold water and feed mostly in rocky areas on crayfish and small minnows. 3) Bass tend to concentrate in groups. 4) Large bass seem to prefer a large mouthful.

Smallmouth bass are quite catchable at first ice. Although few anglers seek smallmouths, those that do often have trouble finding them, because they spend most of their time fishing walleye—instead of smallmouth—spots. There's often a distinct difference. Sure, smallmouths and walleyes both often relate to rock drop-offs, rock humps or deep rock, clay and sand flats. But while walleyes may relate to any such structural elements associated with the deepest water in a section of a lake, smallmouths tend to relate to these areas only in *moderately-deep* lake sections. In other words, walleyes may be many places, while smallmouths are usually only in a few, distinct spots.

The best approach is to learn where smallies are during late-fall, while you are fishing open water. They will be in the same spots at first ice.

PRESENTATION

Most bass are caught by unsuspecting panfish anglers; so, panfish techniques like teardrops and ice flies dressed with grubs, or minnows hooked under the dorsal fin and weighted with a split shot, work. Indeed, if you're catching bluegills, crappies and perch along with an occasional bass, why complain?

But you'll catch more bass on slightly larger baits. Large minnows held down by a larger split shot, or even better yet, a small (⅓ ounce) Swedish Pimple, Acme Kastmaster, or a bare leadhead jig (⅛ ounce) dressed with a lip-

Basic Ice-Fishing Rod and Reel Combo

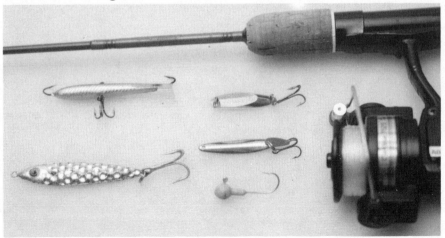

Three types of jigging lures for larger fish like walleyes and bass are: (1) swimming lures like the Jigging Rapala. (2) flash lures like the Spoon, Acme Kastmaster and Swedish Pimple; and (3) bare leadhead jigs.

hooked minnow, usually produce more bass. In addition, a #5 or #7 Jigging Rapala is also a top fish getter. Take it easy when you jig these baits. Simply ease the lure up a foot or two and let it flutter back. Bass inhale these baits during the pause.

You won't consistently land bass on panfish tackle, although it's great sport to try. It's best to have at least 6 pound test line spooled on a spinning reel taped to a light ice-fishing rod. The reel should have a good drag system.

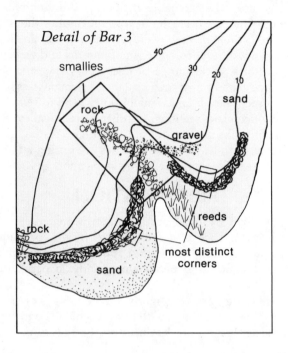

Smallmouths will use the point from its shallowest extension into the lake down to the flat at the base of the drop-off. Bottom content transition areas are dynamite.

Assume we're fishing a point on a rock-bar that drops from 15 to 35 feet of water. Smallies can be terribly spooky in shallow water under ice-fishing conditions, so cut at least 6 holes from the tip of the point, down the drop-off, to the flat at the base of the drop-off.

Start fishing the deep flat by dropping your lure (let's say it's a Swedish Pimple dressed with a fish eye) to the bottom, and raising it up a foot. Smallies seldom hover far above bottom at this time. Lift the bait sharply a foot or so, and let it flutter back into a holding position. Hold the lure stationary, but add an occasional twitch or two to waggle the fish eye riding on the hook below the bait. Basically, that's all there's to it, although you have to search the entire face of the drop-off and check out other potential spots.

Where legal, a second fishing set-up—a small, 3- to 4-inch chub hooked below the dorsal fin and suspended below a tip-up—is also a good bet. Activity usually peaks very early and late during the day, although smallies may be caught all day long. While ice fishing, we have never seen a smallie jump, although we think several have tried!

Tip-Ups

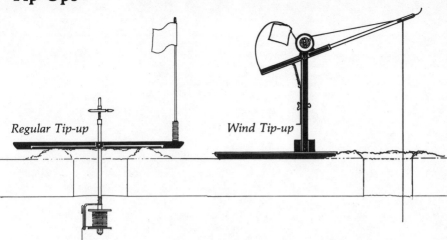

Regular Tip-up

Wind Tip-up

A tip-up is one of the most effective ice-fishing presentations, because it can be stationed and left somewhat unattended, while the bait does its thing. It's like setting a trap.

The two basic types of tip-ups are represented by the two, top tip-ups pictured here. The tip-up has a line spool that hangs below the water, but is attached to a revolving inner core filled with sealed hydraulic fluid to keep it from freezing. A flag flips below extensions on the revolving inner core, and is released when a fish moves off with a bait.

The wind tip-up functions above the ice and consists of a base/stand/arm that can be adjusted to move with the slightest wind. It keeps a bait moving all the time. Even dead bait flips around seductively.

No serious ice angler can be without a set of tip-ups. They apply to almost every type of winter fishing situation.

Chapter 20

GREAT LAKES SMALLMOUTH BASS ACTION ATLAS

While not a lake-wide phenomenon, Great Lakes smallmouth bass fisheries are usually extremely prolific. In fact, in terms of numbers, the Great Lakes and their many connecting waterways offer *some of the best* smallmouth fishing on earth.

Because of the prevailing cold/cool water environments which Great Lakes smallmouths must contend with most of the year, their growth rate and maximum size is limited. A 6 pound fish is indeed a trophy, while top-out size normally just exceeds 4 pounds or so. Yet, incredible numbers of 1¾ to 3¾ pound fish exist, and catches of 100 or more fish averaging 2¼ pounds are not uncommon.

A number of factors ensure the smallmouths' continuing survival on these huge waters. First, with current Great Lakes' sport fishing interest heaped on salmon and trout, many smallmouth populations are actually underfished—or even *unfished*. Second, lamprey infestation, pollution, and the destruction of spawning and rearing habitat, which have been the bane of other Great Lakes fisheries like the walleye and pike, have not as adversely affected this relatively adaptable critter. And third, smallmouths are neither commercially nor tribally exploited. With no market for these critters, they have been pretty much left alone for decades, so very mature populations have developed.

Our research and experience show that where bass populations do exist, they are usually very numerous, healthy and thriving. Moreover, where they are *not* strong, they must be termed very poor. There are very few smallmouth fisheries found in the in between range. Great Lakes, smallmouth bass fishing is either feast or famine.

Interestingly, while smallmouths are confined to shallow shoal areas, they are *not* necessarily found in any and all places where this type of environment exists. Apparently, they are found only in those shoal areas which offer optimum spawning and rearing habitat for small fish. Today, viable smallmouth fisheries occur around offshore islands, as well as along shorelines and in connecting rivers, lakes, canals and backwaters. In fact, some of the fisheries around the far-off, hard-to-get-to islands of Lakes Michigan and Huron offer mind-boggling potential. The Beaver Island Chain of Lake Michigan and the many small islands near Manitoulin Island on Lake Huron are cases in point. In these areas, when conditions are right, you can catch smallies until your arms actually tire!

Since the smallmouth bass is both a bit of a cool as well as a warm water fish, it naturally does better in waters that tend to be cool, rather than prevailingly cold. Smallmouth populations are usually more extensive and numerous in the warmer Great Lakes like Erie.

Perhaps the best advice for fishing Great Lakes smallmouths is not to be intimidated by what may at first appear to be "unusual" conditions. Besides the size of the waters, there is nothing out of the ordinary involved. Smallmouth bass relate to humps, shoals, points, weedbeds, etc., just like they do in smaller inland waters. Fishing methods are also much the same as they are in smaller natural lakes, reservoirs or rivers. True, the larger bays are *huge*, yet they're no more imposing than big waters like Rainy Lake in Minnesota or Lake of the Woods in Ontario. In most cases, you can usually use the same large boats you'd use on inland waters.

The accompanying maps, which are broad in scope, list some of the better known and documented smallmouth fisheries on the Great Lakes. We've included a brief description of each area's general structural condition. The fishing situations and techniques are similar to those used on other waters, and these are fully described in other chapters. But keep in mind that you're usually dealing with extremely clear water so you'll have to minimize the spooking factor.

The smallmouths' seasonal movements shift progressively deeper from the Pre-spawn to the Cold Water Period. Thus, shallow, reed-covered shoals where you might find adult fish in early July will be vacated in September as the fish start to stage off the reefs into deeper water. In each instance, specific smallmouth location must be viewed on a season-by-season basis. Since certain areas have closed seasons, you'll need to check local regulations in advance of any planned trip.

LAKE SUPERIOR

Of the five Great Lakes, Lake Superior has the least number of bass, relative to its overall size. The very cold water and the limited amount of shoal area just do not provide enough proper habitat for the fish to thrive.

The general makeup of this largest of freshwater lakes, with its fast-dropping, granite-walled, very cold (mostly weedless) shorelines is not that hospitable for bass. The whole of the north shore simply does not provide the proper environment for smallmouth development. Therefore, whatever smallmouth bass potential exists, occurs in isolated areas of the warmer, connecting waterways along the south shore.

In some of the bay areas along the south shore, where shoals offer spawning and rearing areas, localized populations of smallmouths have developed. However, in areas like Chequamegon Bay, shoreline development and plain old exploitation have taken their toll, and the bass population is a remnant of what it was—or could be.

Unlike some of the other Great Lakes, Lake Superior has few connecting smaller lakes. Therefore, most of the smallmouth fisheries are restricted to the backs of a few large bays which periodically function as warm or cool water environments, as opposed to strictly very cold ecosystems.

Available prey for bass is also a problem over large areas of Lake Superior—especially for bass in the small and intermediate size ranges. Except for the warmer bay sections, there is generally little select prey for these smaller fish. Therefore, even if larger fish might be able to "hack it" in this harsh environment, so few fish make it to a larger size that populations simply don't develop. Conditions just don't allow the fish the opportunity to spread out and populations to build.

The accompanying map lists Lake Superior's major bass areas. Spring is the best time to hunt lunkers, so most big fish are taken in the Pre-spawn and Pre-summer Periods. While there is good potential for fall fishing in these isolated areas, little is done.

1. St. Louis River/Duluth Harbor/Superior Entryway: A small resident population exists in this estuary.

2. Chequamegon Bay: It's not what it was in the early days, but there are still some fish to be had. With the introduction of salmon and trout, today bass are quite ignored, and the fish population is holding somewhat steady. Specific areas along the old dock pilings of Ashland, Wisconsin, the mouth of the Bark River, and the Sand Cut area hold fish in spring. Later in summer, these fish spread into other parts of the bay and are tougher to locate.

3. Keweenaw Waterway: A prime, big bass fishery exists with some nice fish in the 4 pound plus bracket. However, a health advisory recommends that you not eat fish from these waters. It's strictly catch and release.

4. Presque Isle Harbor: A limited fishery exists around the power station, shoals and pilings in this area.

LAKE MICHIGAN

Lake Michigan sustains excellent (if nonetheless localized) populations of good-sized smallmouth bass. It appears that smallmouth bass have not been adversely affected by the plagues of damming, lamprey infestation, intense angler exploitation and commercial overharvest.

Given areas of Lake Michigan offer very large sections of smallmouth habitat. Therefore, areas may house anything from limited, but fishable smallmouth bass opportunities, to very large numbers of decent-sized fish. Thus, the accompanying map is only a guide to some of the more productive areas. Since it is possible for a smallmouth fishery to develop in any section of the lake with the proper environment, sleeper sections surely exist.

Interestingly, the smallmouth fishery at Waugoshance Point in the northern part of Michigan's lower peninsula was "discovered" by anglers as late as the early 1950's. The reason for this is that common angling boats available before then simply precluded fishing waters other than the close, inshore spots.

As today's modern boats become safer, faster and more sophisticated, off-shore shoal areas, like those around the Beaver Islands in the very northeastern part of the lake are being effectively fished. To be frank, we still don't know the actual extent of the smallmouth bass fishery in many of the shallow reefs in the northeastern portion of the lake. The problem is further affected by totally unrestricted and unregulated tribal netting and its impact on the bass fishing potential. Wildcat netting and incidental fish kills make proper management and scientific investigation impossible.

Beyond this, we also do not know the full extent of summertime dispersal from spawning grounds out into the bays, along the shorelines, or to more distant shoal areas. However, tagged fish have been known to move as far as 10 miles or more from their points of capture. It is known that some far-out reefs have bass and others don't. Current information is either lacking or has not been coordinated with other studies.

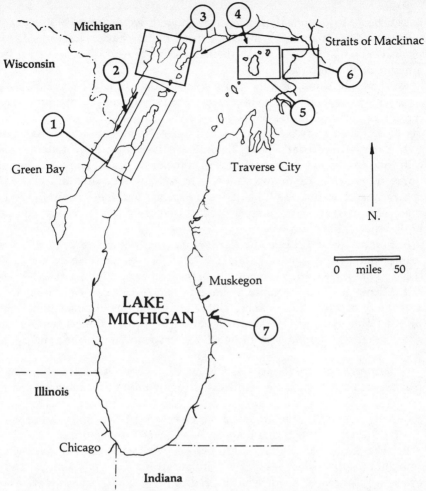

This is both good news and bad news. The good news is that many spots, for all practical purposes, can be considered virgin fisheries. The bad news is that the structural makeup of some of these areas is so huge, diverse and complex that bass anglers must actually go to each area, get local maps, do their own reconnaissance, and ferret out the best areas.

Some of these fisheries, however, are of long standing and have been exploited by anglers in years past. Population levels might be at a low ebb or mediocre state, although some have come back very strong. Again, each of the places listed here has to be viewed on a case by case basis.

Some of the following areas are located well out in the lake. You must ferry your car and boat out to them. Just remember that these are big waters, and you must play it totally safe. Certain places have open and closed seasons for bass, so you must check local regulations. Also remember that many of these fisheries are fragile or are being rebuilt, and catch and release is vital.

1. Door County, Wisconsin, Including Washington and Adjacent Islands: There is a prime, historic, smallmouth bass fishery on the Green Bay side of the Door County peninsula. Many bays, islands and reefs from about Sturgeon Bay north produce anything from a fair to a fantastic smallmouth bass fishery. While mostly smaller fish abound, we do know of great catches taken off Sister Island and Horseshoe reefs. On the Lake Michigan side of the peninsula, only the bays north of Bailey's Harbor produce a fair to decent amount of smallmouths.

Washington Island, and the many smaller adjacent islands and shoals, also produce great bass fishing. With the restricted season and current intense focus on salmon fishing, this fishery is in better shape today than, perhaps, in many decades. This is truly a fantastic, Great Lakes, smallmouth bass fishing area.

2. Bark River/Cedar River/Menominee River Shoreline Stretch: This 40 mile long fishery has come back strong in the past decade, and is still building. Some shoal areas are more conducive to smallmouths than others are. Fish spawn in and around the Cedar River in spring, and then spread out in summer. This close-to-shore, sleeper area can be great fun for those who know how, what, where and when.

3. Summer Island, Little and Big Bay de Noc: Somewhat reduced from its former numbers by mid and late 1970's angling pressure, a decent to good fishery nonetheless exists—especially in the farther out, harder-to-get-to areas.

4. Michigan's Upper Peninsula Shoreline and Adjacent Reefs: The shorelines and shoals of various bays and offshore reefs from about Seul Choix Point to Biddle Point warrant intense investigation by prospecting anglers. There is gold—smallmouth gold—for those willing to spend the time and energy to dig them out.

5. Beaver/Garden/Hog Islands Chain: While continuing tribal netting can play havoc here, there are nonetheless virtually unlimited smallmouth bass opportunities. Reports of limits of 3 to 5 pound fish are too numerous to ignore— especially in some of the farther out and hard-to-get-to islands and reefs. This is a *ferry boat only* trip that takes at least a week to explore.

6. Waugoshance Point: Although a well-known and well-worked smallmouth bass fishery—especially in late spring and early summer (July)— exists in this area, it is not what it used to be or could be; yet there are still many fish to be taken—especially in summer.

7. Port Sheldon: A limited fishery which focuses on the Pigeon River, Pigeon Lake and shoal areas of Lake Michigan offers some nice smallies.

LAKE HURON

Like Lake Michigan, this Great Lake has pockets of super smallie action and then large areas of "Nothingsville." And, just like Lake Michigan, Huron has areas of far-flung, hard-to-get-to sections of smallie waters which somehow survived pollution, nets, pressure from other competing gamefish, and the like. While the "turn of interest" to recently-introduced species like salmon and trout have taken some of the angling pressure off hard-hit populations, others remain at lower or moderate levels. There are also, however, some virtually untouched fisheries, usually because of their hard-to-get-to status.

The smallmouth fishery in this relatively cool/cold water lake is mostly confined to bay-like or island-studded sections. Shallow shoals slow the push of the wind, and allow the water to warm to a point (if only seasonally) where smallmouth bass can proliferate.

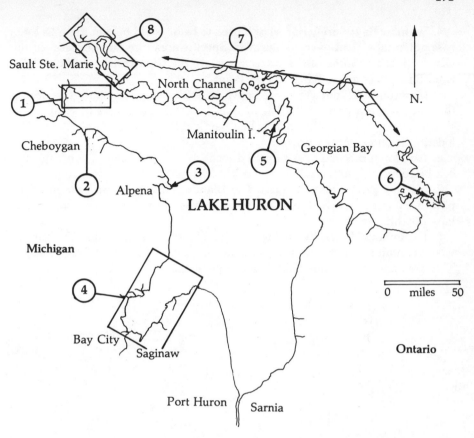

The sites reported here have solid, verifiable reports of fish. We also know of rumored sleeper areas which folks must ferret out for themselves.

Something not common on the other Great Lakes is the chance to get lost in the maze of 30,000 specks of land and reefs that dot the North Channel and Georgian Bay. Also, the ferries that make some of the offshore waters more easily accessible to trailered boats don't exist in the numbers that they do in Lake Michigan. Trips must actually be approached safari-like, and you must take camping gear, food, and extra gas with you if you wish to work the real off-beat spots. But for those with the guts and fortitude, it will be worth it. In some places, 100 or more fish a day are not uncommon. But take care, because unmarked reefs jut out of nowhere, and fog occasionally occurs. This means that a compass and other safety equipment is essential for extensive running to far-flung areas.

1. Les Cheneaux Islands: This sheltered area houses plenty of smallmouths for those who have the know-how. It's more accessible than some far-off areas. It offers exploration along with the comfort of nearby hotels and motels.

2. Cheboygan River/Bois Blanc Island Area: A limited fishery exists, but some nice fish are available for those willing to work.

3. Thunder Bay: The area from Sulpher Island to South Point is a fair to good fishery in late spring/early summer. Later, fish disperse to reefs and shoals, north and south of North Point.

4. Saginaw Bay: Surely not what it used to be or could be, yet there's a lot of bass potential spread over a huge area. Specific areas are more or less seasonally productive. Some of the better areas are the Charity Island Shoal, Wigwam Bay, Pinconning Bar and Fish Point.

5. Manitoulin Island: While we know there are fish in the South Bay area of the southwestern part of the island, we do not know the full extent of the smallie population in other places like Bayfield Sound and Vidal Island. This location is an explorer's dream.

6. Go Home Bay Area: Although a localized limited fishery, some fair fish can be found if you're willing to work.

7. North Channel and Georgian Bay Islands: This area is so vast and complex that it must be fished to be understood. Vast, mind-boggling, smallmouth bass potential exists here.

8. Drummond Island/Sault Ste. Marie: The shoal area behind Drummond Island contains lots of smallies, as do various sections in the St. Mary's River. This area has worthwhile fishing and easy access.

This overall warmest and shallowest of the Great Lakes provides immense smallmouth bass potential. While the aptly-named Bass Islands of the Western Basin are historic fishing grounds, there are also many other less-known and less-expansive, but still quite productive, areas. As a whole, the bass fishery is somewhat exploited. Although still good, the numbers of larger fish appear to be somewhat diminished with the increased bass interest that has developed during the last decade.

While most of the open water areas are the province of either walleye anglers (in the cool sections) or trout and salmon anglers (in colder sections), many of the shoreline shoal areas support smallmouths, sometimes in surprising amount and size.

While localized, isolated populations develop wherever the habitat and water temperatures are even nearly adequate, the most extensive areas exist on the southern part of the lake; more precisely, they're found in the Bass Islands area and the southern and eastern sections of the lake.

In these waters, smallmouth bass must share space and compete for food with other warm and cool water species much more than they do in the other Great Lakes. Walleyes, sauger, sheepshead, rock bass, white bass and the like seasonally mix, meld and move in and out of the smallies' domain. This is one of the few areas we know of where smallmouths are caught on downriggers while anglers fish for walleyes and coho. Reports of fish coming from water as deep as 80 feet during the fall season also give us a wider grasp of the smallmouth's lifestyle.

1. The Bass Islands Area: This 35-mile by 20-mile section of reefs, shoals and islands, extending from Catawba Island on the south shore to Point Pelee on the north, supports smallmouths. Of course, certain sections, certain reefs, and certain shorelines seasonally harbor more or less bass. This area is moderately to heavily fished, at least early in the season, and, in fact, is one of the historic, bass fishing spots on the Great Lakes.

2. Huron River to Avon Point Stretch: Localized populations are scattered in the shallows surrounding the proper-bottomed river mouths that feed Lake Erie along this 30-mile stretch. Try the stretch surrounding Chappel Creek, the Vermilion River, Beaver Creek and the Rocky River.

3. Conneaut River to Caharaugus Creek Stretch: This long stretch spans almost 100 miles and 3 different states. Along this stretch, places like Conneaut, Dunkirk Harbor and Presque Isle Bay all have decent to very good smallmouth populations. Numerous sections like Walnut Creek, Crooked Creek and Six Mile Creek have more or less sizeable populations of fish. In fact, there are localized populations around each of the better bottomed, incoming streams. In summer, they move out into the shoal areas near these streams. Each area has to be viewed on a case by case basis.

4. Niagara River to Grand River Stretch: This is another long stretch that offers "here and there" smallmouth bass opportunities. Dumping of spoil, destruction of habitat due to construction, and pollution have all taken a toll. Yet there are still residual, localized populations.

5. Long Point Bay: Surely not what it used to be, this huge section of water still has smallmouth bass and offers a fishery for those willing to work.

LAKE ONTARIO

With more than 90 different species of fish swimming in the waters of Lake Ontario, smallmouth bass surely have some competition—not only for food, but to a certain extent, living space. Yet, in spite of the odds, smallmouths do quite well in the shallow shoal areas of the lake.

The makeup of the northern shoreline (except for the northeastern area) of Lake Ontario does not provide much conducive, smallmouth bass habitat. The south shore's bays, inlets and numerous incoming streams have better localized (if still limited) populations.

In Lake Ontario proper, smallmouth bass move to inshore sites at a water temperature of about 55°F, and spawn over gravel in 3-15 feet of water at a temperature of about 60°F. Spawning runs also enter the tributaries in the south shore of the lake; these streams are important spawning and nursery

areas. Both young and old move out of the tributaries during summer and fall. Spawning runs do not usually enter streams at the eastern end of the lake, north of Stony Point, however, because the streams in that area lack the proper bottom content. Along the south shore, most spawning occurs in the lower sections of streams, and then the fish move out to the shoal areas of the lake.

Much of the rocky shoreline from Sodus Bay to Salmon River is an important spawning area for smallmouth bass. Several distinct smallmouth bass populations exist in Lake Ontario, each of which spawns in a localized geographic area. Spawning in tributaries and embayments may occur from late May to early June; in the lake proper, spawning may be delayed until late June or July. Sizewise, the fish's growth seems to correspond with growth exhibited in the other Great Lakes, with lots of smaller and medium-sized fish and few larger fish. Top-out size is about 4 to 5 pounds, with a very occasional 6-pounder.

1. Burlington Bay/Bronte Creek/Credit River: Residual, localized populations still exist here. Man-made alterations of habitat, pollution, exploitation and other factors have reduced a once large and extensive fishery.

2. Southern and Eastern Shorelines: Numerous localized populations pivot around some of the main incoming streams, bays and inlets which have appropriate bottom conditions and food sources. While damming and other alterations of water levels and bottom content have reduced some populations, the fishery is quite healthy both in maximum size and numbers of fish.

Each of these individual areas must be viewed on a case by case basis. Because of current angler attention being switched to fish like salmon and trout, the once-reduced smallmouth stocks are building. There are places along this area where catching 100 fish a day is not uncommon.

3. Gallo Island/Chaumont Bay Area: This bay-like section just south of the mouth of the St. Lawrence River (the Thousand Islands Area) contains various smallmouth groups. Some of these groups are very numerous; others less so.

Fish tend to spawn in shoal areas of the islands or in shallow, rock-bound bays and inlets, and move out into the larger bays and lake in summer.

4. The Mouth of the St. Lawrence River: This part of the Thousand Islands area, including sections in the lake like Amherst Island Bar, Charity Shoal, Collins Bay, Mc Shoal, Simcoe Island, the west face of Wolf Island, and the like, is fully discussed in the following sections on connecting waters. (See Thousand Islands Area.)

5. Bay of Quinte and Waters of the Prince Edward County Peninsula: The shoal areas around this huge tract of land and connecting waterways all have smallmouths where the correct bottom content and food sources are present. In fact, the smallmouth population is building. Because of the vast size of this area, each individual spot must be viewed on a case by case basis. Some sections are generally better than others, so hunting is in order. All in all, this is a terrific area for the knowledgeable bass angler to go exploring.

CONNECTING WATERS OF THE GREAT LAKES

Between each of the Great Lakes, connecting them as they drain to the sea, are huge river systems and even a huge lake—all of which support smallmouths in varying quantities. In fact, some of the these areas are *prime* smallmouth waters.

Because of resultant, physical makeup and just plain geography, most of the waters in these sections are shallower or warmer than the "big water," are bounded by shoal areas and shallow cover, and provide (at least seasonally) some of the very necessary ingredients that smallmouths use. Some of these sections held large numbers of bass in the past, but because of development, they no longer support the numbers of fish they formerly did. Yet, there are smallmouth bass to be had in some of these waters—at times, lots of them, and sometimes even lots of lunkers.

The main waterways leading to the Atlantic Ocean are: the St. Mary's River, which connects Lake Superior with Lakes Michigan and Huron (which are at the same level); the St. Clair River, which drains Lake Huron into Lake St. Clair; the Detroit River, which drains Lake St. Clair into Lake Erie; the Niagara River, which flows over Niagara Falls into Lake Ontario; and the St. Lawrence River, which flows to the Atlantic Ocean.

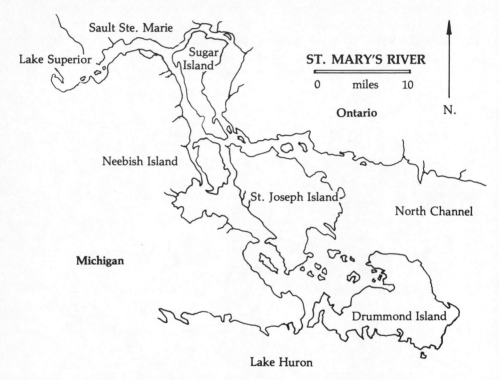

1. St. Mary's River: The section (actually a part of Lake Huron) under the Sault Ste. Marie locks has a resident population of smallmouths. While the fishery can't be considered large or extensive, it still harbors some good fish. In spring, spawning takes place in bays and shallows throughout the river and in places like Bay Mill's Point, Cedar Point, The Duck Lake Cut, the Moon Island area and Marks Bay. These sections primarily serve as spawning and nursery areas for young-of-the-year fish, as well as a growth area for small and intermediate-sized bass. The large and lunker bass, however, operate somewhat differently. After spawning, they relate more to areas of flow during the summer and fall season.

A prime area exists around Drummond Island. Potagannissing Bay, Scott Bay, Sturgeon Bay on one side, and some of the coves around the other side of the island, like Huron Bay, offer surprisingly good, if nonetheless limited, localized populations of smallmouth bass.

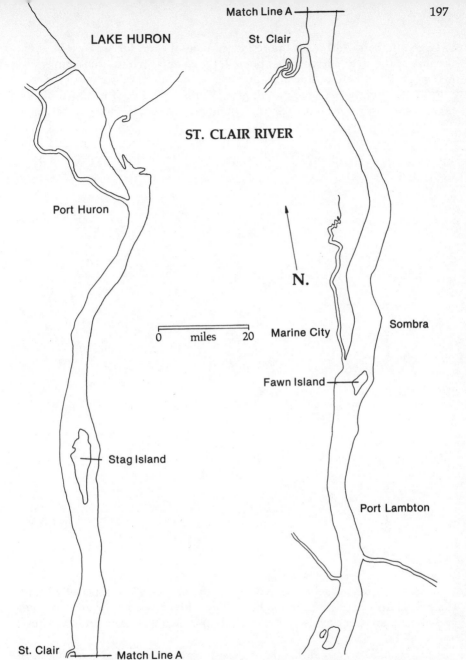

LAKE HURON
St. Clair

ST. CLAIR RIVER

Port Huron

N.

Sombra

0   miles   20   Marine City

Fawn Island

Stag Island

Port Lambton

2. St. Clair River: The St. Clair River, together with Lake St. Clair and the Detroit River, forms the connecting waterway between Lake Huron and Lake Erie. This river and its tributaries are important spawning and nursery areas for many species that support major fisheries in the waterway and in Lake Huron and Lake Erie.

Of the almost 90 species of fish treated here, 22 species are native to the St. Clair River. Most of the native species probably spawned (or spawn) in tributaries to the river or in the shallow embayments and shoreline areas.

The river is an important migration route for larvae which move through it in large numbers. Although the residence time of most larvae may be short, because of the swift currents that prevail, the river is an important nursery for many species of fish, and seasonally hosts many adults of various species.

A limited number of smallmouth groups utilize the river for spawning purposes, and an even more limited number can be considered residents. Throughout the year, the seawalls, pilings, piers, shallow shoals and other structural elements see some smallmouth use. Spots around Stage and Fawn Islands, as well as the St. Clair River plant, are the more productive sites.

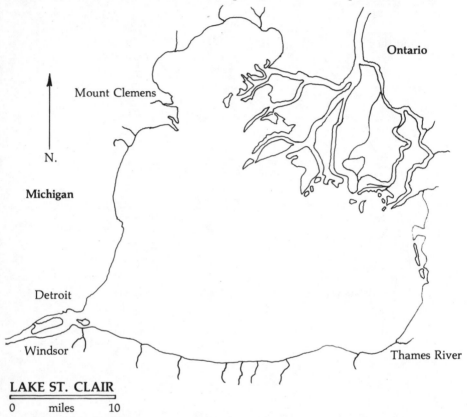

N.

Michigan

Mount Clemens

Ontario

Detroit

Windsor

Thames River

LAKE ST. CLAIR

0   miles   10

3. Lake St. Clair: The bays and wetlands of Lake St. Clair, especially the St. Clair Flats area at the mouth of the St. Clair River, are important spawning and nursery areas for many species that support major fisheries in Lake Huron and Lake Erie.

More than 70 species of fish have been recorded as residents, or migrants. Most of these 28 species that are native to the lake spawn in the shallow, productive, St. Clair Flats area, along shore, or in tributaries to the lake.

The countless seawalls, cut channels, submerged pilings, cribs, metal and concrete ruins, shallow rocky shoals and rush banks occur in such profusion that a short listing of smallmouth bass locations is not even possible. For years, smallmouth bass were almost ignored as a fishery, but with the bass-boom craze that started in the 1960's, increasing fishing pressure has deleted some of the easy pickings. Yet, there are countless fish to be had—and some good ones—in this fantastic body of water.

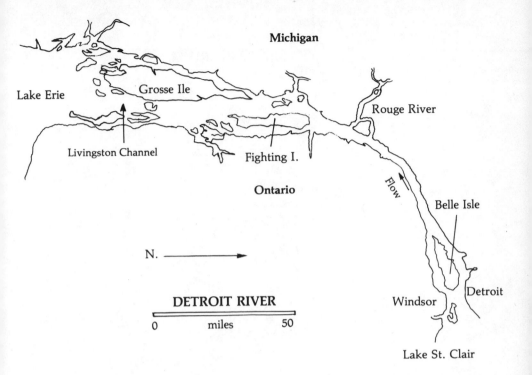

Michigan

Lake Erie

Grosse Ile

Rouge River

Livingston Channel

Fighting I.

Ontario

Belle Isle

N. ⟶

Flow

DETROIT RIVER

Detroit

Windsor

0   miles   50

Lake St. Clair

4. Detroit River: A localized, resident population exists, but the overall makeup of the river, with its ultra-fast current and developed shorelines in the upper portion, precludes much use. More fish can be found in the wider, more obstructed, down river portion, where the current is more reduced and is broken by islands, seawalls, cribs, breakwaters and the like. Livingstone Channel, Stoney Island, Sturgeon Bar and Grosse Ile areas are most productive—particularly early in the year.

5. The Niagara River: The Niagara River forms a connecting waterway between Lake Erie and Lake Ontario. Niagara Falls, approximately 15 miles downstream from Lake Erie, divides the river into upper and lower sections. The lower river is deep and swift, with narrow zones along each shore supporting rooted aquatic vegetation—especially along the U.S. side from the river mouth upstream to Lewiston. In the upper river, aquatic weeds are present, especially in the shallow bays and shoal areas around Grand Island.

The abundance of young fish and low numbers of adults in the upper river sections indicate that the young fish move out of the upper river and the upper water in Lake Erie. This river has changed during ensuing years due to dredging, man-made construction, pollution and the like. Nonetheless, the river supports both resident and immigrant populations of smallmouth bass. The best fishing occurs early in the year (late spring), usually around Grand Island. Yet, various upstream sections also hold fish in cut channels, seawalls, cribs, submerged pilings and other protective structures.

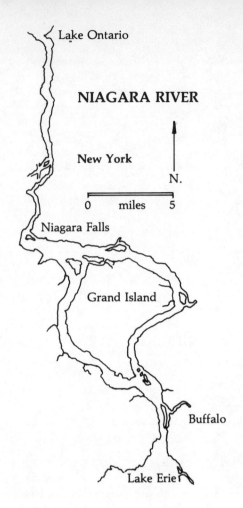

NIAGARA RIVER

Lake Ontario

New York

N.

0 miles 5

Niagara Falls

Grand Island

Buffalo

Lake Erie

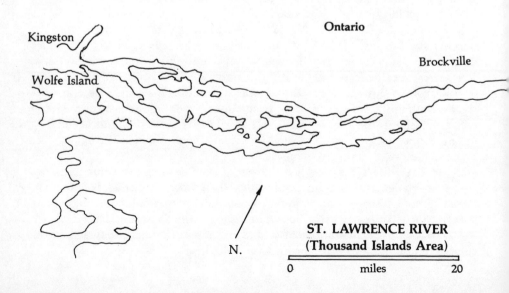

Ontario

Kingston

Brockville

Wolfe Island

N.

ST. LAWRENCE RIVER
(Thousand Islands Area)

0 miles 20

6. St. Lawrence River/Thousand Islands Area: The St. Lawrence River forms the connecting waterway between Lake Ontario and the Atlantic Ocean. Historically, it contains important spawning grounds for many species which often run long distances upstream. Young fish remain in the creek mouths for some period of time before moving into the river. Heavily-used tributaries include the Oswegatchie River, Raquette River and St. Regis River. The habitats and migration patterns of many of the St. Lawrence River fish groups have been drastically altered by extensive dam construction on the river. In the early 1930's, dams were reported to have stopped spawning runs in certain areas.

In the upper St. Lawrence River, smallmouth bass move inshore to depths of 3-15 feet to spawn over gravel shoals and rock ledges. Large spawning runs enter tributaries, where most spawning occurs near the mouths. Historically, the spawning period in the upper river extends from mid-May to July. In the tributaries, spawning occurs during late May to early June; in the colder St. Lawrence River waters, spawning occurs later and can continue into July.

This huge area hosts and boasts a major, Great Lakes smallmouth fishery. Because of the vast area involved and the wide distribution of smallmouth bass habitat all through the river system, it is impossible to pinpoint specific areas in this 140-odd mile long system. Numerous, localized and migrant fish groups range throughout the river. Along with the resident fish, lake populations periodically move into the river mouths during different seasons. Because of the large distances involved and the vast amount of area and habitat considered, you must be willing to move around to find fish. But rest assured that there are many nice bass sometimes caught at depths of even 50 feet.

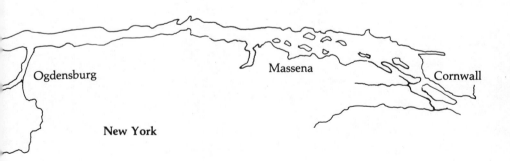

Ogdensburg

Massena

Cornwall

New York

Tony Portincaso and Ron Lindner (right) with several Great Lakes smallmouths kept for a shore lunch with the filming crew. These fish were just a small portion of the 100-odd fish caught that day.

Chapter 21

FLY FISHING FOR SMALLMOUTHS THE ULTIMATE EXPERIENCE

Combine the most sporting method of catching fish with the scrappiest, most aggressive fighter and the result is fresh water fishing's ultimate experience—catching smallmouth bass on a flyrod.

The equipment needs are simple. The best length for rods is 8½ to 9 feet. The minimum line rating is #6, maximum #9. Lines should be weight forward or Bass Bug Taper. Use #20 dacron for backing. Leaders can be from 6 to 9 feet long, and should be tapered to a #6 - #12 tippet, depending upon the size of fish and type of cover. Reels can be either single action or multiplier.

Casting a bass fly is not as easy as using other fishing equipment, but is not as difficult as you may have been led to believe. Read the following section carefully and try to visualize what is being described.

Useful Knots

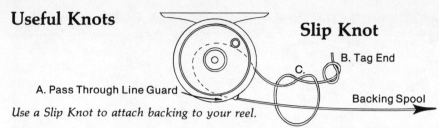

Slip Knot

B. Tag End

C.

A. Pass Through Line Guard

Backing Spool

Use a Slip Knot to attach backing to your reel.

Backing To Reel: *A simple knot for attaching backing to the reel is shown above. Pass the tag end of the backing around the reel arbor and bring it out again. Tie an overhand knot in the end and tighten it. Now tie a second overhand knot around the standing part of the line and draw it tight. Pull on the line to slide and jam the knot against the arbor.*

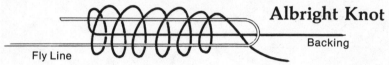

Albright Knot

Backing

Fly Line

Fly Line To Backing: *Now you are set to join the fly line to the backing with the Albright Knot. Unwind a foot or so of line from its plastic spool. Form a loop in the line end. Insert the tag end of the backing through the loop from the rear, and wrap six turns of backing around the loop, from left to right. Tuck the tag end of the backing through the front of the loop. Hold coils securely between left thumb and forefinger. Slowly pull on the standing part of the backing until the coils snug up into a tight, even knot. Trim tag ends.*

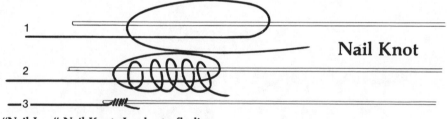

1

2

—3—

Nail Knot

"Nail-Less" Nail Knot: Leader to fly line.

1. *Hold the line tip over the leader butt. Form a loop in the leader in front of the line.*
2. *Pass the leader end through the loop and over the line five or six times.*
3. *Pull on the leader end to snug up the wraps evenly and tighten the knot. Trim tag ends.*

1

2

3

4

Surgeon's Knot

To connect new tippets (sections of leader) to your leader, use either a Surgeon's Knot or a Blood Knot.

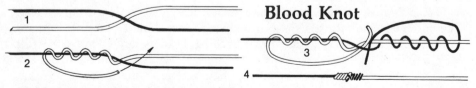

1

2

3

4

Blood Knot

Blood Knot (Barrel Knot): Tippet to leader.

1. *Lay one end of the tippet over the leader end to form an X. Allow about four to six inches of each to tie the knot.*

In bait or spin casting, the weight of the lure loads the rod. When the rod casts the lure, the line is pulled out. In fly casting, the weight of the line loads the rod. The rod casts the line, and the line carries the fly along with it.

In fly casting, the bigger or heavier a fly is, the more difficult it is to cast. The key to casting big, wind-resistant, bass bugs is to learn to control your fly line.

A fly cast consists of a back cast and a forward cast. In order to accomplish these casts effectively, a good "stroke" is necessary. A good stroke develops enough line speed to carry a fly to the target. With a good stroke, your line will form a narrow loop on both the fore and back casts.

Timing is also important. On both the fore and back cast, you must maintain control and line speed. Here are two examples which illustrate a good stroke and proper timing.

Imagine you have a towel in your hand. Now twirl it as you hold it by one end. Next, go through the motion of snapping someone with the towel. To develop speed, you must make a brisk, linear motion with a CRISP STOP at the end of the stroke. If you make the same motion with the towel overhand, the towel will uncurl in the same "U-shape" as fly line displays in a properly executed fly cast. That's the basic fly casting stroke.

The following example illustrates the timing required for casting. Imagine that you have a pull toy on a 20-foot string and you're standing in the middle of a basketball court. The toy and string rest parallel to the line which bisects the court. You want to move the toy from a point 20 feet in front of you to a point 20 feet behind you and then back again. The line must be tight before you give it a tug, and you must wait for the toy to travel far enough behind you to straighten the string, before you try to snap it back again. If you let go of the string just as it straightens in front of you, it will continue to travel forward.

Combine the stroke of an overhand towel snap with pull-toy timing and you can fly cast. But let's consider a few other basic pointers.

Bass bugs don't come out of the water easily, so do this: Don't just think about lifting the bug. Try lifting the line first, then the leader, and finally the fly from the surface.

Keep your wrist stiff and straight—try not to break it—as you lift the line and fly. If you break your wrist too much and allow the rod to fall too far back, the back cast loop won't be tight. It won't develop enough line speed, and the fly won't be carried behind you.

Casting line back and forth without letting the fly touch water is called false casting. The object is to work out more line by letting 2 to 6 feet of line slip out at the end of each stroke. Once you have 25 or 30 feet of line in the air, it has enough weight to carry (or shoot) a fly to a target, 60 feet away.

The weight-forward variety of fly lines are best for casting bass bugs. A "bass bug taper" is a particular, weight-forward line which is especially easy to cast with minimum line in the air.

HAULING FOR ADDED VELOCITY AND DISTANCE

"Hauling" is a technique fly casters use to get extra distance. A haul is accomplished by a pull of the line with your hand. Hauling as a fly is snatched from the water is called a single haul. The length of line pulled down in a single haul is let out at the top of the back cast as the line straightens behind you. "Double hauling" refers to a downward pull on the line with the left hand as you apply power on the forward stroke.

Hauling greatly increases your ability to cast great distances and to cast accurately during windy conditions, because it accelerates the line and increases the loading of the rod, thus allowing it to gain maximum velocity. Like twirling a ball on a string, if you abruptly shorten the string as the ball is twirling its speed is greatly increased.

Single hauling is a down/up motion. Double hauling is a down/up/down motion with the release of the line immediately following the final down haul.

STRIPPING IN LINE, SETTING THE HOOK, AND CONTROLLING FISH

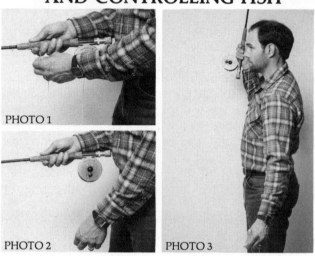

PHOTO 1

PHOTO 2

PHOTO 3

Photo 1

If you're right handed and have the rod in your right hand, reach down with your right index finger and grip the fly line. Now grasp the fly line with your left hand at a point between your right hand and the fly reel.

Photo 2

Strip in line by pulling it in with your left hand; allow the line to slide behind your right index finger. Work the fly with flips of the rod tip as you take up slack by stripping line. Keep the tip of your rod low enough to allow for a hook set. Excess, stripped line can fall into your lap or on the floor of the boat.

Photo 3

To set the hook, raise the rod sharply as you haul down on the line with your left hand. Release your fly line from behind your right index finger at the same time or you'll have a line burn.

Once the bass is hooked and the line is tight, place the line back behind your right index finger to maintain tension. Continue to strip line in or play it out until you land the bass. It's true surface-to-hand action.

Effective Retrieves for Smallmouths

Steady Swim

Good search routine. Effective when fish are moving.
Good motion to move fly from one ambush point to next.

STEADY SWIM

The key is not to move the fly too far each time you pop it. This retrieve works well when you cast parallel to cover, but requires stripping line fast to avoid slack line.

Intermittent Swim

Pause several seconds, pause again   Steady pull   Stop

Repeat and pick-up for next cast

Good basic shoreline extended cover and/or 6 feet and less depth technique.

INTERMITTENT SWIM

Try not to make your pops too aggressive. A short flip of the tip, combined with a short line strip, works fine. Concentrate on keeping the tip pointed at the fly. Use a period of no movement to regain slack line and bring your rod tip back to a 9 o'clock position. Try not to move the fly while you're regaining slack line.

Pop/Slide/Dive

Done with diver only. Works when fish are particularly stubborn.
Most strikes come when fly stops while submerged or when rising.

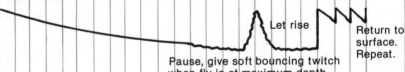

Let rise

Return to surface. Repeat.

Pause, give soft bouncing twitch when fly is at maximum depth, pause, slow jiggle swim.

POP/SLIDE/DIVE

This is probably the most effective method to trigger reluctant bass, and is also a good method for covering plenty of water. Our favorite fly pattern is a fur-strip diver, but standard divers also work. Use a brightly-colored fly to make underwater strikes easy to detect. You may not feel a tug when a bass takes a fly, but you'll see it disappear.

"Stationary" Retrieve

Lift tip as fly enters water making it "pop" to attract attention.
Let sit for a long period.

Good when fishing deep cover or right over a bed of shallower water.
At times, this is your #1 retrieve.

STATIONARY RETRIEVE

The secret is to wait twice as long as you can stand to! This retrieve often is the only one that turns big fish on. Keep the slack out of your line and pay attention, because bass have a habit of striking when you're gazing at eagles, bears, otters, etc. If you tend to daydream, at least keep your ears open; you'll hear 'em strike.

SELECTED SURFACE FLIES
FOR A SMALLMOUTH BASS

Surface flies fall into three basic categories: *sliders, poppers* and *divers.* *Sliders* make a minimum of water disturbance and imitate injured baitfish or small mammals. Sliders are generally smaller than divers or poppers, and this as well as their design make them the easiest surface flies to cast.

The sliders pictured in *Row 1* include from top to bottom: Dahlberg Floating Minnows and a Dahlberg Dilg. White, yellow, black and chartreuse are important slider colors.

Poppers should range from 6 to 1/0, but their heads shouldn't be much larger in diameter than a penny or they're too difficult to cast. They're designed to "pop" when they're twitched, and may imitate struggling insects, minnows or frogs. Some poppers have rubber legs, while others are more streamlined. Rubber-legged poppers are best suited to slow retrieves or calm water. Streamlined poppers are best for tough casting situations, fast retrieves or fishing in current. Definitely avoid using poppers that twist in the air or in the water. *Rows 2* and *3* are examples of various, deer-hair, popping bugs.

Divers are probably the best all 'round surface choice because they both pop and dive. They pop when they're twitched but dive during a steady retrieve. A pause brings them back to the surface where they can be popped again.

Divers imitate the same prey as sliders and poppers but offer a sub-surface option which often triggers fish when other, surface-only flies fail. Some divers are tied with feather tails, while others feature fur strips. *Row 4* features standard and a fur (rabbit) strip Dahlberg Diver. White, yellow and chartreuse are easiest to see under water but but sometimes fish prefer more subtle colors.

These flies and many others are available to your dealer from Umpqua Feather Merchants, Idleyed Park, Oregon 97447.

TIP

Bass often follow a surface fly a great distance, and the acceleration of the lift often triggers the fish into making a move which you can see directly behind the fly. Force yourself to leave the fly in the water to tease the follower into striking, especially if you're using a diver. If you take the fly away from a follower, your odds of catching the fish are drastically reduced, because you have pulled the fish away from his ambush point.

To ensure that deer-hair bugs float well, dress them with a paste-type float-ant before wetting them. Even though you've dressed them, after you start catching fish, they may get soggy and won't float well enough to pop. Squeeze excess water out of the fly with your thumb and forefinger; then apply a crystal-type fly drier. This will restore the "float" to your fly.

SELECTED UNDERWATER FLIES FOR SMALLMOUTH BASS

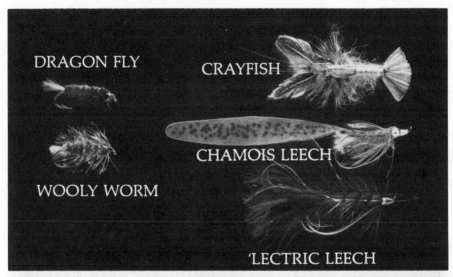

DRAGON FLY

CRAYFISH

CHAMOIS LEECH

WOOLY WORM

'LECTRIC LEECH

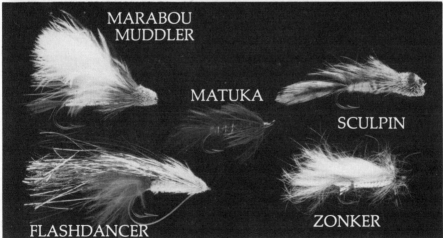

MARABOU MUDDLER

MATUKA

SCULPIN

FLASHDANCER

ZONKER

Although surface flies offer the greatest thrill, underwater flies are often more ef-fective. These can be fished almost anywhere. Choose flys with snag guards if you're fishing on bottom. Minnow imitations are deadly for smallmouth bass; favorites are the Marabou Muddler, Zonker, Matuka, Sculpin and Flashdancer. Best size are 1/0-4.

NYMPHS represent immature aquatic insects. The Wooly Worm and Dragon Fly Nymph are two of the best for smallmouth bass. Best sizes are 2-6. This is the least "fun" fly to fish because you rarely see the strike, but if fished properly, is extremely effective.

CRAYFISH and LEECH FLIES imitate some of a smallmouth's favorite food. There are many fly patterns designed to imitate crayfish and leeches, but our favorites are the Whitlock patterns. Pictured here are: Whitlock Crayfish, Whitlock Chamois Leech, Whitlock 'Lectric Leech. Best sizes are 2-6.

RETRIEVES FOR SUB-SURFACE FLIES

Underwater flies are retrieved with the same, basic mechanics as surface flies. With underwater flies, it is even more essential to keep the rod tip low and avoid excess slack. When a bass takes an underwater fly, there is no surface explosion to wake you up, so you must *pay attention.* Often the smallmouth just sucks in the fly, then spits it out without actually tugging on the line. The slower you retrieve, the harder it is to detect strikes. Any movement in the leader or line should prompt you to set the hook. In good, bass territory, when fishing a particular spot that JUST HAS to have a fish on it, the best fly rodders often set hooks on pure intuition.

MINNOW IMITATIONS can be retrieved in an infinite variety of ways: fast, slow, steady, erratic, long or short strips. Experiment to find out which works best.

Sculpins and marabou muddlers are very effective when fished right along the bottom. To accomplish this, add one or two small split shot ahead of the fly, or use a sinking tip line. Zonkers and matukas present a very realistic silhouette because of their raised dorsals. These are excellent, big fish flies and stay down well in fast water because of their streamlined design.

The flashdancer, in terms of producing pure tonnage, is the most universally effective smallmouth bass fly we have ever used. It is extremely visible in the water, which is probably why it is so effective. It is absolutely deadly, fished in swift, shallow pools when water temperatures are high (78°F+). This fly is also the best choice in dark water, where visibility is a factor. Except in very dingy water, a very fast retrieve with pauses is usually most effective with this fly. This makes it ideal for "searching" large areas.

NYMPHS are the most difficult, underwater flies to use for bass. The common mistake is to move them too far. A natural insect cannot lurch through the water in two or three foot spurts. For example, a dragon fly nymph propels itself by blowing water out of its anus. It moves along on short, 1-inch jerks. To imitate this motion, strip in line with quick, short, 1-inch pulls.

A wooly worm should be fished similarly, but occasionally try a slow, steady, 2-3 foot pull; then pause to let the fly sink.

When fishing a nymph in current it is often necessary to present the nymph with what is known as a "drag-free" drift. This means that the fly should drift in the water as though it was not connected to line. In order to accomplish this, you must adjust the fly line on the water so that current doesn't cause it to pull the artificial fly faster than than a natural would drift. This adjusting is called "mending" line.

Because nymphs are smaller than minnows, smallmouth bass usually will not travel very far to get them. You must "put them right on the beam." Where smallies always align themselves parallel to current, a nymph, dead drifted right on a fish's nose, will trigger the bass 999 times out of 1000. This applies to all smallmouths, regardless of size. The key is that the fish can't be spooked, and the fly has to be right on the fish's nose and traveling at the same rate as the current. When a bass takes a nymph, the strike is very subtle, and without good concentration you may miss the majority of strikes.

CRAYFISH and LEECHES should be retrieved to imitate the naturals. Fish them where the naturals exist. Because of their bulk and water resistance, crayfish patterns, when fished in flowing water, work best fished with the current. Only in slack water should they be retrieved upstream.

Leeches made of fur, feathers, or chamois can be fished deep, shallow or in between. A slow, steady, swimming retrieve is usually the best. If you have trouble hooking fish with a chamois leech, switch to one made of another material. Sometimes the chamois gets balled up ahead of the hook, which prevents the hook from getting to the fish.

SMALLMOUTH BASS! TOPWATER TERROR!

Fly fishing in calm, shallow water with a topwater bass bug is one of life's ultimate thrills. A topwater bass bug is a red flag to a bull, smallmouth bass.

In honesty, there are times when you can't buy a smallie on the surface. Usually, however, throughout most of the season, they'll respond. And there are many times when surface bugging with a fly rod is absolutely the most effective way to catch them.

Without doubt, there is great surface action for smallmouths in many lakes and reservoirs throughout the U.S.A. and southern Canada. However, few anglers get into this explosive action. Here's how *you* can!

Bass can be caught on top through September, but one of the best times to introduce yourself to fly fishing is from May through mid-June. The action can last all day long, and it is common to catch and release lots of smallies. On some waters, there's a fair shot of taking a lunker. Whether you're fishing a Canadian shield lake, an early meso lake or a clear, southern reservoir, the basic principles are the same. Simply locate the proper, shallow water habitat, present the lure, and hang-on!

How deep are the bass during the early season? That often depends on water clarity. Many lakes have stained water, and you won't be able to see bottom in more than 4 feet of water; others are gin-clear with bottom visible at 20 feet or more. As a rule, bass spend more time shallow in stained lakes. But you can still spend the majority of your time searching water less than 6 feet deep in spring, no matter what type of lake you're on.

Regardless of the depth they're found at, smallmouths are *cover-oriented* and instinctively align themselves with darker colors, shapes and shadows on the bottom. The lighter color of surrounding shelf-rock contrasts sharply with cracks, boulders and tree branches—shadow areas—and this helps to make the spots that smallies lie in obvious.

The best areas usually have lots of cracks, corners and edges that provide cover for both predators and prey. Broken rock, medium-sized boulders or fallen timber on the shelf help make it a magnet for spring bass.

All total, spring smallies can often be caught on surface bugs in less than one foot of water. This is especially common in stained water. The clearer the water, the deeper they *might* be. But never rule out shallow water, especially if cover is present.

Good cover makes the difference. On the other hand, when it's absent, bass in clear water may spawn on shelves 15-feet deep. But when it's calm, they may still come up and smash a surface bug. In essence, if you combine prime cover with calm, shallow water, you're in business.

Use polaroid glasses for this type of vision-oriented fishing, and pay close attention to irregularities in the bottom. You must probe each nook and cranny, thoroughly.

Sound slow? It's not with a fly rod. A fly rod lets you pick up a lure and lay it down with pinpoint accuracy in far less time than it takes to cast, fish and retrieve a lure with spin or bait casting equipment. You're fishing where the bass are, all the time.

Some of you may think it's difficult to learn to fly fish. Nahh! With a little practice you'll be making 60-foot casts with accuracy. That's all you need for 90% of all the fly fishing in the entire world. With a little more work, you'll be able to "shoot" a tight loop under the branches of an overhanging tree, cast around corners, and generally do all sorts of things that you could never do with a spinning or bait casting rod.

STREAM STRATEGY

Unlike trout, smallmouths are seldom selective in their feeding preferences. In most of the streams we fish, minnows and small fish make up most of a smallmouth's diet. However, smallies will eat almost anything that comes along, including snakes, frogs, mice, worms, leeches, crayfish and insects that are plentiful or large enough to be of interest.

We prefer seeing and hearing a fish take the fly. Fishing flies close to, or on the surface is not always the most effective way to rack up strikes, but it *is* the most fun, requires the most casting skill, and will almost always produce fish. The key to success is locating fish that are susceptible to shallow-water, fly techniques.

LOGS AND BRUSH

Depending upon the bottom type, logs and brush can provide shade, added depth or both. When we look for good, smallmouth, log/brush locations, we like to see a fairly swift current, moderately clear water and a light-colored sand or gravel bottom. Most of the time, bass hold directly beneath the deep brushpiles. When they are active, they move toward the upstream or top end of the banks. In flat, sandy stretches of river, these banks often have a long, tapering cut of deep water at the head, above which we start casting. Our first choice of flies in this situation is a standard, deerhair popper or diver, large enough to interest big fish.

The trout angler is concerned with a delicate presentation, but the bass angler needn't worry about *splatting* the fly onto the surface. In fact, we think this often attracts the fish. The key to presenting a fly in the brush is accurate casting and a thorough retrieve. The cast should be *inches* from the target. If the fish are holding under the bank, the fly must be as tight against the bank as possible. Work the fly in a series of gentle swimming pops, parallel to the cover. We like to cast from just slightly upstream and alternate a foot or so of swimming pops with two or three feet of dead drift, to get the fly close to the cover.

On your first cast to a prime spot *always* retrieve the fly well out from the bank or visible logs to give either fish holding deep or following fish a shot at it. We like to keep the fly on the water until it "turns the corner" on the retrieve. Like trout, bass are often triggered by this direction change. The diver is especially effective "on the corner" where it can be twitched and slipped in the current, using seductive twitch-and-dead-drift combinations. When working from a boat on the upstream side of a log or brushpile, be sure to maintain an upstream position. This angle allows you to keep a fish away from the brush after it's hooked. In brush/log cover we use nine-foot leaders with 10-pound tippets, for pressuring a snag-bound 3-pounder or for pulling an errant cast from the limbs of an overhanging maple.

UNDERCUTS/GRASS BANKS

Although we've seen some great bass—especially big fish—near undercut grass banks, such places are seldom consistent producers. Most undercut banks are "clay-based" and lack the dense cover necessary to consistently support large numbers of fish. But when additional features are found, such as brush, beaver runs or zig-zags in the shoreline, clay undercuts are likely to hold fish. We fish such banks from a much closer distance (30-40 feet) and with a shorter retrieve (10-12 feet) than we would a long/brush bank. The proximity allows us to get many more casts tight to the bank, and the fish are not likely to strike more than 6 to 8 feet from the shore. If the fish are striking short, our fly would be either a diver or a slider.

One of the most effective tactics we use in pools is something we call "one fish, two fish." Here's how it works; the moment you hook a fish and have it under control, your fishing partner casts three feet or so upstream from the hooked fish, letting the current take the fly as close to the hooked fish as possible (the best fly is a white, sinking fly). Often a hooked bass disgorges its stomach, and the rest of the fish in the school scramble for the "free lunch." By immediately presenting a fly near a hooked fish, another fish in the pool often will nail it. Bring fish #1 quickly to the boat while fish #2 does what it pleases. Quickly release fish #1 and cast near hooked fish #2 which may result in fish #3. Your partner quickly boats and releases fish #2 and repeats the process for fish #4.

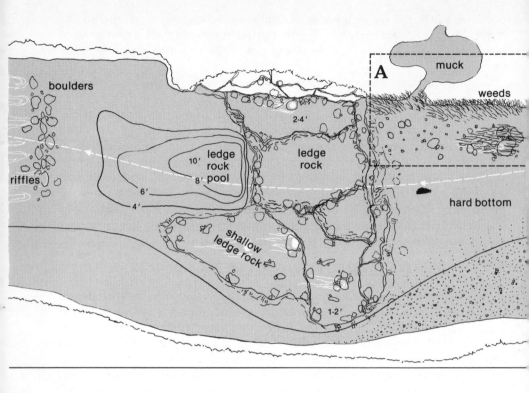

TYPICAL SMALL, ADULT RIVER STRETCH

Here's a stretch of river showing many features found in typical, small, adult rivers. Obviously, in order to show as many elements as possible, many features were compressed into this short stretch. Remember, rivers are viewed by stretches, because rarely is a stream the same from beginning to end. Different stretches of the same stream may have different personalities. Consequently, different fish species are present.

River stretches, like this one, consist of alternating riffle/pool/riffle areas. The stream bed is composed of sections of sand, gravel, rocks and some boulders. In addition, ledge rock outcroppings may be present in some rivers.

Rocks provide a current break and cover for the fish. Pools, both shallow and deep, can be located between the riffle areas. Sometimes, humps or even islands can be present, and provide another form of current break.

Hard-bottomed bays or areas behind islands can provide opportune spawning habitat and may be a super smallmouth area early in the year. Occasionally, a muck-bottomed bay may be attached to the river, and weeds may grow

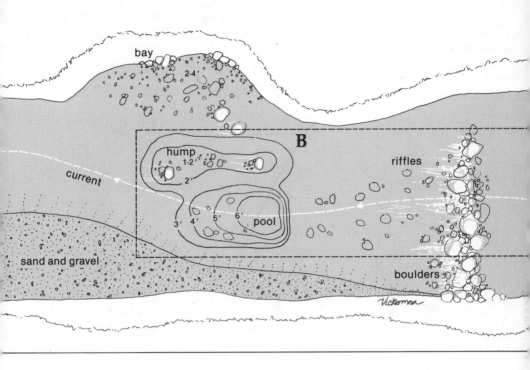

in adjacent areas at the mouth of the connecting channel. These weedy areas can be an overlooked hot spot. Shallow ledge rock areas, when present, can offer smallmouths another shallower water area—especially if a good ledge rock pool is nearby.

While the overall depth of the water depends on many factors (rain, melt-water, etc.), the average depth normally ranges from 3 to 10 feet, depending on the river.

Most pools following a rapids are 6 to 10 feet deep, and occasionally, deeper. Larger, deeper pools may function as a home area for smallmouths throughout the year. Smallmouths could exist in a very limited area *if* all their needs are met, seasonally.

In general, smallmouths relate to the darker-bottom areas of any river. So, if you're faced with a stretch of water with a sandy, lighter-bottom condition, skip it and move to an area with a darker bottom.

Obviously, not all rivers will have all of the features discussed, but the basic principles are the same. Simply read the water! Your eyes and a little river saavy will lead you to the smallmouths.

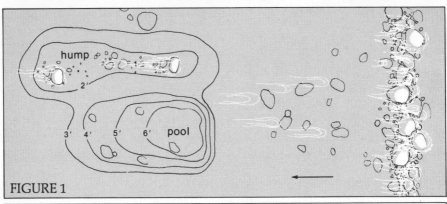

FIGURE 1

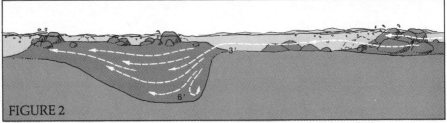

FIGURE 2

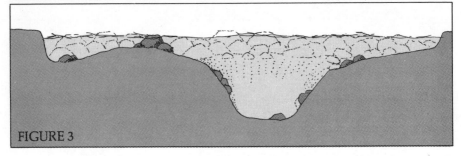

FIGURE 3

Detail of AREA B

AREA B depicts a deeper midstream pool adjacent to a rocky hump which is located near a shallow water riffle. This is a typical situation found on many, if not most, small adult rivers.

In *FIGURE 1*, note the shape of the pool and the sharper drop-off on the upstream end of the pool. Smallmouths would only have to move a few yards to forage on the sunken hump or shallow water riffle.

FIGURE 2 shows patterns of current flow in the pool area, under normal water level conditions. Note the boils located downstream from the boulders; this is a key to locating underwater structure!

FIGURE 3 represents a cross-section of the river, looking upstream. This should help you visualize exactly what this area looks like and will aid you in identifying the pool boundaries.

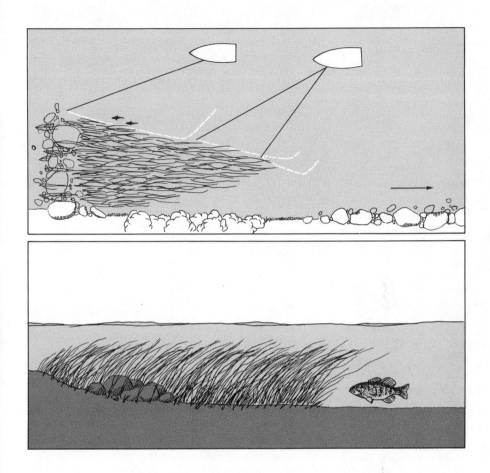

WEEDS

Almost every old-time, smallmouth angler we know hates weeds, but to exclude weed cover from the list of places to fish can be a costly error. Stream smallmouths are not likely to frequent stagnant weed patches in a slough or back eddy, but weedgrowth adjacent to swift water and a bit of strewn rock is prime cover. The best way to keep weeds from upsetting your day is to use flies equipped with an effective weed-guard. If you dislike weed-guards, you can reduce your snags by fishing from downstream, casting up.

The best areas in a river weed patch are under the downstream canopy formed by the current that stretches the weeds out. The most aggressive fish will be under the upstream end of a canopy, at the outside weed edge next to the best current flow. Our favorite surface fly for this location is a slider (Dahlberg Dilg), although a dragonfly nymph, dead drifted along these patches, is deadly.

As weather, water conditions and the seasons change, the cover in which bass are vulnerable to a fly changes, also. By identifying the various types of cover and fishing them thoroughly, you can usually establish a daily pattern.

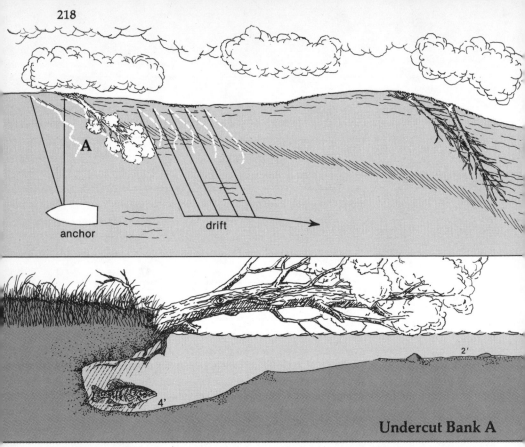

Undercut Bank A

Log Bank

Note on the cross-sections A, B, and C that the top portion of the bank is deeply undercut and that this undercut becomes less as the bank comes out of the corner. This is caused because a river does most of its forming during high water levels, and the maximum force of the current strikes the beginning of the river bend.

Position A
Start fishing at the very top portion of the bank. This is the number one spot for aggressive fish.

Allow the boat to drift parallel to the bank and slow enough to allow unhurried presentations. Combine long, thorough, calculated drifts over structure extending out from the bank, and thoroughly cover all shoreline targets.

Position B
In order to facilitate hooking and controlling a hooked fish, stay upstream from the brush piles. Be careful not to allow the current to accelerate your fly too rapidly as it approaches the end of the quarter. Don't swim the fly upstream.

Allow the line to belly slightly to give the fly a downstream tack.

Position C
After working a brush pile from above, allow the boat to drift below it and work it some more, still focusing on presenting the fly parallel to the cover. Do not overlook the tailing ends of this type of bank. Often where the bank is no longer deeply undercut, it will begin to shallow and form an apron containing scattered logs and brush. These areas can be very significant and may produce several good fish.

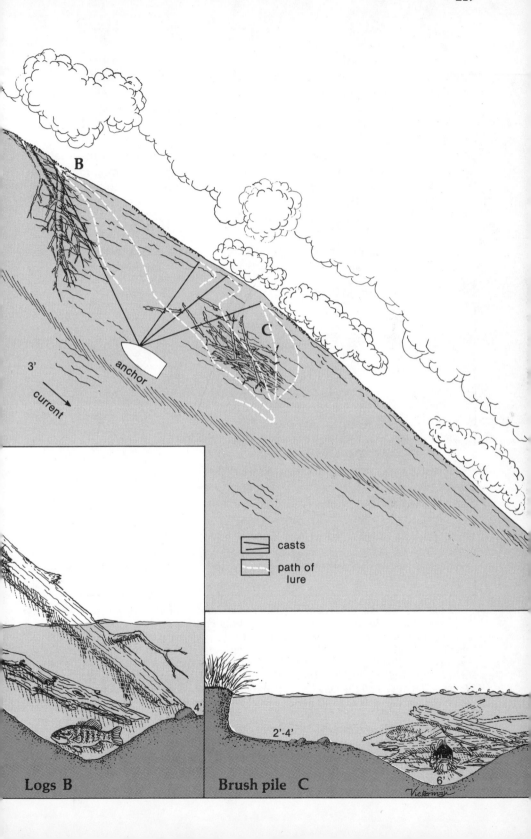

3'

current

anchor

B

C

casts

path of lure

Logs B

Brush pile C

4'

2'-4'

6'

Vickerman

ROCKS

On most smallmouth rivers, rocky cover takes one of two basic forms—banks or pools. The ideal rock bank involves an outside bend lined with rocks of assorted sizes from softball size up to the size of small automobiles. Our approach on such banks is similar to the grass undercut approach, except that we work the fly out into the river as far as the rocks extend—even if that means 60-70 feet or farther.

Experimenting with retrieve speed and length is important in this situation, as is varying the length of dead drift you allow between swimming and popping. We often work the best rock banks two or three times, to be certain we have covered them thoroughly.

LEDGE ROCK AND POOLS

Though the bass may be smaller, for sheer numbers of fish there is no substitute for ledge rock and pools. The bottom often is composed of intermittent

Shallow Ledge Rock Pool

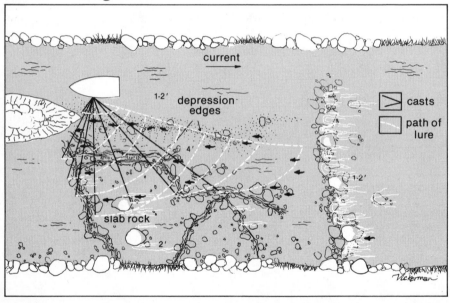

The pool in the diagram is bordered on top and bottom by riffles and on the sides by ledge rock faults. Ideal depth for the heart of the pool would be around four feet. The shallow ledge rock and riffle areas adjacent to the pool would be two feet deep or less. Smallmouth will hold in much shallower water in this situation than they normally do because of the protection and camouflage offered by the dark bottom and the surface riffles. This pool is fished best from either top corner, starting with short casts quartered down and stripped all the way back upstream, gradually lengthening the casts until they reach the far side and tail out above the downstream riffles.

The corner of the pool, adjacent to the downstream island point, would be our choice for an initial anchoring point. This allows the retrieve to run parallel to the long break on the edge of the pool. Even with an upstream direction on the fly, the fish can be teased into striking, by letting the fly hang and drift back in the current. This position also causes followers to stack up on the break below the boat, making them very susceptible to the "one fish, two fish" routine.

bedrock with scattered boulders and rubble, as well as cracks and fissures where smallmouths hold. The pools are formed either by large cracks in the bedrock where the bottom simply "falls away," or by the damming effect of a shallow riffle, immediately downstream. Frequently, these areas will occur in a riffle-pool-riffle-pool sequence, custom tailored for the wading fly fisherman.

The real trick to effectively fish such spots is to first identify their boundaries. Once you have established these boundaries, position yourself to work all the edges of the pool.

Our first choice of surface flies for this situation is a slider fly we call the Dahlberg Dilg. We like to start at the upstream corner of the pool, beginning with short casts to the upstream edge, letting the fly skate and quarter across the current. We gradually lengthen our casts until the fly reaches the opposite edge of the pool. We continue working in this same manner all the way down the pool, shifting position 15 or 20 feet at a time, until the fly's downstream path brings it along the pool's tailout. If we are unable to produce fish in this manner, we'll repeat the process using a Flashabou Muddler, Matuka or diver, concentrating on the fastest or deepest water.

Are float trips fun? You betcha! An airborne smallie shows how this fish fights—high, long and hard!

Chapter 22

WORLD RECORD SMALLMOUTH BASS

Will the current world record smallmouth bass of 11 lbs. 15 oz. ever be challenged? If so, where, when and how will it be caught?

The world record smallmouth was caught in Dale Hollow Reservoir on the Kentucky/Tennessee border in 1955! Certainly, this record has stood the test of time; however, nothing lasts forever, and even this time-honored record could be broken. If this interests you—read on!

If you study the accompanying world record listings, a few interesting facts become evident concerning monster smallmouths. Approximately 75% of the state record fish were caught from rivers or reservoirs! This is not surprising, since the smallmouth's native range was originally limited to the Great Lakes/St. Lawrence drainage system, and the Ohio, Tennessee and upper Mississippi River systems. Obviously, these river systems provide the proper combination of environmental factors to produce immense smallmouths.

A reservoir is simply a dammed up river which, in many cases, previously contained native smallmouth bass. The fish did quite well in these "artificial" lakes, and due to a number of factors (such as increased habitat, more stable environment and prey) grew to mammoth size.

Interestingly, all of the current 10 pound plus record fish were taken from a relatively small geographical area. The waters are: Wheeler Dam, Alabama; Dale Hollow Reservoir, Kentucky/Tennessee; and Hiwassee Reservoir, North Carolina. These waters are situated at approximately 36° north latitude, which is the southernmost extent of the smallmouth bass range. In addition, it also marks the northern limit of the threadfin shad range, which is a primary prey for the smallmouth. Apparently, the reservoir environment, forage base and extended growing season *in combination* are key factors for growing 10 pound plus smallmouths. We suspect these factors may be even further enhanced by the genetic potential of the native fish in this region to reach huge proportions, although there is presently no scientific evidence to support this theory.

Top-notch smallmouth bass fisherman, Billy Westmorland, has more 8 pound plus fish to his credit than anyone we know. Westmorland's largest fish was a 10-pounder taken from Dale Hollow; however, he's convinced that he lost a 12 to 14 pound smallmouth! In his book, *Them ol' Brown Fish*, Bill states that he believes that if the record is broken, the record-breaker will be caught in Dale Hollow again. Wherever it's caught, the person is either going to have to be very, very persistent—or lucky—or both!

Odds-wise, the best shot for a world record fish would be in the Tennessee River TVA Impoundments like Pickwick Lake, Wilson Lake, and Wheeler Lake. In addition, Dale Hollow would have to be another top candidate. How about the sleepers? Well, Hiwasee Reservoir, NC is one; Clair Engle Lake, CA and Trinity Lake, CA are others.

The Fall Cold Water Period, followed by the Pre-spawn Period of spring, are probably your best bets for catching a monster smallmouth. Experience indicates that the fish would probably be caught on 4 pound test line with a tiny jig, or else on a crankbait or spinnerbait presentation, at night. However, we suspect that a light line/live bait presentation, like a live bait rig and a leech, shiner or shad would be a prime candidate. This approach is common in the North, but has yet to be used extensively in the deep, clear reservoirs of the South.

Perhaps the record will fall to some enterprising Yankee, escaping the snow and ice-bound lakes of a northern winter. It may take a real die-hard, fishing one of these reservoirs in November, December or January when most of the locals are snuggled warm inside their homes, to crack the elusive 12 pound mark!

For those of you who are willing to make the sacrifices in time and effort to try to break the record, good luck! To the rest of you, look up your state's smallmouth record, and try to put together a big fish game plan. After all, 4-8 pound smallmouths would be a record in many states, and are definitely within your reach. Everyone is entitled to one for the wall!

Billy Westmorland with a 10 lb. trophy smallmouth caught in Dale Hollow Reservoir, TN/KY.

U.S. Smallmouth Bass Records

STATE	WEIGHT lbs. oz.		WATERS	YEAR
Alabama	10	8	Wheeler Dam	1950
Alaska	No Record			
Arizona	6	14	Roosevelt Lake	1980
Arkansas	7	5	Lake Bull Shoals	1969
California	9	1	Clair Engle Lake	1976
Colorado	5	5	Smith Reservoir	1979
Connecticut	7	12	Shenipsit Lake	1980
Delaware	4	7	Unknown	1983
Florida	No Record			
Georgia	7	2	Lake Chatuge	1973
Hawaii	3	11	Lake Wilson	1982
Idaho	7	5½	Dworshak Reservoir	1982
Illinois	6	5½	Farm Pond	1980
Indiana	6	8	Stream	1970
Iowa	6	8	Spirit Lake	1979
Kansas	4	12	Milford Reservoir	1983
Kentucky	11	15	Dale Hollow Lake	1955
Louisiana	No Record			
Maine	8		Thompson Lake	1970

U.S. Smallmouth Bass Records

STATE	WEIGHT lbs.	oz.	WATERS	YEAR
Maryland	8	4	Liberty Reservoir	1974
Massachusetts (Tie)	7		Lovell's Pond	1972
	7		Hamilton Reservoir	1982
Michigan	9	4	Long Lake	1906
Minnesota	8		W. Battle Lake	1948
Mississippi	7	5	Pickwick Reservoir	1976
Missouri	6	12	Bull Shoals	1983
Montana	4	11½	Horseshoe Lake	1975
Nebraska	6	1½	Merritt Reservoir	1978
Nevada	2	15	Lahontan Reservoir	1981
New Hampshire	7	14½	Goose Pond	1970
New Jersey	6	4	Delaware River	1957
New Mexico	6	8¾	Ute Lake	1972
New York	9		Friends Lake	1925
North Carolina	10	2	Hiwassee Reservoir	1953
North Dakota	5		Sakakawea	1982
Ohio	7	8	Mad River	1941
Oklahoma	5	10	Broken Bow	1983
Oregon	6	13	Brownlee Reservoir	1978
Pennsylvania	7	4	Youghiogheny River	1983
Rhode Island	5	15	Washington Pond	1977
South Carolina	5	4	Toxaway River	1971
South Dakota	4	6	Fort Randall Tailwaters	1982
Tennessee	11	15	Dale Hollow Reservoir	1955
Texas	6	2	Canyon Reservoir	1982
Utah	6	11	Lake Borham	1983
Vermont	6	12	Lake Champlain	1978
Virginia	8		Claytor Lake	1964
Washington	8	12	Columbia River	1967
West Virginia	9	0¾	South Branch	1971
Wisconsin	9	1	Indian Lake	1950
Wyoming	4	12	Stater Ash Creek	1982

REGION 4:   REGION 5
Alaska & Canada   GREAT LAKES AND TRIBUTARIES

REGION 1

REGION 3

REGION 2

In Search of . . . Smallmouth Bass

Here's a slate of selected smallmouth bass waters. Simply, locate the geographical region you want to fish. Then select a lake, river or reservoir and go fishin'!

REGION #1

MAINE
LAKES: Big, Sebago, Graham, Great Moose, Dramariscotta, plus numerous ponds
RIVERS: Sandy, Kennebec, Penobscot

VERMONT
LAKES: Champlain, Harriman, Somerset, St. Catherine
RIVERS: Connecticut, Black, White, Otter

RHODE ISLAND
LAKES: Indian, Stafford, Watchaug

DELAWARE
RIVERS: Brandywine Creek

CONNECTICUT
LAKES: Lillinonah, Bantam, Brookfield
RIVERS: Housatonic, Connecticut, Thames

MASSACHUSETTS
LAKES: Quabbin, Wachusetts, Small kettle ponds
RIVERS: Connecticut, Merrimack

NEW YORK
LAKES: Cayuga, Champlain, George, Chautauqua, New Croton, Pepacton
RIVERS: Susquehanna, St. Lawrence, Hudson, Mohawk, Delaware

NEW JERSEY
LAKES: Hopatcong, Round Valley, Greenwood, Swartswood
RIVERS: Delaware, Raritan (south branch), Ramapo

PENNSYLVANIA
LAKES: Youghiogheny, Ryerson Station, Wallenpaupack, Raystown, Kinzua Dam

228

RIVERS: Allegheny, Youghiogheny, Monongahela, Susquehanna, Delaware
OHIO
LAKES: Strip pits
RIVERS: Mad, Big Darby, Kokosing, Little Miami, Stillwater
INDIANA
LAKES: Maxinkuchee, Freeman, Wawasee, Potoka
RIVERS: St. Joseph, Elkhart, Sugar Blue, Indian
MICHIGAN
LAKES: St. Clair, Cisco, Charlevoix, Bear, Gull, Union, Cass
RIVERS: Kalamazoo (north branch), Chippewa, Huron, Looking Glass, Cass
WISCONSIN
LAKES: Geneva, Lac Court O'Reilles, Shell, Tomahawk, Grindstone
RIVERS: Wisconsin, Black, St. Croix, Red Cedar
MINNESOTA
LAKES: West Battle, Lake Vermilion, Rainy, Lac La Croix, Pokegama, Basswood, Green, Crooked
RIVERS: Mississippi, St. Croix, Rum, Cannon, Root, Ottertail, Rainy
IOWA
LAKES: Spirit, West Okoboji, Big Creek
RIVERS: Upper Iowa, Middle Racoon, Cedar, Mississippi, Des Moines, Cedar
NEBRASKA
LAKES: McConaughy, Red Willow, Enders, Box Butte, Merritt, Gravel pits near I-80
RIVERS: Missouri
SOUTH DAKOTA
LAKES: Fort Randall Tailwaters
NORTH DAKOTA
LAKES: Sakakawea

REGION #2
VIRGINIA
LAKES: Smith Mountain, Clator, Philpott
RIVERS: James, New, Rappahannock, Shenandoah
WEST VIRGINIA
LAKES: Summersville, Tygart, Sutton, Stonecoal, R.D. Bailey
RIVERS: New, Potomac (south branch), Shenandoah, Cacapon, Ohio, Greenbrier, Elk
TENNESSEE
LAKES: Dale Hollow, Pickwick, Percy Priest, Center Hill, Cherokee, Tims Ford
RIVERS: Tennessee, Buffalo, Cumberland, Duck, Harpeth, Sequatchie
KENTUCKY
LAKES: Dale Hollow, Cumberland, Green River, Carr Fork, Barren River, Kentucky
RIVERS: Elkhorn, Barren, Pitman, Drakes, Nolin, Stoner, Slate, Silver, Hinkston

ALABAMA
LAKES: Wheeler, Wilson, Pickwick, Little Bear Creek
RIVERS: Tennessee

MARYLAND
LAKES: Liberty, Deep Creek, Prettyboy, Lock Raven, Triadelphia, Rocky Gorge
RIVERS: Potomac, Youghiogheny, Susquehanna

NORTH CAROLINA
LAKES: Bear, Fontana, Chatuge, James
RIVERS: New, Elk, Little Tennessee, Pigeon, Watauga, Cane, Wilson, Mitchell

GEORGIA
LAKES: Blue Ridge, Chatuge
RIVERS: Tennessee

TEXAS
LAKES: Canyon, Meredith, Travis, Belton, Amistad, Stillhouse Hollow, Greenbelt, Spencer
RIVERS: Guadalupe

KANSAS
LAKES: Wilson, Milford

MISSOURI
LAKES: Stockton, Table Rock, Bull Shoals
RIVERS: Niangua, Gasconade, Big Piney, Current, Meramec

ARKANSAS
LAKES: Bull Shoals, North Fork, Greers Ferry, Greeson, DeGray
RIVERS: Crooked, Buffalo, Big Piney, Ouchita, White

REGION #3

WASHINGTON
LAKES: Osoyoos, Shammamish, Potholes, Banks
RIVERS: Snake, Columbia (mid), Okanogan, Yakima

OREGON
LAKES: Billy Chinook, Prineville, Brownlee
RIVERS: Columbia, Snake, Umpqua, John Day, Owyhee

CALIFORNIA
LAKES: Trinity, Shasta, Folsom, Berryessa, Merle Collins, New Hogan, Don Pedro, Nacimiento, Pine Flat
RIVERS: Russian, Kings, Cache, Putah

IDAHO
LAKES: Dworshak, Snake River Impoundments
RIVERS: Snake, Clearwater, Salmon

WYOMING
LAKES: Flaming Gorge, Strip pits

ARIZONA
LAKES: Apache, Roosevelt, Bartlett
RIVERS: Verde, Colorado, Black

NEW MEXICO
LAKES: Ute, Conchas, Navajo
RIVERS: Rio Grande

REGION #4

CANADA
LAKES: Ontario/Minnesota Boundary Waters; Falcon, Crowduck, George
      (Manitoba); Menphremagog (Quebec)
RIVERS: Winnepeg (Manitoba); St. Lawrence (Ontario & Quebec);
      Kawarthas chain (Ontario)

HAWAII
LAKES: Wahiawa/Wilson on Oahu
RIVERS: Wailau system on Kauai

REGION #5

GREAT LAKES
Detailed information is included in Chapter 20 - Great Lakes Fishing.

Chapter 23

CATCH & RELEASE

Strategies for Smallmouth Survival

"What do you mean let 'em go—are ya nuts? I'm gonna keep 'em all!"

In the good ol' days, the "meat-is-neat" philosophy was common. Most individuals kept nearly every smallmouth bass they caught. Unfortunately, this overharvesting led to the demise of many, many smallmouth bass fisheries. In his book, *Bass 'n Objects*, Bill Dance states that there was a time when he believed that status was measured by the size of the stringer he tossed on the dock. He stringered fish—lots of them—and so did many others. However, quite a few years ago, he realized that a fish is too important a commodity to be caught only once. Dance states, "Catch a lot of fish, keep what you can use, and release the rest." Today, expert, conservation-minded fishermen like Bill Dance, Al Lindner and others are striving to ensure an abundance of fish for generations to come.

Throughout this book, catch and release fishing has been emphasized. Hopefully, by now you'll understand why this practice is critical in maintaining some smallmouth bass populations. Yes, a smallmouth bass population can be destroyed by a few knowledgeable, greedy anglers.

Chances are good that some of you already practice catch and release in some situations; that's great! However, for a vast majority of anglers, the concept of catching and releasing fish is new—especially *big* fish.

This chapter gives a few tips on how to successfully release fish—*alive*. In addition, we've provided a simple calculation you can use to accurately estimate the weight of smallmouth bass.

How do you know when to keep or release fish? State or provincial regulations, which are almost always designed on a general basis, rather than on a water by water basis, cannot always indicate whether or not to take smallmouths. Regardless of the legal limit, there are numerous waters where *no* smallmouth bass should be taken! In these waters, catch and release is essential for the survival of even a remnant population of smallmouths. Most of these waters are small to medium-sized natural lakes, small reservoirs, strip pits, and sections of some rivers.

On the other hand, there are some waters where a few smallmouths may be kept for food. Many Canadian shield lakes would qualify. Certainly, sections of the Great Lakes, like the Bass Islands area of Lake Erie, have exceptional smallmouth bass populations. In addition, there are innumerable small rivers and streams throughout the country that are teeming with smallmouths. Sections of larger rivers like the Upper Mississippi and St. Lawrence also offer super fishing. Yet, even in such waters with healthy smallmouth bass populations, the fishery *must be protected* by using sensible, selective, catch and kill practices. Remember, nothing lasts forever, so don't exploit the fishery. Take only one personal trophy, or just a few fish for dinner.

Size Distribution Comparisons
Depending on Fishing Pressure

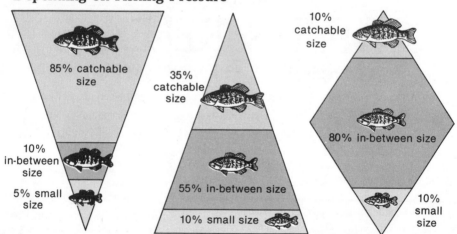

Fishing pressure has a profound effect on gamefish populations. As the amount of intelligent fishing pressure increases, the numbers of larger, mature fish decreases! For example, consider the following chart based on size distribution of 1000 fish:

Fishing Pressure	Approximate Number of Larger Fish	Lunkers
Virgin Waters	850	85
Moderately Fished Waters	350	35
Heavily Fished Waters	100	10

If we place the theoretical number of lunkers at 10% of the larger fish, the result gives you an idea of how few lunkers are present. For this reason, all anglers have the responsibility to release as many fish as possible.

HOW TO RELEASE FISH

There is more to the subject of catch and release than meets the eye. It's a complex subject that involves minimizing stress, using proper handling techniques and recognizing injured fish. Let's discuss the issue and see just how to put 'em back alive.

The basis for successful release is a knowledge of stress and how it can cause shock in fish. Stress and shock are two related physical conditions. Stress, from a biological point of view, includes anything that adversely affects fish. Every act involved with catching, handling and releasing fish can cause stress.

There are also varying degrees of stress, depending on how the fish fares while out of its natural environment. The poorer a fish is handled, the higher the degree of stress. Stress can cause shock which occurs when the fish's circulatory system shuts down. Keeping fish from going into shock is a balancing act with the fish's life hanging in the balance! Successful fish release depends on attention to details.

Basic Factors Affecting Fish Release

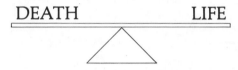

DEATH   LIFE

The Balancing Act

STRESS	STRESS MINIMIZERS
1. Lack of oxygen	1. Constant oxygen source
2. Lactic acid build-up	2. Minimal lactic acid build-up
3. Slime removal (handling infection)	3. Minimal handling
4. Hooking injury	4. Careful handling
5. Temperature change	5. Protection of sensitive body parts
6. Injury to sensitive body parts	
7. Other poor handling techniques	

Now that you're aware of the factors affecting successful fish release, just how do you put 'em back alive?

When you catch a fish, simply reach down, grab the hook and shake the fish loose without ever touching it. Immediate release is the best tactic and should be used whenever possible. However, sometimes a fish is badly hooked and necessitates careful hook removal. This procedure requires time and subjects the fish to stress. If you work quickly and carefully, though, the fish usually can be released successfully.

Fish hooked in the gills and gullet experience higher death rates than those hooked in other mouth areas; therefore, assess the hook damage immediately. Scientific studies show that even with gill- or gut-hooked fish, the hook should be removed, and not left to rust away. Do the best job you can, removing the hook and releasing the fish. A hemostat or similar hook-out tool is a big help. Obviously, use discretion in this matter by keeping a severely injured fish, rather than wasting it by an unsuccessful release.

What about tournaments? The growth of competitive fishing tournaments has been accompanied by an increase in live release catches. Standard tourney procedure calls for: (1) bagging the fish, (2) taking them to the weigh-in, (3) waiting in line, (4) weighing the fish, (5) holding them and (6) releasing the fish. If it's not possible to fish-for-inches rather than pounds, or to calculate weight using a length-to-weight ratio, then proper handling is critical.

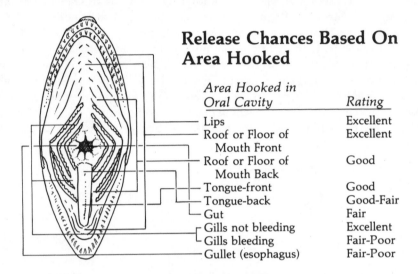

Release Chances Based On Area Hooked

Area Hooked in Oral Cavity	Rating
Lips	Excellent
Roof or Floor of Mouth Front	Excellent
Roof or Floor of Mouth Back	Good
Tongue-front	Good
Tongue-back	Good-Fair
Gut	Fair
Gills not bleeding	Excellent
Gills bleeding	Fair-Poor
Gullet (esophagus)	Fair-Poor

The survival rates of fish that cannot be immediately released is increased by using various substances. Two common, effective compounds are ice and salt.

During warm water periods, use ice to lower the water temperature in your livewell to between 56°F and 60°F. Caution: Do not use chlorinated water, because it will harm the fish.

When you use the other effective treatment, salt, use plain old rock salt or an aquarium salt; do not use a table salt which contains toxic iodine. Any dosage from 1/10 to 1 tablespoon of salt per gallon of water is safe and effective.

In addition, quinoline, a tranquilizer, is available from well-stocked aquarium shops. It works!

Recently, a few innovative people have formulated specific, catch and release chemicals which are available in sports shops. These chemical treatments don't compensate for rough handling, but they can be a real plus in enhancing fish survival. These products are a combination of ingredients which have the following effects on fish: slightly tranquilizes; neutralizes build-up of blood acids; kills bacteria and fungus; stimulates protective slime coat production; and neutralizes chlorine, heavy metals and toxins in water. In summary, these products are easy to use, and they're beneficial. Use them if you're a tournament buff.

ESTIMATING WEIGHT

To calculate a smallmouth's approximate weight, measure the fish's length (round off to nearest 1/4 or 1/2 inch) and multiply length X length X length.

Divide the answer by 1600, and the result will be very close to the actual weight of the average bass. However, since not all fish are "average," you should take this fact into account for your own personal use.

Length to Weight Ratio

Smallmouth bass weight (lbs.) = $\dfrac{\text{length}^3}{1600}$

Here's an example which shows the calculation for an 18-inch smallmouth bass:

1) 18 X 18 X 18 = 5832

2) 5832 ÷ 1600 = 3.6 lbs., or approximately 3 lbs. 10 oz.

Simple, isn't it? And surprisingly accurate!

OUR INDIVIDUAL ROLE

Outdoor writers, among others, tout phrases like, "10% of the anglers catch 90% of the fish," with little data to back up their statements. If it ever was true, it's probably not true now. A minority of anglers still do most of the catching, but today more anglers have sufficient knowledge and experience to catch fish consistently. The information in this book, combined with on-the-water know-how, will allow YOU to catch smallmouth bass regularly.

Individual release efforts may appear futile. What can one person accomplish by releasing a few fish? The easy answer is "Not much." However, small groups of good anglers can have an important impact. Knowledgeable and effective anglers have a great responsibility for catch and release. As part of this fraternity, you can influence other anglers by your example. *Please*, practice sensible catch and release. Put 'em back alive!

CONCLUSION

This is the fourth book in the *IN-FISHERMAN* Masterpiece Series. *SMALLMOUTH BASS: A Handbook of Strategies* takes an indepth look at smallmouth bass and how they operate in many waters. Understanding the how's and why's of fish behavior will help you catch more smallmouths regardless of where you live and fish.

While this book is comprehensive it is not "complete," because as further research is conducted, more nuances of the smallmouth bass personality and lifestyle will be discovered. However, the information contained in this book is an up-to-the-minute compendium of the most productive, smallmouth bass fishing methods—they're dynamite.

In addition to this book, we encourage you to read the other books in our *IN-FISHERMAN* Masterpiece Series: *WALLEYE WISDOM: A Handbook of Strategies, BASS: A Handbook of Strategies,* and *PIKE: A Handbook of Strategies.*

Because of the vast scope of each volume, no one man has enough knowledge to tackle such an undertaking. Instead, we took another avenue; each book is written by a collective group of top anglers. Each of these writer's background, experience and expertise qualifies him as a true expert. And they tell all; they hold nothing back.

If you are truly interested in becoming a top-flight angler, we urge you to subscribe to our *IN-FISHERMAN Magazine,* the foundation of this knowledge. We offer a brochure free of charge which lists the books and magazines we publish. Simply write to *IN-FISHERMAN,* Box 999, Brainerd, MN 56472, and ask for the free brochure.

In closing, the staff wishes you tight lines and good fishing. Remember, catch a lot of fish; keep a few to eat and release the rest.

Confessions of a Former Meat-Hog

In the old days, for a variety of reasons, I participated in the demise of a superb, smallmouth bass fishery. It only took two seasons of "catch and keep" to bring the smallmouth population of that particular lake to its knees. And now, 16 years later, the lake still hasn't come back to anywhere near its former glory. Perhaps it never will.

To my discredit, I did some heavy damage on other lakes as well. However, when I finally realized what was happening, I stepped back and did a fast "180 degrees." In my defense, however, the prevailing belief in those days was that a lake couldn't be fished-out, which is true. You probably won't be able to take every last fish, but we now know that a species can be fished-down to such an extent that it's no longer worth fishing.

The realization that intelligent fishing pressure can—and does—cripple many waters for a decade or more is no longer a question, but fact! And the fact that this is happening with increasing regularity all across North America must be recognized!

There is no question that the time has come for anglers to recognize the importance of conserving our fisheries resources, and to do something about it!

So when you're confronted with fragile fisheries (like most smallmouth bass fisheries), take a trophy for your wall or a couple fish to eat, but put the rest back. You'll be able to go back and catch fish over and over again.

Ron Lindner

the In-Fisherman
GLOSSARY

ADAPTATION: The process of getting used to or fitting into a particular set of environmental circumstances.

AGGREGATION: A group of gamefish or prey fish holding in an area, but not moving together in a school. See *school*.

ALGAE: Simple, one cell plants usually having the ability to photosynthesize sunlight into energy. Initial step in a food chain.

ALLEY: Parallel openings between patches of emergent weeds (usually bulrushes), or emergent weeds and the shoreline.

APPETITE MOODS: The three basic attitudes of fish toward feeding. See *positive, neutral and negative feeding moods.*

BACKTROLLING: A system of boat control, simultaneously moving a boat slowly in reverse and using lure or bait presentations (casting or trolling).

BASIC NATURE: A species' inherent makeup or tendencies which determines its niche in an environment.

BASIC NEEDS: The three basic survival requirements of any fish species; namely reproduction, suitable habitat and food. A favorable environment fulfills these needs.

BASIN ZONE: A lake zone. The area lying below the Deep Water Zone, beginning where hard bottom ends and soft bottom begins. This zone includes the deepest water areas.

BIOLOGY: The study of living things.

BITING: The feeding action of a hungry fish. See *striking.*

BOAT CONTROL: Boat use to aid bait or lure presentation. See *backtrolling, controlled drift, front trolling, speedtrolling.*

BOTTOM-BUMPER: A lure or rig which strikes the bottom (i.e. jig).

BOTTOM CONFIGURATION: A locational factor; the relative make-up (shape, size, depth, islands, etc.) of the bottom.

BOTTOM CONTENT: Bottom types in a body of water (rock, sand, gravel, silt, muck, submerged cribs, brush and/or trees, etc.).

BREAK: Any change in otherwise regular terrain.

BREAKLINE: That point in a body of water where there is a definite increase in depth—sudden or gradual—or a change in cover, like a weedline or brushline; edge of channel or hole; where two layers of water meet and differ in temperature, oxygen and/or turbidity; the limit of effective light penetration, etc.

BREAKLINE, SECONDARY: A second or auxilary point of change. For example, a second definite increase in depth after the first drop-off.

BRUSHLINE: The inside or outside edge of a line of brush.

CABBAGE: Any of the pondweeds (Potamogeton); usually attractive to gamefish.

CALENDAR, IN-FISHERMAN: A calendar based on ten identifiable periods of activity for various species of gamefish. These ten periods constitute a *fish cycle.*

CALENDAR PERIOD: Any of the ten periods of fish activity in the IN-FISHERMAN Calendar.

CLEAN BOTTOM: The bottom (usually hard bottom) of a body of water that is free of debris, etc.

CLIMATE: The average weather conditions for a region.

COLD FRONT: The line of impact when cold air forces the warm air upwards. As a cold front moves, cold air beneath is slowed down by contact with the ground, and piles up. This pile of cold air forces warm air up very rapidly, often causing storms. See *post-front.*

COLD WATER PERIOD: A period of the fish cycle which occurs twice—in early spring between the Frozen Water and Pre-spawn Periods, and in late fall between the Turnover and Frozen Water Periods. Most times applied to the fall season.

COMPETITIVE SPECIES: An aspect of *social condition* involving the relationship of species within a body of water, particularly in regard to available food and spawning areas.

CONTROLLED DRIFT: A system of *boat control* using an outboard, electric trolling motor or oars to keep a boat moving along a specific course.

COSMIC CLOCK: The sun's effect on water and local weather factors, such as barometric pressure, wind, cloud cover, seasonal change, etc.

CRANKBAIT: A lipped diving plug.

DEEP WATER ZONE: A lake zone. Hard bottom lying below the first major drop-off and below the open water zone. It ends where soft bottom begins.

DEPTH CONTROL: One of two primary factors in successful bait or lure presentation.

DISSOLVED OXYGEN: (DO). Oxygen chemically bound into water by forces such as wind and plants. It is utilized by fish.

DROP-OFF: A point where there is definite increase in depth.

ECOLOGY: The branch of biology dealing with relations between organisms and their environment.

ECOSYSTEM: A system formed by the interaction of a community of organisms and their surroundings.

ELECTROPHORESIS: A process that can determine the genetic make-up of fish.

EPILIMNION: The warmer layer of water above the *thermocline.*

EROSION: The process by which the surface of the earth is being constantly worn away. The most important elements responsible for erosion are rivers and streams, wind, waves and glaciers.

EUTROPHIC: *A lake classification* or lake type used to describe bodies of water characterized by high levels of nutrients in proportion to their total volume of water.

FANCAST: To make a series of casts systematically covering an area.

FISH CONTACT: Locating fish—usually by catching them. Includes visual observation.

FISH CYCLE: All ten Calendar Periods. See *Calendar,* IN-FISHERMAN.

FISHING PRESSURE: The number of anglers using a body of water.

FLAT: An area characterized by little or no change in depth.

FOOD CHAIN: A step-by-step representation of feeding relationships in a community. Food chains originate with the sun's energy and each link in the chain represents energy transfer. All the food chains in a community make up a food web.

FOOD PRODUCING AREA: Any area that seasonally produces forage for fish.

FRONT TROLLING: A system of *boat control* with the boat moving forward.

FROZEN WATER PERIOD: A period of the fish cycle when a body of water is mostly or completely covered by ice. In Southern waters, which rarely freeze, the sustained period of coldest water.

GEOLOGY: The science dealing with the earth's physical history.

HABITAT: The place where a plant or animal species lives.

HARD BOTTOM: Firm bottom areas (sand, clay, rock, gravel, etc.).

HIGH PROTEIN FORAGE: High-fat content, soft-rayed forage species such as ciscoes and whitefish.

HOLDING STATION: Any specific position regardless of depth where fish spend much of their time.

HYPOED LAKE: A body of water stocked with a species of fish to bolster its natural fishery.

HYPOLIMNION: The colder layer of water below the *thermocline.*

IMPOUNDMENT: A confined area where water accumulates, usually the result of damming a river. See *reservoir.*

INFILLING: The process by which higher surrounding terrain tends to fill in lower terrain.

INSIDE EDGE (OF WEEDS): A line of weeds between the shoreline and the weedline. See *outside edge* (of weeds).

JUNK WEEDS: Any type of weed usually not attractive to gamefish.

LAKE CLASSIFICATIONS: Broad categories of lake types; oligotrophic (infertile), mesotrophic (fertile), eutrophic (very fertile).

LAKE MODIFICATION FORCES: Forces such as ice action, wave action, erosion, etc., which change bodies of water.

LAKE TYPE: A group of bodies of water whose characteristics are similar enough to one another that they can be approached from an angling standpoint in much the same manner. See *lake classifications.*

LAKE ZONES: Four designated IN-FISHERMAN water zones: *shallow water, open water, deep water and basin zones.*

LIMNOLOGY: The study of the biological, chemical, geographical and physical features of bodies of water.

LITTORAL ZONE: Shallow water zone.

LOCAL WEATHER FACTORS: The prevailing weather conditions affecting the day-to-day locational patterns of a fish species.

LOCATIONAL PATTERN: Where, why and how a species positions itself to take advantage of its surroundings.

LOOSE ACTION PLUG: A lure whose side-to-side movements are wide and distinct.

MARL: Deposits of sand, clay and silt with a high concentration of shells (calcium carbonate).

MESOTROPHIC: *Lake classification* used to describe fertile bodies of water between the late-stage *oligotrophic* and early-stage *eutrophic* classifications.

MIGRATION: The movement of fish from one area to another. Migrations generally occur on a seasonal basis, from one set of distinct environmental conditions to another, such as from winter habitat toward spwaning areas. They would not be confused with *movements.*

MORAINE: A mass of rocks, sand, etc., deposited by a glacier.

MOVEMENT: The locational shift of fish from one area to another, generally on a daily or even hourly basis. Also can refer to fish changing from a neutral to a positive feeding mood, with fish shifting only a few feet from a resting to an advantageous feeding position. A *directional* movement is one which is made from one specific area to another specific area, usually at a fast rate of speed. A *random* movement is the slow milling activity made within a specific area.

NEGATIVE FEEDING MOOD: An *appetite mood* in which the attitude of fish is negative toward biting. Fish also are said to be inactive.

NEUTRAL FEEDING MOOD: An *appetite mood.* The attitude of fish which are not actively feeding but could be tempted through refined presentation. See *striking.*

NICHE: Based on a species' characteristics, and depending on competing species, an organism assumes a particular role and a set of physical surroundings within an ecosystem.

NURSERY AREA: Areas where fish species are reared to the fingerling stage.

OLIGOTROPHIC: *Lake classification* used to describe bodies of water characterized by low amounts of nutrients in proportion to their total volume of water. Infertile.

OPEN WATER ZONE: A lake zone. The upper water layer from the outside edge of the first major drop-off down to the deep water zone.

OUTSIDE EDGE (OF WEEDS): The *weedline.* The outside edge of a line of weeds.

PATTERN: Any consistently reoccurring locational/presentational situation.

PHOTOSYNTHESIS: Green plants have chlorophyll which allows them to synthesize organic compounds from water and carbon dioxide using the sun's energy. This is called photosynthesis, and produces oxygen.

POPULATION DENSITY: The number of individuals occupying a certain area. For example, the number of bass per acre.

POSITIVE FEEDING MOOD: An *appetite mood.* The attitude of fish which are actively feeding.

POST-FRONT: That period after a weather front. Usually used in reference to a cold front when the atmosphere becomes clear and bright, and is accompanied by strong winds and a significant drop in temperature.

POST-SPAWN PERIOD: The period immediately following spawning characterized by poor fishing because fish are recuperating and relocating.

POST-SUMMER PERIOD: A period of the fish cycle following the Summer Period. It can mean about a week or more of terrific fishing.

PRECAMBRIAN SHIELD: The Canadian Shield. A geological rock formation covering much of eastern and central Canada and some of the north central U.S.A.

PREDATOR: An organism which feeds on another.

PREDATOR/PREY RELATIONSHIP: An interrelationship between a species and an accessible and suitable forage.

PREFERRED FOOD: Food or forage best suited to a species' basic needs.

PRE-SPAWN PERIOD: The period of the fish cycle immediately before spawning when fish position themselves near their spawning grounds.

PRE-SUMMER PERIOD: The period of the fish cycle immediately following post-spawn. Fish mood is often positive, but fish establish a wide variety of patterns.

REEDS: Bulrushes or rushes.

RESERVOIR: Impoundment. A place where water is collected and stored.

RIG: A fishing boat; the hook, snell and other terminal tackle for live bait fishing; assembling tackle.

SADDLE: A site where a structural element narrows before widening again.

SCHOOL (OF FISH): A number of fish of the same or similar species grouped together and moving as a unit to benefit from the defensive and/or feeding advantages associated with coordinated activity.

SHALLOW WATER ZONE: *A lake zone.* The area out to the first major drop-off.

SHIELD WATER: Body of water located on the Precambrian or Canadian Shield. Specifically, a body of water in an area where the basin and surrounding terrain has had their nutrient-producing rock and sediment layers eroded away by glaciers.

SLICK: A sand or clay bar, point or drop-off devoid of weeds, brush, rock or boulders, etc.; a section of calm surface water in a river.

SOFT BOTTOM: Bottoms (silt, mud, muck, marl, etc.) which are not hard.

SOCIAL CONDITION: One of three elements helping to determine a species' locational pattern. It includes population density, food availability, and competitive species and how these interrelate.

SNAKETROLLING: A system of *boat control* in which a lure or bait is trolled in a weaving manner to cover a wide area and a range of depth levels.

SPAWN PERIOD: A brief period of the fish cycle directly linked to seasonal progression and a range of suitable temperatures. When a species reproduces.

SPECIES: A group of closely-related organisms which can produce offspring.

SPEED CONTROL: One of two primary factors in bait or lure presentation. The other is depth.

SPEEDTROLLING: A system of *boat control* in which a lure is trolled behind a boat moving at fast speed.

SPOOKING: Frightening or "turning off" one or more fish.

STRAGGLERS: Fish lingering apart from others of their species after a movement.

STRIKING: An involuntary reflex action prompted by a bait or lure. Fish are made to bite. See *biting.*

STRUCTURAL CONDITION: One of three elements helping to determine a species' locational patterns. It includes bottom configuration, bottom content, water characteristics, vegetation types and water exchange rate.

STRUCTURAL ELEMENT: Most any natural or man-made, physical features in a body of water. See *bottom configuration.*

SUMMER PERIOD: A period of the fish cycle when fish generally hold to patterns established during the last part of the Summer Peak Period.

SUMMER PEAK PERIOD: A short period of the fish cycle which begins after the first hot spell that remains for several days and nights. Fish begin establishing summer patterns at the latter portion of this period.

SUSPENDED FISH: Fish which are hovering considerably above the bottom in open water.

TAPER: An area that slopes toward deeper water.

THERMOCLINE: The center area of temperature stratification in a body of water. Specifically, the division between the epilimnion and hypolimnion. Temperature changes very quickly.

TIGHT ACTION PLUG: A lure whose side-to-side movements are short and distinct.

TOPWATER PLUG: A floating lure designed for use on the water's surface.

TOTAL ENVIRONMENT: The body of water a species lives in, and any outside stimuli influencing it.

TRANSITION (BOTTOM): The point where one type of bottom material changes to another.

TRIGGER: One of eight lures or bait characteristics designed to stimulate positive responses from fish (action, color, size, shape, scent, sound, vibration, texture). Triggers appeal to the sensory organs of a species.

TURNOVER PERIOD: A very brief period of the fish cycle when some lakes or reservoirs are in turmoil. A mixing or "turning over" of the water takes place as cold water on the surface settles and warmer water from below rises. This turnover homogenizes lakes that have thermoclined (layered according to water temperature) in summer and reoxygenates the water.

TWO-STORY LAKE: A body of water in which warm water species inhabit the upper portion while cold water species inhabit the deeper portion.

WATER CHARACTERISTICS: The characteristics of a body of water, usually referred to in terms of mineral content (soft, few minerals; medium, some minerals; hard, many minerals). The amount of minerals determines fertility.

WATER EXCHANGE RATE: The rate at which water enters or leaves a body of water.

WORKING METHOD: An aspect of presentation consisting of triggers, controls, gear selection and technique.

Here's IN-FISHERMAN, Gary Roach, with a 5 pound class smallie. He caught the fish in the Bass Islands area of Lake Erie during the Pre-spawn Period. The bait? A Fuzz-E-Grub and minnow.